IMAGES
of America

FRANKLIN PARK

On the cover: The bear dens were the first attraction to open in Franklin Park's zoo in October 1912. The bear dens were a popular attraction until 1971, although they were located in the Long Crouch Woods and away from the body of the zoo. (Courtesy of Historic New England.)

IMAGES
of America

FRANKLIN PARK

Julie Arrison

ARCADIA
PUBLISHING

ISBN 978-0-7385-6531-6

Published by Arcadia Publishing
Charleston, South Carolina

Printed in the United States of America

Library of Congress Control Number: 2008940188

For all general information, please contact Arcadia Publishing:
Telephone 843-853-2070
Fax 843-853-0044
E-mail sales@arcadiapublishing.com
For customer service and orders:
Toll-Free 1-888-313-2665

Visit us on the Internet at www.arcadiapublishing.com

Frederick Law Olmsted and his design firm shaped thousands of American landscapes and, in turn, shaped millions of lives. If it was not for such a poignant figure in American history, I may have never been inspired to pursue the life of a historian.

CONTENTS

Acknowledgments

This book would not have been possible without the cooperation of my "Olmstedian" network. Christine Poff and the Franklin Park Coalition provided me with park-related objects and contacts within the community. Ilya and Murray Cooper, Mike and Suzanne Monk, Diane Rogers, and Shep Wolsky took time out of their lives to tell me about their stories of their time in Franklin Park. Mark Swartz and the staff of the Frederick Law Olmsted National Historic Site, as well as the Friends of Fairsted, helped me gain an appreciation for the man behind the designs. Arleyn Levee was kind enough to review my work.

Michele Clark of the Olmsted National Historic Site and Aaron Schmidt of the Boston Public Library Print Department gave me an opportunity to delve into their amazing collections. Margaret Dyson of the Boston Parks and Recreation Department guided me in the early stages of the project with the annual reports of the parks department. Earl Taylor of the Dorchester Historical Society provided a rare postcard collection. Peter Drummey and Elaine Grublin of the Massachusetts Historical Society provided me with access to the Arthur Shurtleff collection, while Kathy Griffin uncovered the Good Government Association newspaper clippings. Barry Gaither of the National Center of Afro-American Artists provided rare pictures of the playhouse in the park. Emily Gustanis and Lorna Condon of Historic New England provided the cover for this work and other requests toward the end.

Jerry Burke has been not only an invaluable resource of history and ephemera, but he has become a great friend through this process. William Fowler, Harvey Green, and Ballard Campbell, all of Northeastern University, provided me with an exceptional educational experience. A fellow graduate student and friend, Jennifer Jovin, convinced me to pursue this project. Erin Rocha of Arcadia Publishing was always there to provide guidance and advice.

My family and friends have been listeners and supporters throughout this project. Whether it was indulging me in a walk in the park where I droned on about the history, spending time panicking about a deadline, or simply asking how the book was coming, I could not ask for a better network of people in my life.

INTRODUCTION

In 1869, the citizens of Boston, likely after hearing about the successes of other large urban parks, requested that the City of Boston design and construct a park system. On June 7, 1876, a group of Bostonians called a public meeting at Faneuil Hall to discuss the importance of public parks. In a handbill to the citizens and taxpayers of Boston, these men highlighted the issues that were bound to harm Boston's ever-growing population, including an increased death rate, a lack of fresh air, and the eventual scarcity of available property on which to build pleasure grounds. The result of this meeting was an increase in government action to plan for and construct a system of city parks that would be unsurpassed in usefulness and beauty.

On November 9, 1876, the common council and the board of aldermen committed to research the feasibility of Boston's park system. One of the aldermen was Hugh O'Brien, who would eventually become the first Irish mayor of Boston in 1884. His Roxbury residential status afforded him the prejudice to speak in favor of using the area of land then referred to as West Roxbury Park. In a speech given on May 21, 1877, O'Brien stated,

> Nature has already prepared the scenery by the great variety of trees, the beautiful lawns, and the extensive views of the surrounding country. No expensive grading would have to be done there, for that work has already been accomplished by the great landscape Architect on High. I repeat that West Roxbury Park, about the geographical center of the city, is the cheapest of all our Parks, notwithstanding its large area, and no scheme will be complete without it.

The area known as West Roxbury Park was nestled between Dorchester, Jamaica Plain, Mattapan, and Roxbury. Many of the earliest settlers came to "Rocksborough" or "Rocksberry" around 1630 from Nazing, Essex County, England. The Town of Boston dispersed land in 50-acre plots for any man who came over from England at his own costs. One of the earliest owners of land in the vicinity of West Roxbury Park was Humphrey Johnson. His land was located in the area between the Wilderness and the north-facing side of Schoolmaster Hill. Other residents included Robert Williams, whose family owned about half of today's park; Samuel Hagbourne; Increase Summer; John Piermont; John Scarborough; Lucius Manlius Sargent; and Joseph P. Ellicott. The annexation of Roxbury in 1868, Dorchester in 1870, and West Roxbury in 1874 added to the political reach of the City of Boston. There were more constituents with a variety of needs to be addressed in many different neighborhoods.

The City of Boston hired Frederick Law Olmsted, the father of American landscape architecture, and his firm, which eventually included his sons John Charles and Frederick Law Jr. to complete the design, engineering, and construction of the Emerald Necklace—Boston's modern park system. The area known as West Roxbury Park would be considered the crown jewel of the system. The 1881 annual report of the Boston Parks Commission stated that the area was chosen for "the topographical advantages for a particular class of park purposes which nature has there provided." About 485 acres were at the city's disposal, and additional land was purchased from occupants between 1881 and 1886 to bring the total acreage of designable areas to 527 acres.

Olmsted and his firm worked meticulously to study the history of the land, learn about the patterns of users, and design a space that would appeal "to a different class of human sensibilities" and allow men a relief from the evil of "artificial conditions." Olmsted was enamored with the views of the Blue Hills, the sloping valleys within the parkland, and the history that was encompassed in the 527 that were his to design. He named areas of the park for families that occupied the property or events that happened in a given area. For example, Revolutionary soldiers returning to the Boston area after the Battle of Lexington and Concord in 1775 used the Resting Place as a camp. The firm viewed parks as a refining art that could bring together all classes of people in relative harmony by providing places for both passive and active recreation.

In the 1884 annual report, the board of the park commissioners, following the lead of Mayor O'Brien, decided that monies from the Franklin Fund, left to the City of Boston by Benjamin Franklin upon his death in 1791, would be used to clear the debt of the majority of the $500,000 in eminent domain land purchases for the park when the fund matured in 1891. The 1885 annual report stated, "The park thus purchased should be called 'Franklin Park' in honor of the testator who has so generously endowed his native town . . . in perpetual recognition of the generosity of the great Bostonian to his native city." The courts would eventually rule that the intended use of the funds was inappropriate, and Franklin Park was never funded with money from the Franklin Fund.

Instead the taxpayers of Boston paid not only for the construction of Franklin Park but also for the maintenance of the newly designed landscape. The park was constructed between 1885 and 1898, at a time when there were high levels of immigration into Boston by Irish, Italians, and Jews. This inexpensive immigrant labor was part of what made construction of the park only possible in the late 19th century. Taxpayers also funded the park police that would assist in ensuring public safety within the borders of the park.

The grounds opened on May 1, 1883, and it was reported that "great numbers of people visited them during the summer. Several large picnics of school-children and charitable societies took place and games of ball and lawn tennis were frequent, suitable grounds being specifically designated for those purposes." During this time, Olmsted and city engineers surveyed the land, established a field office at the old Ellicott House, and prepared to present their plans and designs to the City of Boston. In December 1884, Olmsted submitted his "Report on Franklin Park" to the board of park commissioners. The goals he listed, including a wish to keep the large part of the lands as natural as possible and to create places for active recreation, were highlighted and submitted with his 1885 preliminary sketch of Franklin Park.

After close to a year of deliberation concerning funding, designs, and construction, the formation of Franklin Park was finally under way. In the first year, grounds were cleared of boulders and trees that did not work into Olmsted's plan. Driveways were constructed to facilitate the ease of movement for men and construction vehicles. Refreshment stands were set up on Refectory Hill and at the corner of Williams and Walnut Streets. The average daily attendance in the summer was approximately 11,000 persons. In 1887, the area that would be known as the Playstead was cleared of rocks, leveled, and graded. Structural construction was completed on the wall that would become the overlook. The focus of 1888 was the area of the Country Park known as Ellicottdale. The year 1889 would witness the dedication of the Playstead, the completion of the Valley Gates, and continued planting efforts. Sheep were introduced to maintain the Country Park in this year as well.

The next decade would bring the completion of Scarboro Pond, the Refectory, and the park as a whole under the guidance of Olmsted. Olmsted retired in 1895 and passed in 1903. Following his death, many plans for construction were not completed according to his plans. Although both of his sons and the firm remained entrenched in the continued construction of the Boston Park System, financial woes and decreased visitation plagued design plans. In 1895, John Pettigrew was appointed as the superintendent of the Boston Metropolitan Parks Commission. He and Charles Sprauge Sargent, the director of the Arnold Arboretum, made major changes to Olmsted's plans. The firm was usually consulted to discuss changes to the original design. The sons' opinions carried significance in future planning, but political and economic issues altered Frederick Law Olmsted's original plans. The Greeting, the most important plan that was never realized, called for parallel drives and walkways under American elms that formed a promenade and meeting ground about half a mile in length. It was to reach from Blue Hill Avenue along Seaver Street and along the Playstead. Attractions dedicated to the enjoyment and entertainment of parkgoers were to be developed along the Greeting, including a music theater and Little Folks Fair. Where Olmsted planned his Greeting, Pettigrew planned a "long, grassy glade extending from Blue Hill Avenue to the Playsted, surrounded on both sides by a meandering path." The estimated costs for Olmsted's plans were upward of $175,000 to complete, whereas Pettigrew's plan was estimated at $15,000. Much of Pettigrew's plans used trees, shrubs, and plants that were native to New England and would have a better chance for survival, with little maintenance.

The total cost for Franklin Park's construction was $2,314,130.14. Attendance dropped off significantly in the early 20th century due to restrictions on active recreation, automobiles, and the distance from waterways. In order to attract users, evolutions in park plans would include a golf course in the Country Park, a toboggan run on Schoolmaster Hill, and an increase in the number of tennis courts in Ellicottdale. John Pettigrew and his successor Robert Peabody were responsible for advancing plans for a zoological garden in Franklin Park in order to boost faltering attendance.

The park commission hired Arthur Shurtleff, a former apprentice in the Olmsted firm, in 1910 as the chief landscape architect for the planned zoological gardens. Shurtleff worked closely with the Olmsted Brothers firm, beginning in 1911, to plan the zoo along the area originally intended to be Frederick Law Olmsted's Greeting. The zoo stretched from the Long Crouch Woods and followed the lines of the original Greeting plan. The Olmsted brothers were responsible for plantings along the zoo's walkways and for consultation with Shurtleff in regard to their father's original plans for the area. Shurtleff began his work in the Long Crouch Woods area, which was the area that Olmsted Sr. had proposed as a site for bear dens. In 1912, the bear dens opened and were soon followed by the birdhouse and flying cage.

In the first two decades of the zoo's existence, the goal of increasing visitation to Franklin Park was met with 20 million visitors accounted for in 1920. In 1926, Franklin Park was deemed to be the second most beautiful park in the world, behind Unter Den Linden in Berlin. Visitation of the park and the zoo were impacted by a variety of factors throughout the 20th century. Major declines in park visitation are first noted during the Great Depression of the 1930s. Likewise, expenditures on the zoo and park proper also declined due to the Depression. Rationing during World War II allowed for limited supplies for both the park and the zoo. The neighborhoods that originally surrounded Franklin Park in the 1890s underwent several dramatic demographic transitions. These transitions had a difficult impact on park space, and many feared their safety as the area was neither well maintained nor policed in the 1960s and 1970s. Discussion ensued about closing the zoo. Tim Anderson, an activist in Roxbury, stated, "The removal of the zoo would be an act of contempt to black Roxbury." Many other activists were involved with the zoo, including Elma Lewis, who sat on the board of directors. Together these activists fought to keep the zoo open and financially stable.

Elma Lewis has also been credited with the revival of Franklin Park through the 1960s and 1970s. Although a controversial figure, she broke many barriers and rallied neighbors in Mattapan, Roxbury, Dorchester, and Jamaica Plain to be a presence in Franklin Park. She is best known for starting the long-standing Playhouse in the Park program. The program gave local students and dance troupes the opportunity to showcase their talents and also attracted nationally renowned acts, such as Duke Ellington and George Clinton, to offer free concerts to local residents on summer evenings.

The tradition of advocacy started by Elma Lewis has been carried on since 1978 through the Franklin Park Coalition. Started by a group of concerned citizens infuriated with the lack of police presence, the growing piles of refuse, and the less-than-desirable activities occurring within the 527 acres of pleasure grounds, they came together to fight for Boston's forgotten landscape. Through neighborhood cleanups, the Summer Youth Crew—which still provides jobs for deserving youth from the neighborhoods around the park—an active board of trustees, and an even more active constituency, Franklin Park is once again worthy of its designation as the crown jewel of the Boston Park System.

Franklin Park is a place that provides the same tranquil beauty and opportunity for recreation that it did when designed by Frederick Law Olmsted. Yet the history that has occurred both in and around the park has added to the value of Boston's largest open space. The history of the park and the people who have used the park have enhanced the understanding of Olmsted's principles and design ideals and, therefore, our understanding of history.

Unless otherwise noted, images are courtesy of the author's collection.

One

Planning and Construction

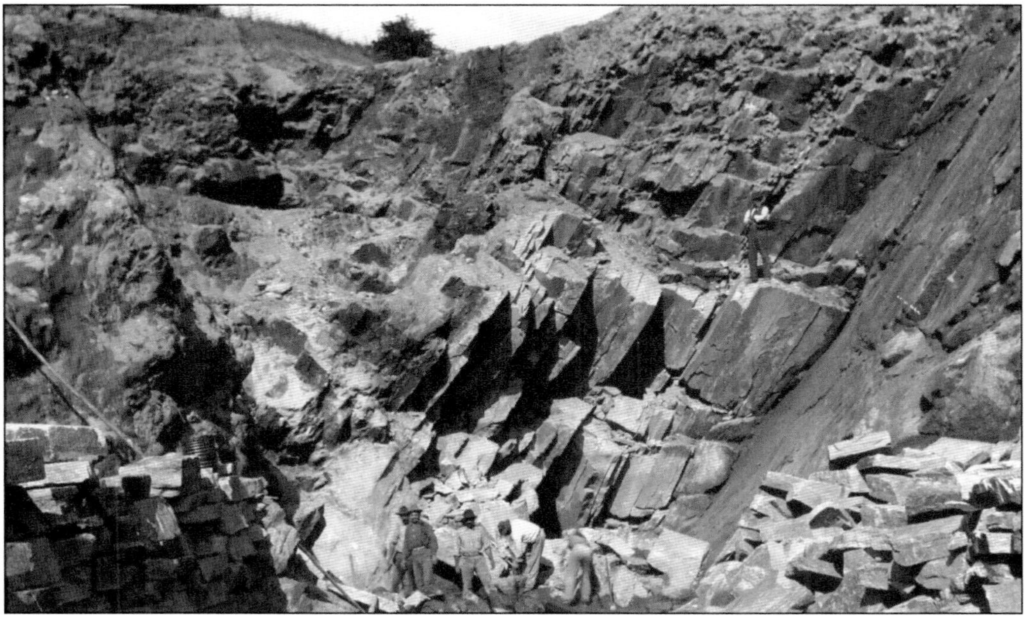

The planning and construction of Franklin Park was approximately a 20-year process, inspired by the wishes of the citizens of Boston to have an urban park system to meet the needs of the public. Hundreds of workers were employed in a variety of capacities from 1884 through the early 20th century. Pudding stone quarries supplied construction materials for the entire Boston Park System. The quarry was filled in 1971.

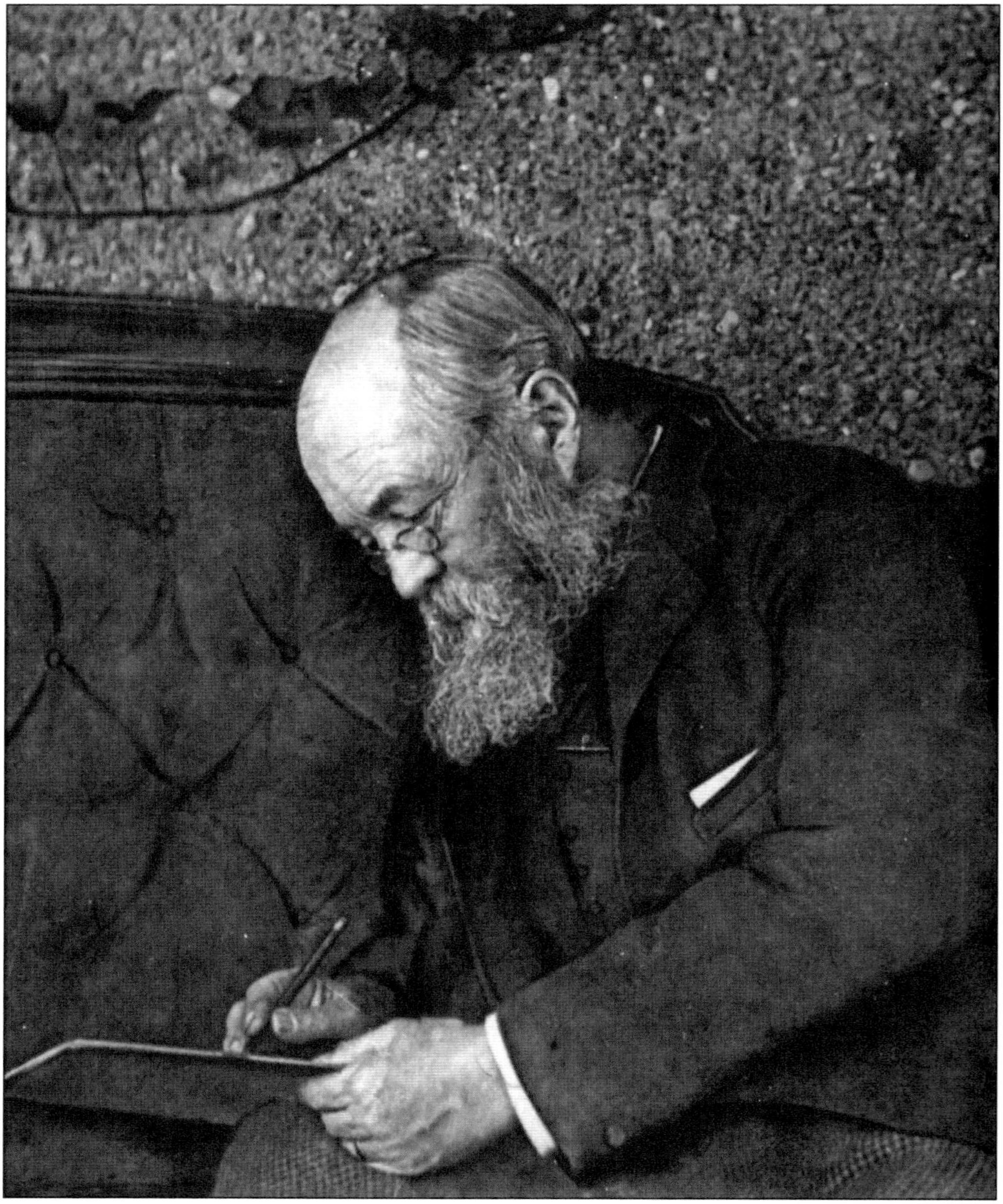

Frederick Law Olmsted was hired as the chief landscape architect for Boston's park system in 1878. Olmsted was born in Hartford, Connecticut, in 1822. He spent much of his life traveling around the world and the United States, writing about those experiences in books and newspapers, and working in a variety of occupations that would ultimately influence his thoughts and designs. Some of Olmsted's famous designs include New York City's Central Park, the Stanford University campus, and the Biltmore estate in North Carolina. He was designated as the landscape architect for the 1893 World's Columbian Exposition in Chicago as well. Olmsted eventually settled in Brookline in 1883 and spent the remainder of his life and career at Fairsted, his home and architectural firm's office. Fairsted remained the firm's office until the late 1970s. It was here that he would plan the elements that would create Boston's Emerald Necklace. (Courtesy of the National Park Service, Frederick Law Olmsted National Historic Site.)

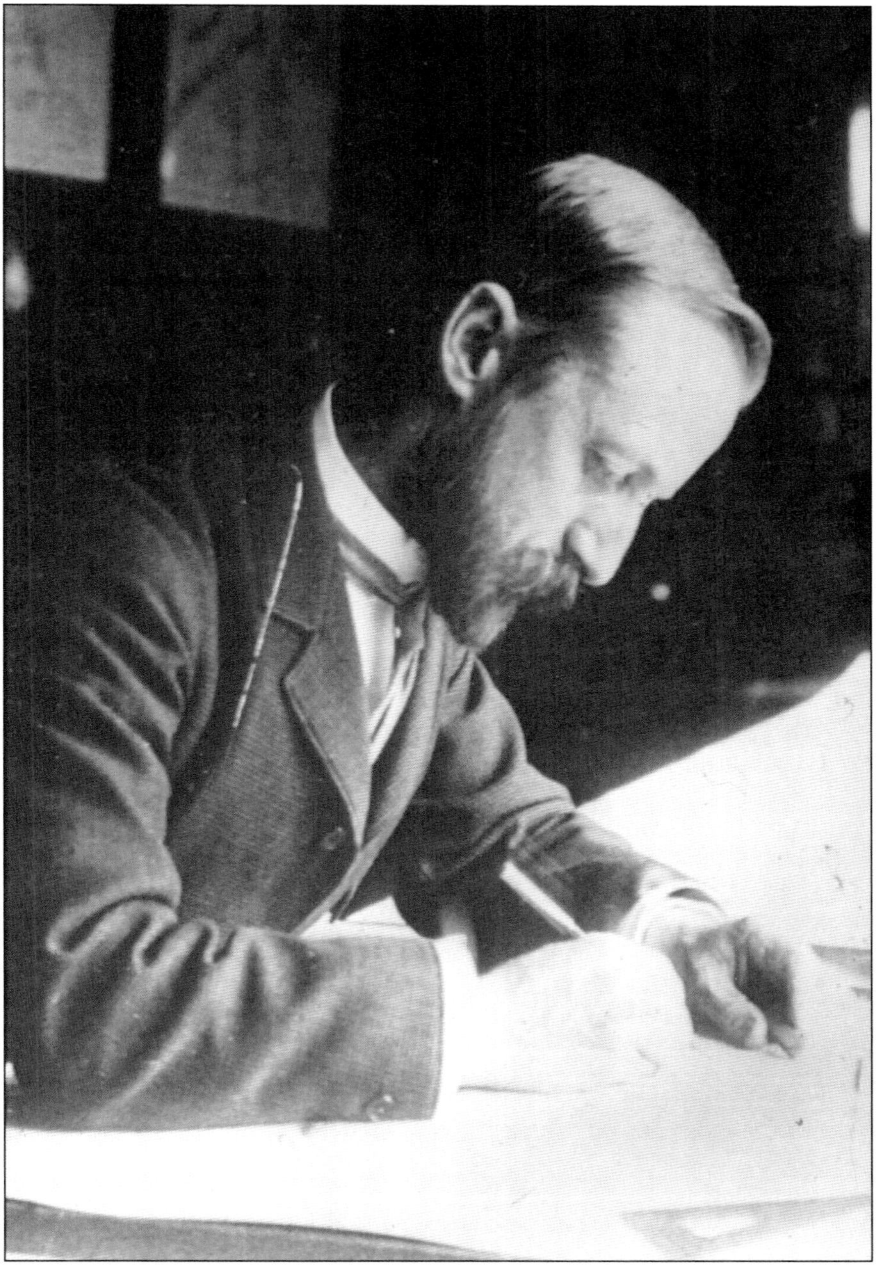

John Charles Olmsted, the adopted son of Frederick Law Olmsted, was responsible for designing various elements in Franklin Park, including roadways, the Ellicott Arch, and the Schoolmaster Hill terrace and shelter. After his father's death in 1903, he continued the firm's legacy with his brother Frederick Law Olmsted Jr. John Charles Olmsted was the founder of the American Society for Landscape Architects. He continued to design integrated park systems in Portland, Oregon; Seattle, Washington; and Essex County, New Jersey. Although he spent a great deal of time traveling on business for the firm, he remained involved in the continued design and construction of the Boston Park System. His 1905 report—released 10 years after Olmsted Sr.'s retirement—was monumental to ensuring that many design features would remain intact. (Courtesy of the National Park Service, Frederick Law Olmsted National Historic Site.)

OBSERVATIONS. *Divisions of the plan are outlined in the adjoining diagram, which for convenience of discussion are named as follows:*

A	The Country Park	E	The Little Folk's Fair	I	Long Crouch Woods
B	The Playstead	F	The Deer Park	J	The Steading
C	The Greeting	G	Refectory Hill	K	The Nursery
D	The Music Court	H	Sargent's Field		Border Grounds

A The Country Park. The entire property has been bought by the city because of its special advantages for one purpose. That purpose is to provide opportunity for a form of recreation to be obtained only through the influence of pleasing natural scenery upon the sensibilities of those quietly contemplating it. The larger part of the property, being the division designated "The Country Park," is proposed to be set apart with absolute exclusiveness, for this purpose. That is to say, if this part of the Park is to have value for any other purpose, it is designed that it shall occur but incidentally, and at no appreciable sacrifice of advantages for the quiet enjoyment of natural scenery. The division is a mile long and three quarters of a mile wide. Natural scenery of much value for the purpose stated cannot be permanently secured on a tract of land of diversified surface of these limits, with a great city growing about it, if the essential elements of such scenery are to be divided, belittled, diluted, or put out of countenance by artificial objects at all more than is necessary to its protection and to the reasonable convenience of those seeking the special benefits offered. The plan proposes, therefore, that nothing shall be built, nothing set up, nothing planted as a decorative feature; nothing for the gratification of curiosity, nothing for the advancement or popularization of science. These objects are provided for suitably in the Public Garden, the Arboretum, and other public grounds. To sustain the designed character of the Country Park, the urban elegance generally desired in a small public or private pleasure ground is to be methodically guarded against. Turf, for example, is to be in most parts preferred as kept short by sheep, rather than by lawn-mowers; well known and long tried trees and bushes to rare ones; natives to exotics; humble field flowers to high-bred marvels; plain green leaves, to blotched, spotted and fretted leaves. Above all, cheap, tawdry, cockneyfied garden toys are to be eschewed. But a poor, shabby, worn, patchy, or in any way untidy rurality is equally to be avoided with urban and suburban finery and fussiness. The site of the Country Park is in most parts rugged, everywhere undulating. Where there are no outcropping ledges, solid rock is often close under the surface, and where it is not, there is in many places almost a pavement of boulders. Compared with that of most public parks, the surface soil is poor; while the subsoil is stony, compact and hard. For these reasons, when the natural surface is much trampled and worn it becomes an inert dust, pernicious to vegetation. It cannot be prepared to resist the wear of athletic sports without undue expense. Under wise regulations and with considerate customs of use, for the establishment of which the good will of the people must be engaged, the site of the Country Park will be found happily adapted to its special distinctive purpose. But it can be wisely used for no recreations which would tend to the destruction of its verdant elements; for none, not of the class of those in which women and children may not, and do not, customarily take part. The plan looks to its being maintained in quietness; quietness both to the eye and the ear. A grateful quietude may be enjoyed in it by many thousand people at a time if they are not drawn into throngs by spectacular attractions, but allowed to distribute themselves as they are otherwise likely to do.

The intention of the plan of the Park as a whole, is that from no part of this Country Park division of it shall anything in any other of its divisions be visible, or at most, be noticeable, except rock, turf and trees, and these harmoniously composing with the natural scenery of the Country Park. The fitting of other divisions for the several purposes to be indicated below, is planned with a view to lessen the difficulty of constantly and lastingly preserving the Country Park for its exclusive purpose. A large part of the Country Park is to be wooded, and adapted to the use of picnic and basket parties, especially small family parties. Various conveniences for these are to be prepared. Tennis Courts, Croquet Grounds, Archery Ranges, and small lawns for little children's festivities, are provided for in near connection with the various picnic grounds.

B The Playstead. This is a field of turf thirty acres in extent (the most nearly flat ground on the property, little broken by rock), to be used for the athletic recreation and education of the city's school boys, and for occasional civic ceremonies and exhibitions. The Overlook on its left, is an elevated platform for spectators. It is eight hundred feet long, covering a barren ledge which would otherwise be disagreeably prominent. It is built of boulders obtained in clearing the Playstead, which are to be mainly overgrown with vegetation befitting the form and material of the structure, adapted to harmonize it with the natural scenery, and make it unobtrusive. In its rear, obscured by existing trees, is to be a large low roof for the shelter of visitors during showers. The Overlook will be in the shade of existing trees during the afternoon.

C The Greeting. Parallel and contiguous Drives, Rides, and Walks, under rows of trees, forming a Promenade or Meeting Ground of the Alameda type, half a mile in length. Monumental, architectural and various decorative adjuncts are here admissible but not essential. The Playstead and the Greeting are to be without underwood, and adapted, with electric lighting, for night as well as day use. Together they will form an unenclosed ground reaching across the Park, a mile in length.

D The Music Court. A sylvan amphitheatre adapted to concerts.

E The Little Folk's Fair. A division for childish entertainments, to be furnished with Swings, Scups, Seesaws, Sand Courts, Flying Horses, Toy Booths, Marionettes, Goat Carriages, Donkey Courses, Bear Pits, and other amusing exercises and exhibitions, mostly to be provided by lessees and licensed purveyors.

F The Deer Park. Range for a small herd, to be seen from the Greeting. Most of the ground, owing to the thinness of the soil over a flattish ledge, is little adapted to other Park uses.

G Refectory Hill. Refreshments to be principally served out of doors, under a large pergola or vine clad trellis, upon a terrace formed in the manner of the Playstead Overlook. Horse Sheds on the east side. Extended sylvan prospects from the terrace.

H Sargent's Field. Ball and Tennis Grounds.

I Long Crouch Woods. A Rambling Ground, with sheltered southwestern slopes, to be held subject to lease to a suitable organization, for a Zoological Garden.

J The Steading. A rocky, sterile knoll reserved for the Commissioners' offices.

K The Nursery. Depressed ground, to be used, when adequate drainage outlets for this part of the city shall have been provided, for a service garden.

Border Ground. Bounding streets are generally laid down on this plan as if moderately enlarged from the present thoroughfares (which at various points are but narrow lanes) and with a sidewalk on the Park side, at such varying distances from the wheelway as may be necessary to avoid, in forming them, the destruction of fine trees and excessive grading. This arrangement is made practicable by setting back Park fences and other obstructions fifty to eighty feet from the wheelways. Thus, also, a much larger widening of the wheelways than is suggested by the drawing can be made whenever public convenience will be served by it, without inordinate cost. In a few cases, for short distances, streets are shown as they may be improved by a slight taking of private land. This is to avoid heavy outlay for grading and the destruction of fine natural features on the Park side of the present roads. Forest Hills Street, at one point, is thrown wholly into the Park for greater directness. To avoid interruption of pleasure travel by funeral processions, and to improve passage around the Park, a short cross road is planned opposite Forest Hills Cemetery, tunneling under the Park drive (L.L. in the index map). A short new street in extension of Sigourney Street is suggested, to facilitate passage around the Park. A small piece of land is proposed to be taken into the Park at the corner of Sigourney Street, to avoid awkward complications. The land proposed to be thrown out of the Park property for all these purposes of street improvement is much larger than that to be taken in. Other roads within the Park being intended only for pleasure travel and Park work, one road is carried across it for the passage, day and night, of common street travel. It follows the line between the Country Park and the adjoining districts on the east, which is nearly the line of the present Glen Road.

GENERAL PLAN O

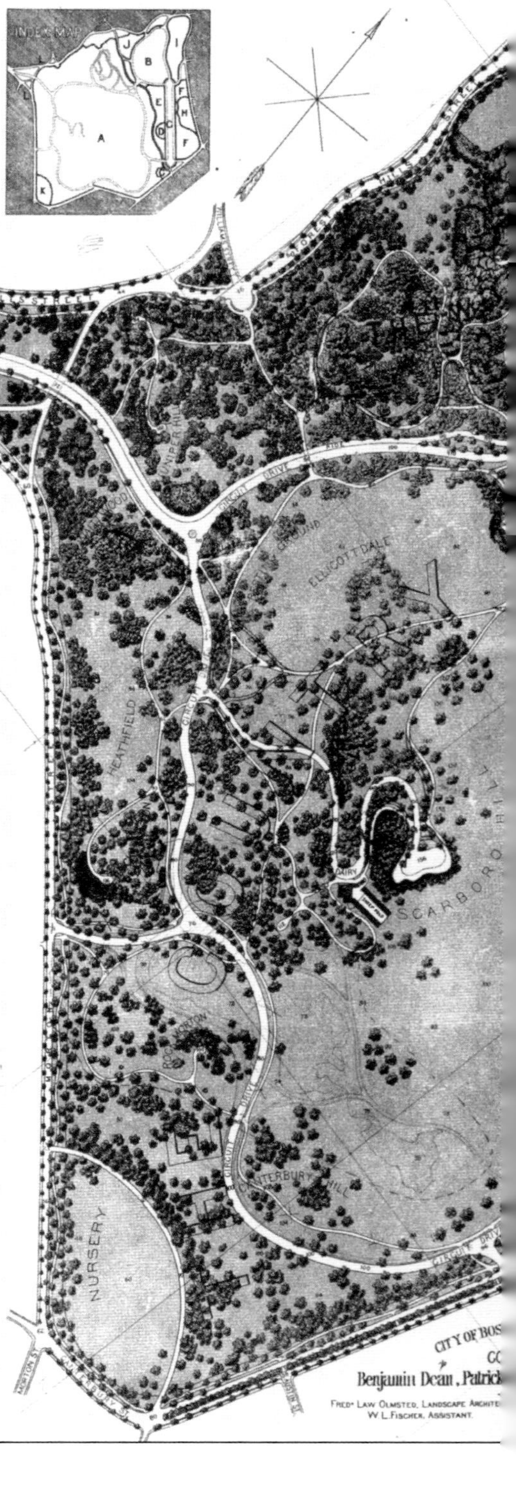

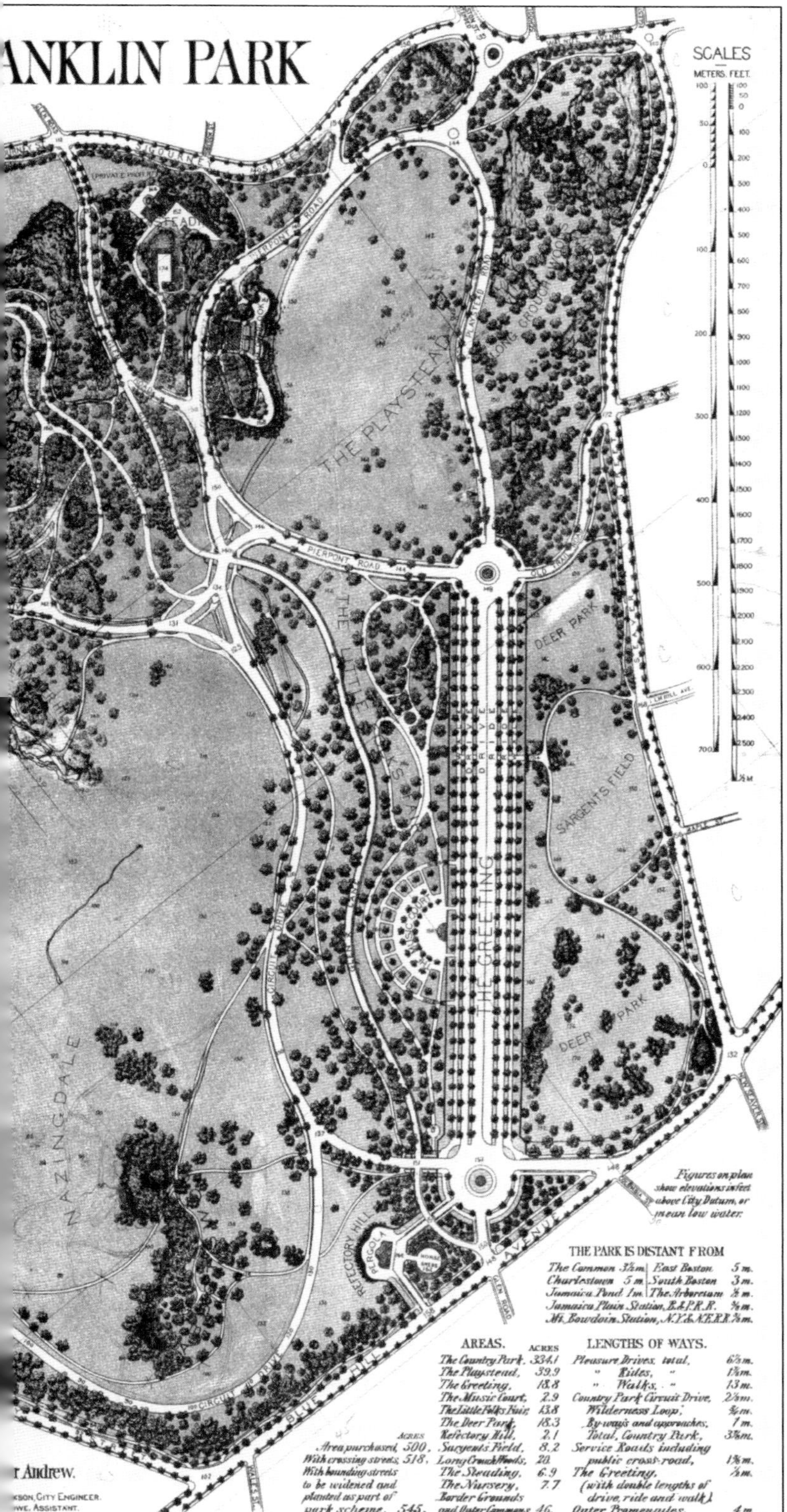

Frederick Law Olmsted worked on a number of projects in addition to the Boston Park System from 1878 to 1895. His studies of the West Roxbury Park landscape lasted through the early 1880s. The "General Plan of Franklin Park" was submitted to the Boston park commissioners in 1885. The general plan was sensitive not only to the design of the lands but also to the history of those who lived on it. Olmsted named many of the features and places for families that had long held property within the 527 acres of what would become Franklin Park. These areas include Schoolmaster Hill, Scarboro Pond, Hagbourne Hill, Ellicottdale, and Nazingdale. The general plan included Olmsted's intention for the major landscapes, including the Country Park and the Playstead, and smaller areas such as the Long Crouch Woods and Sargent's Field. (Courtesy of the National Park Service, Frederick Law Olmsted National Historic Site.)

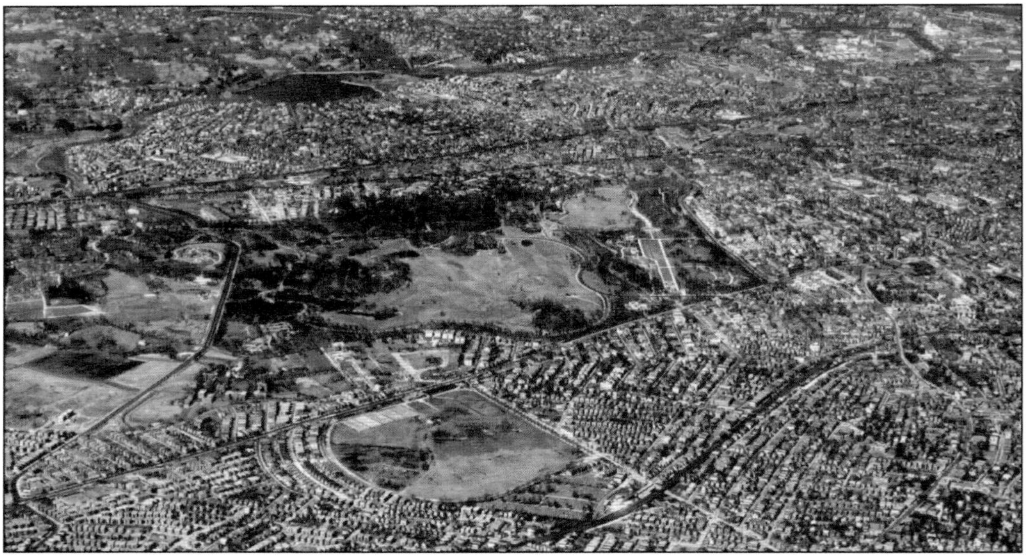

The Franklin Park Coalition and the City of Boston designed brochures for park visitors for various events, including the bicentennial and Boston 200. These maps were designed to allow visitors to take a self-guided tour of the features of the park. This map shows historical landmarks around the park, and the entire pamphlet shared information on the history of the park. These were handed out at park events and at visitors' centers around the Boston area. In the aerial shot, taken in 1925, it is obvious that Frederick Law Olmsted's basic designs were followed meticulously. (Above, courtesy of the Boston Public Library Print Department; below, courtesy of the Franklin Park Coalition.)

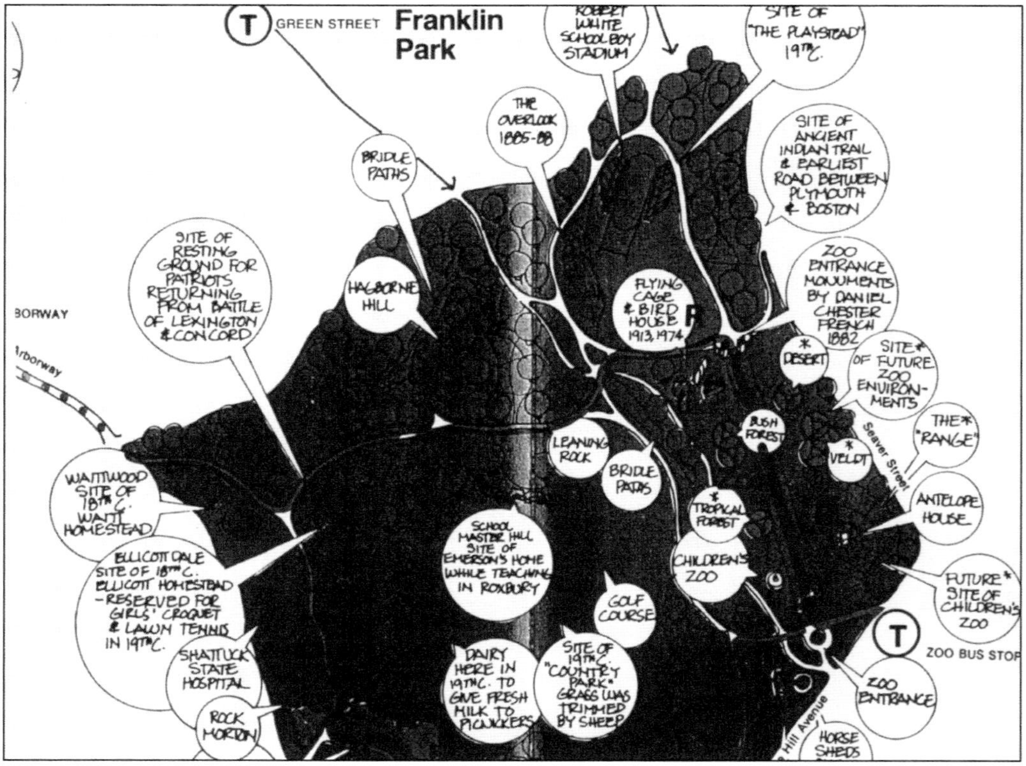

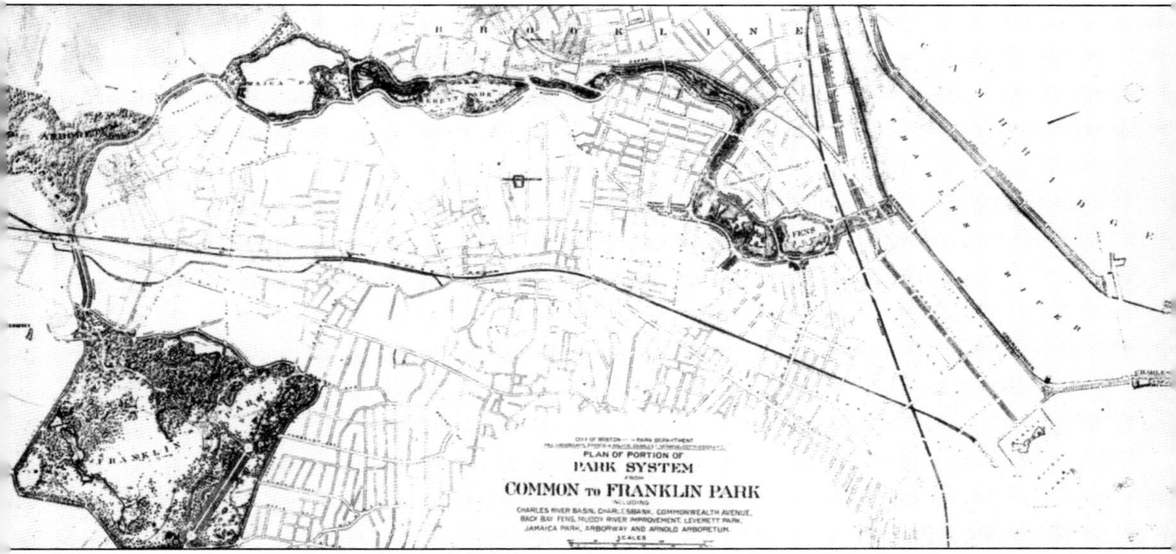

In designing the Boston Park System, Olmsted used a variety of existing elements, such as bodies of water and open space, in juxtaposition with engineering, architecture, science, and urban planning. The ultimate goal was to create a system of parks and parkways that could accommodate an array of users, including pedestrians, bicyclists, and carriages, with ease and provide all with urban respite. It is debatable whether another firm could have accomplished some of the feats completed in the Emerald Necklace. The Back Bay Fens, once a dumping ground and marsh, were turned into walking paths and tidal river pools for the fashionable Back Bay. Jamaica Pond, once a prominent location for ice harvesting, was designed with paths for meandering and a boathouse to rent rowboats and sailboats. The Arnold Arboretum, owned and operated by Harvard University, proved to be a marriage of scientific study and aesthetics. (Courtesy of the National Park Service, Frederick Law Olmsted National Historic Site.)

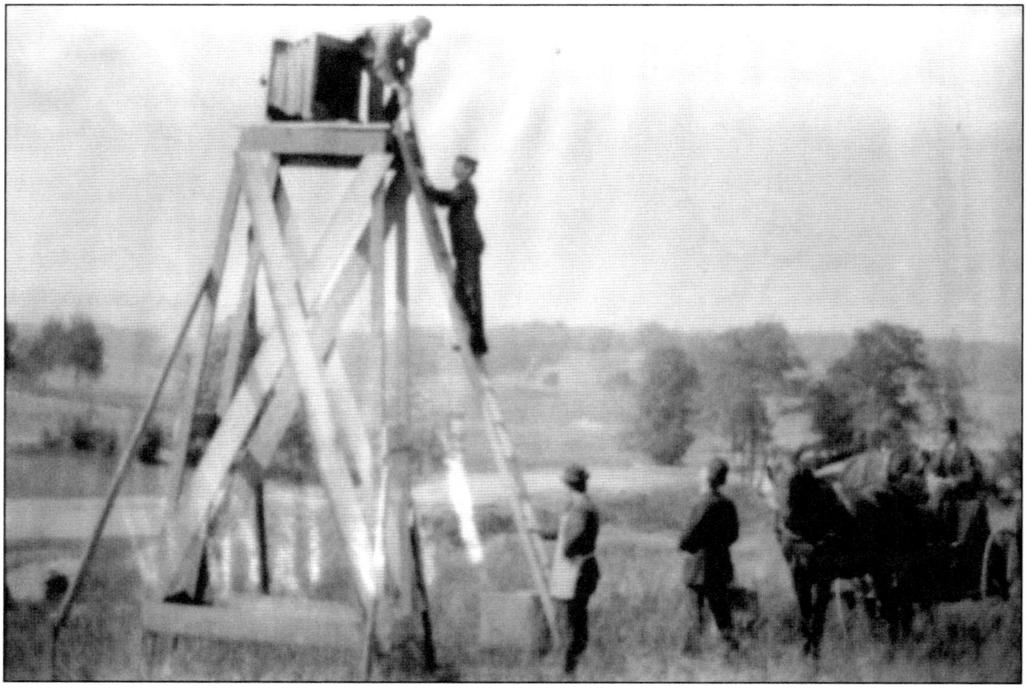

The Olmsted landscape architecture firm kept detailed records of plans in all forms, including photographs. Most projects were chronicled from the initial planning phases through the completion of construction. On October 18, 1892, D. W. Butterfield of Cambridgeport photographed Refectory Hill. Butterfield was one of the photographers throughout the 1890s in Frederick Law Olmsted's firm. (Courtesy of the National Park Service, Frederick Law Olmsted National Historic Site.)

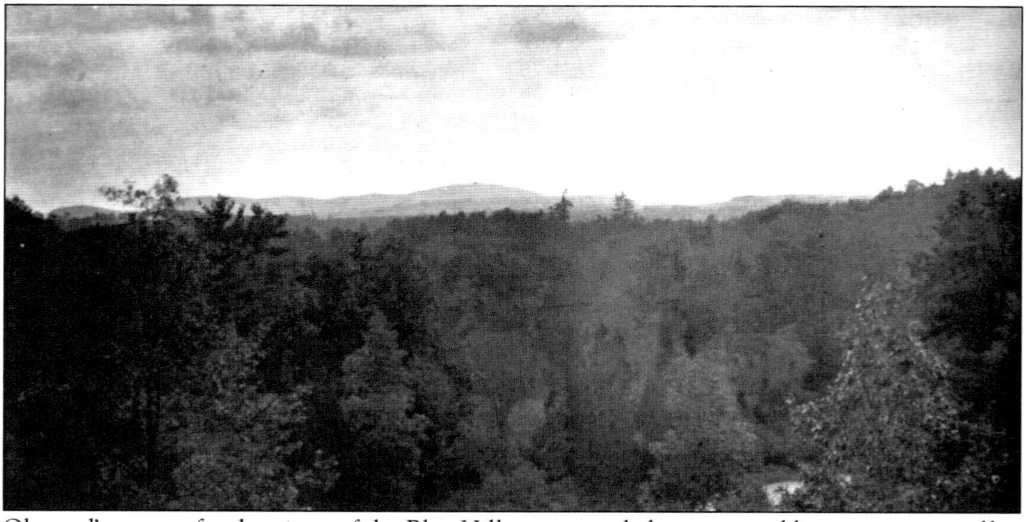

Olmsted's respect for the vistas of the Blue Hills was regarded in many publications as one of his finest design achievements in Franklin Park. Olmsted was enamored with the view. According to his "Notes on Franklin Park," he incorporated "them into the scenery with the greatest effect from many points of view, their noble, mountain-like undulations presenting in the stateliest of backgrounds." (Courtesy of the National Park Service, Frederick Law Olmsted National Historic Site.)

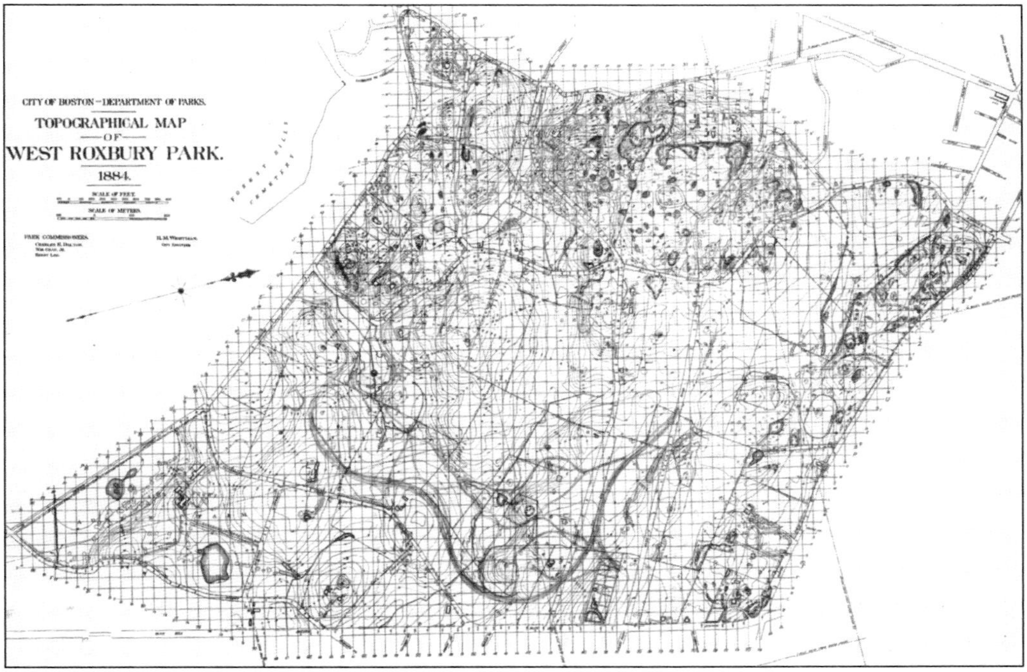

Olmsted wanted to keep aspects of the New England scenery while planning for future development around the park. His design included plantings along the roadsides. Soil had to be brought in to support this. Topographical surveys were completed in 1883. (Courtesy of the National Park Service, Frederick Law Olmsted National Historic Site.)

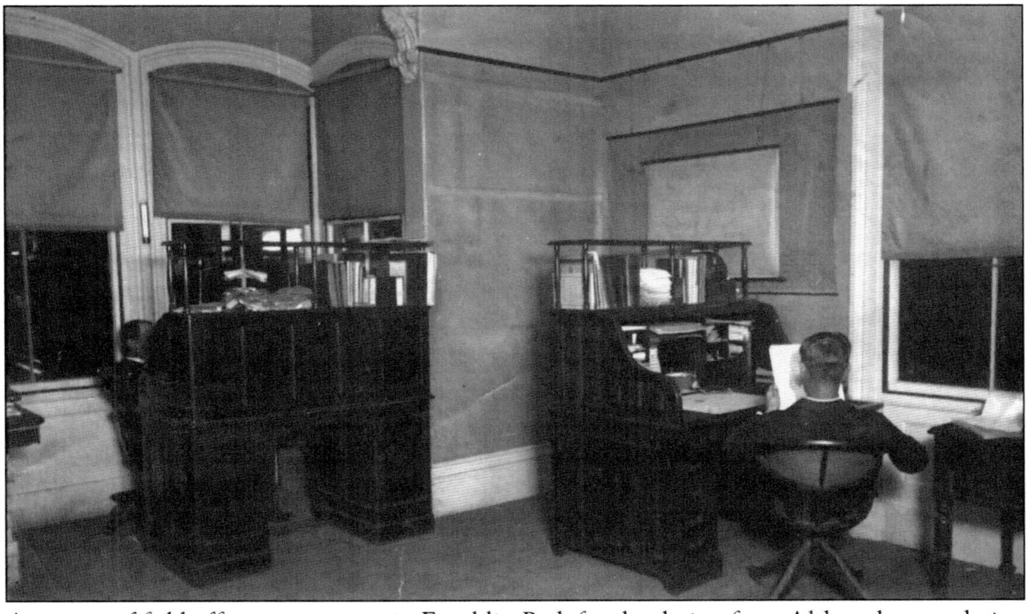

A variety of field offices were set up in Franklin Park for the design firm. Although most design work was completed at Fairsted, implementation was easiest from field offices. This office was located inside the Williams House that served as offices for both the Olmsted firm and various construction companies from 1886 to 1898, when it was razed.

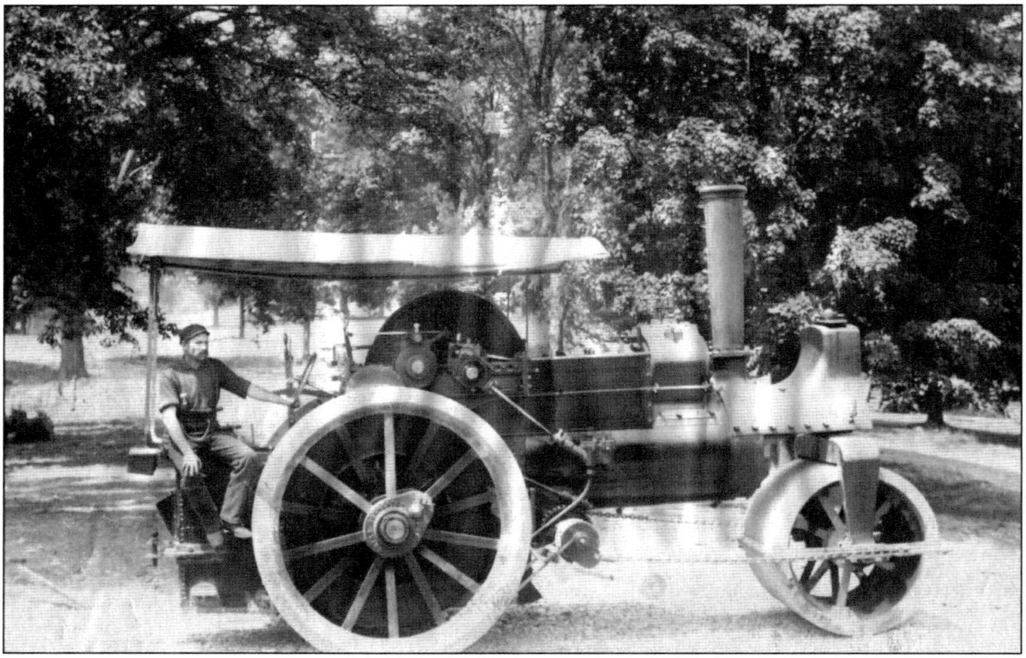

The ease of construction for the Boston Park System was due to a variety of factors, including burgeoning technology and an influx of immigrant laborers. According to the 1890 annual report of the Boston park commissioners, this 15-ton steamroller was purchased and was "of great assistance in the construction of roads and walks." (Courtesy of the National Park Service, Frederick Law Olmsted National Historic Site.)

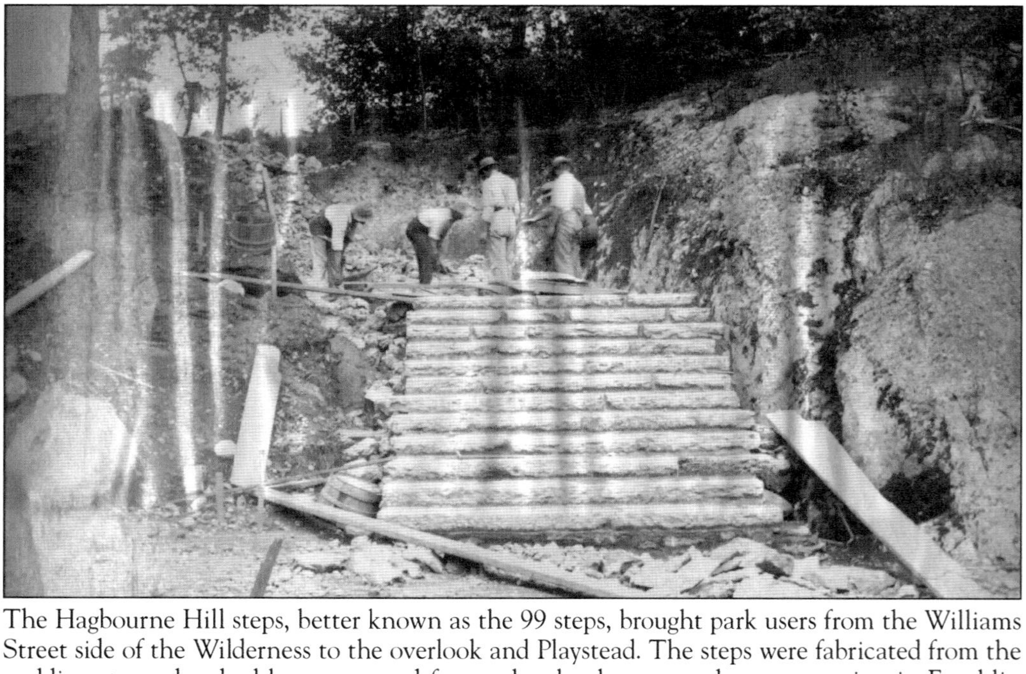

The Hagbourne Hill steps, better known as the 99 steps, brought park users from the Williams Street side of the Wilderness to the overlook and Playstead. The steps were fabricated from the pudding stone that had been removed from other landscapes under construction in Franklin Park. Construction was completed in 1892. (Courtesy of the National Park Service, Frederick Law Olmsted National Historic Site.)

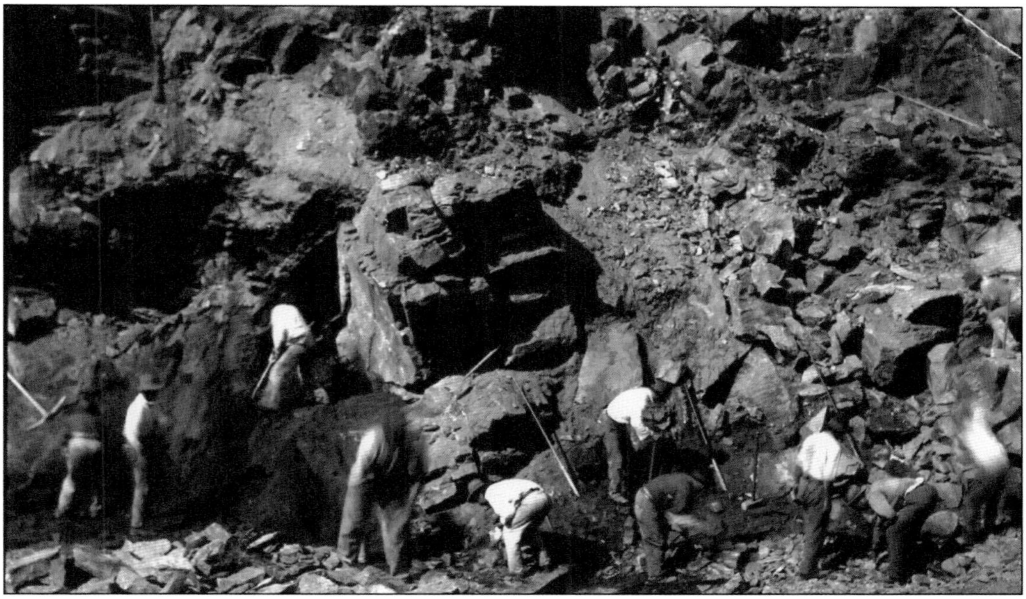

Roxbury pudding stone was used to enhance the rustic features of Franklin Park. This type of conglomerate is only found in this part of the world. Oliver Wendell Holmes immortalized pudding stone in his poem "The Dorchester Giant." "They flung it over to Roxbury hills, They flung it over the plain, And all over Milton and Dorchester too; Great lumps of pudding the giants threw; They tumbled as thick as rain."

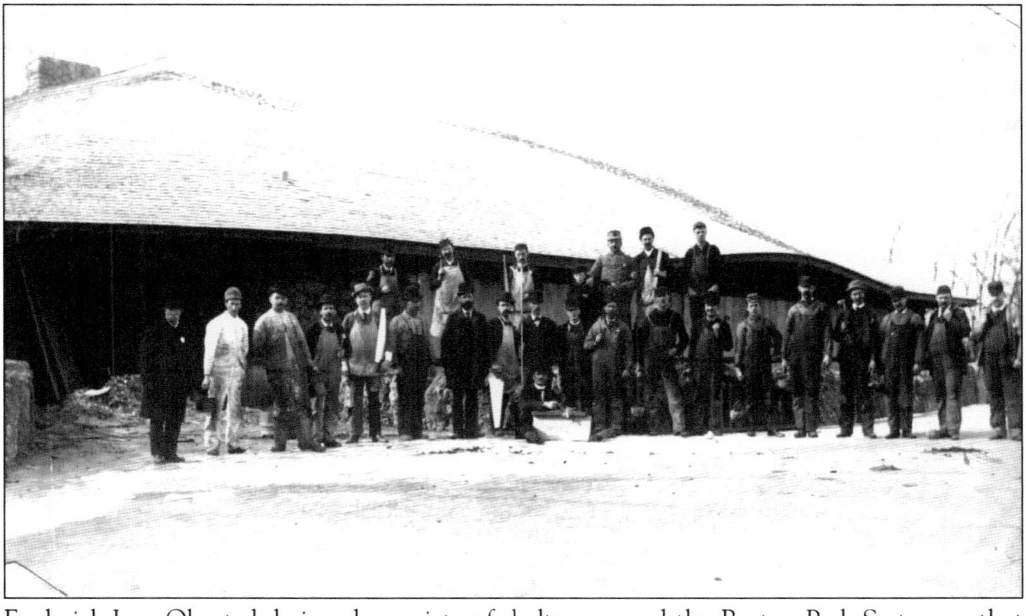

Frederick Law Olmsted designed a variety of shelters around the Boston Park System so that users could have access to a variety of conveniences. His designs included multiuse facilities, such as the overlook shelter, that were appropriate to whichever park they were located in. These facilities provided lavatories, locker rooms, refreshments, places to rent equipment, and headquarters for park police.

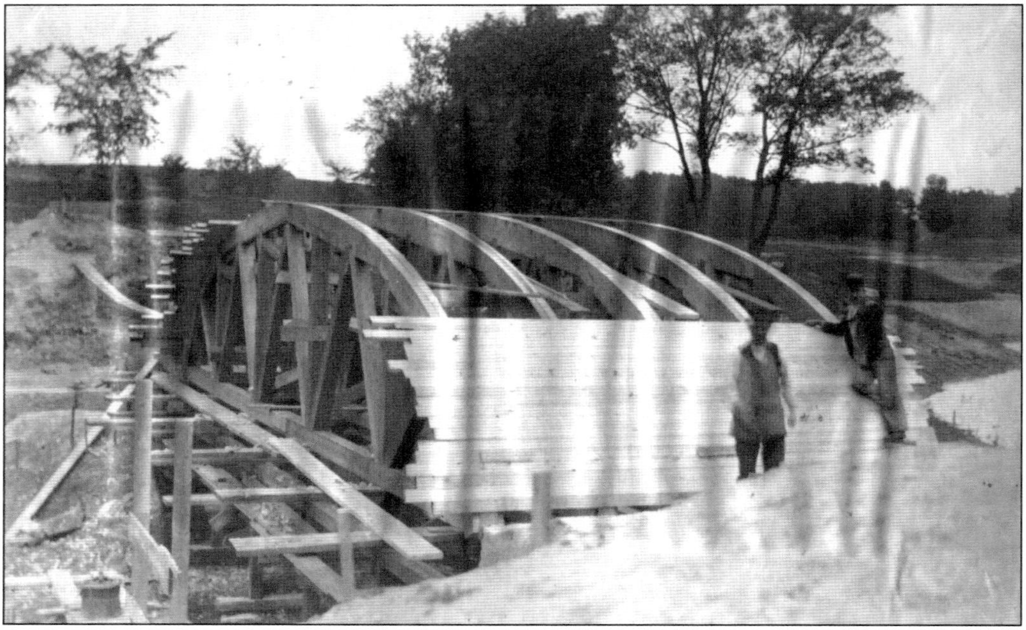

H. H. Richardson was a Boston architect famous for his use of the Romanesque style. He and Frederick Law Olmsted shared a close relationship, and it is believed that Richardson influenced Olmsted's move to Boston. His successor firm, Shepley, Ruttan, and Coolidge, designed the bridges over Scarboro Pond and the Funeral Bridge in Franklin Park. (Courtesy of the National Park Service, Frederick Law Olmsted National Historic Site.)

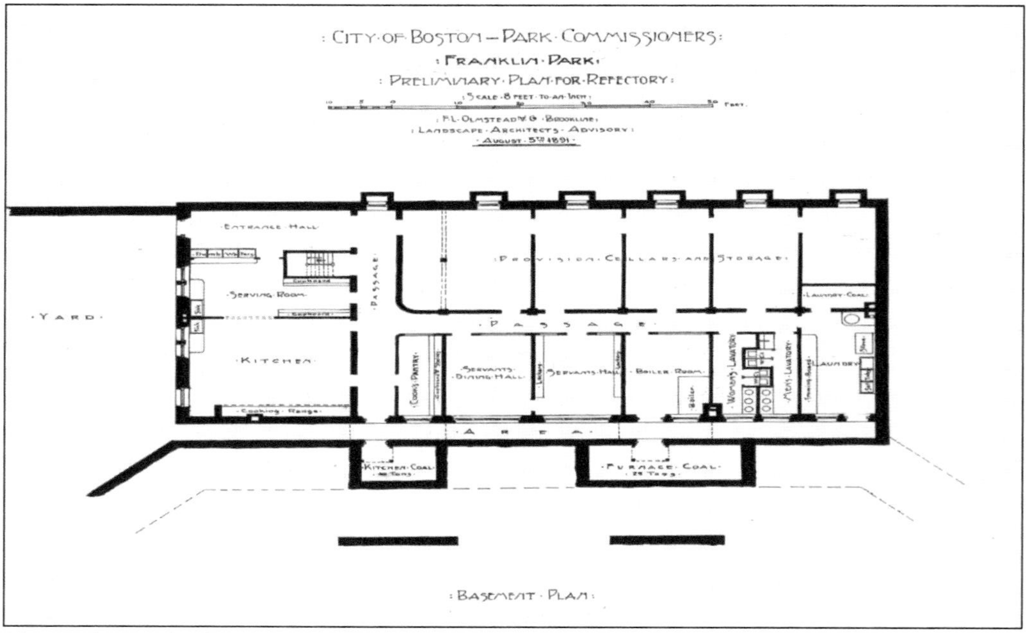

The Refectory building served a multitude of purposes for the Franklin Park community in its 80-year history. The building served as both a public library branch and an open-air home for sick children in the early 20th century. It was mainly used for its intended design and purpose—as a place for refreshments—until 1974. (Courtesy of the National Park Service, Frederick Law Olmsted National Historic Site.)

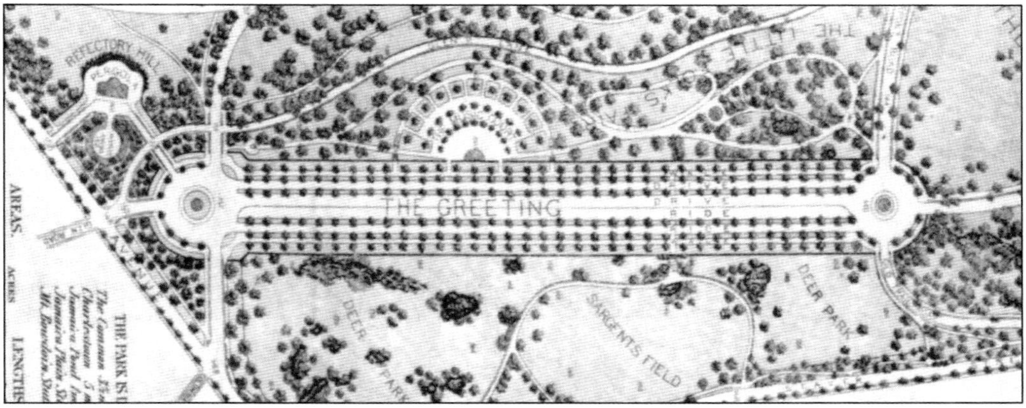

The Franklin Park Zoo was the last major change to Olmsted's plans. Arthur Shurtleff designed the zoo. The first exhibits opened in October 1912, and construction based on the original plans lasted into the 1930s. Further renovations in the latter part of the 20th century have changed the zoo dramatically from its initial design. (Courtesy of the Massachusetts Historical Society.)

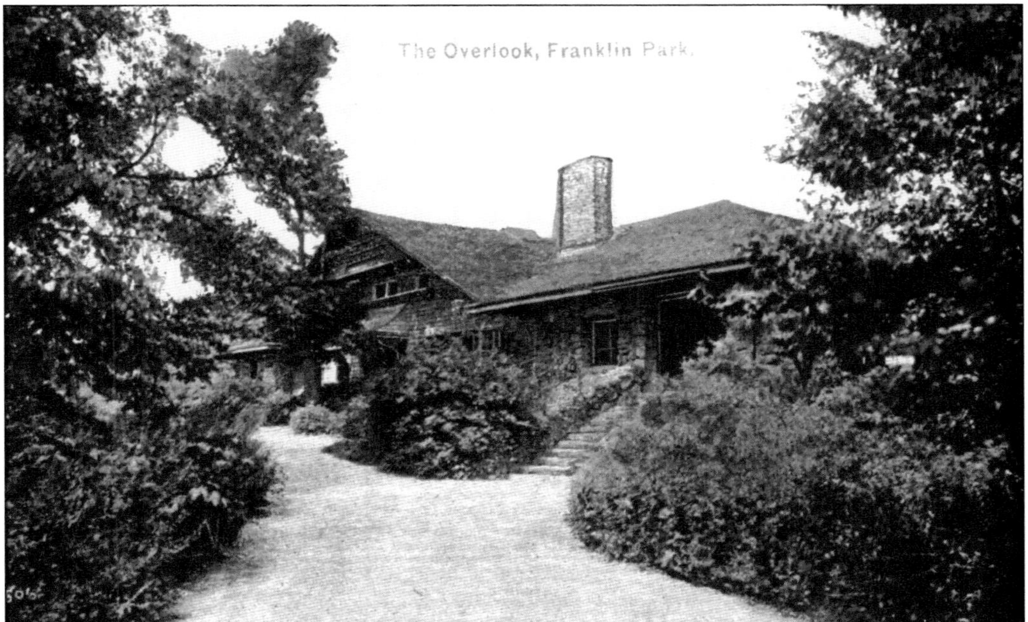

Before the designs in the park were fully realized, Franklin Park was a destination for local Bostonians and many New Englanders. On the back of this postcard, Etta writes, "We have been in this building more than once. Wish you could be here to go with me this summer. It is lovely in this park. Will send you another view of the same park."

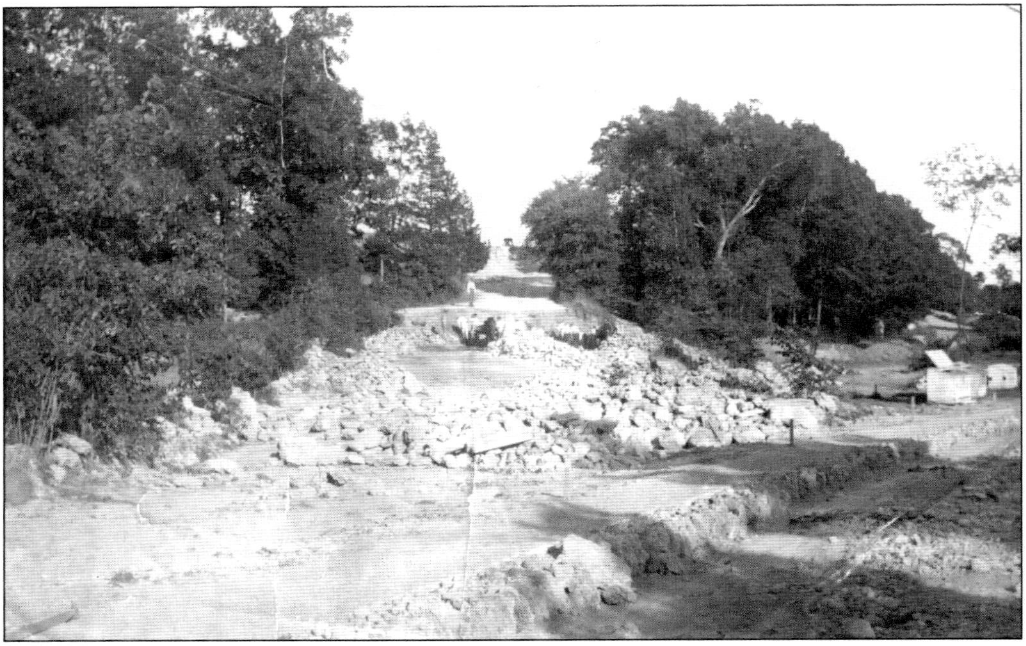

Tons of rocks were removed from various areas of the park. Much of the refuse was used to build walls, steps, and bridges. Drinking fountains on the overlook, in Abbotswood, and on Schoolmaster Hill were designed using blasting refuse from around the park and planted with native vines. The 99 steps were constructed with crushed rocks that were removed from the Playstead. The bridges over Scarboro Pond were reinforced with pudding stone that was removed from Ellicottdale and the quarry. The rocks were removed using large chains pulled by horses or oxen. Balanced Rock is considered one of the most famous rocks in Franklin Park. Its bottom rests on a ledge of pudding stone.

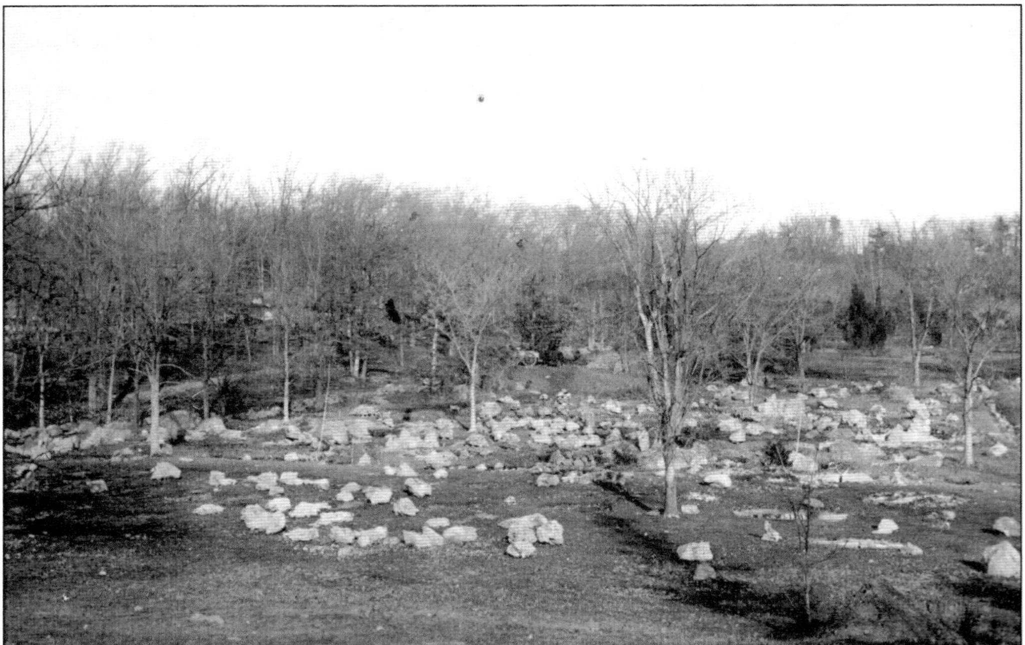

Two

The Country Park

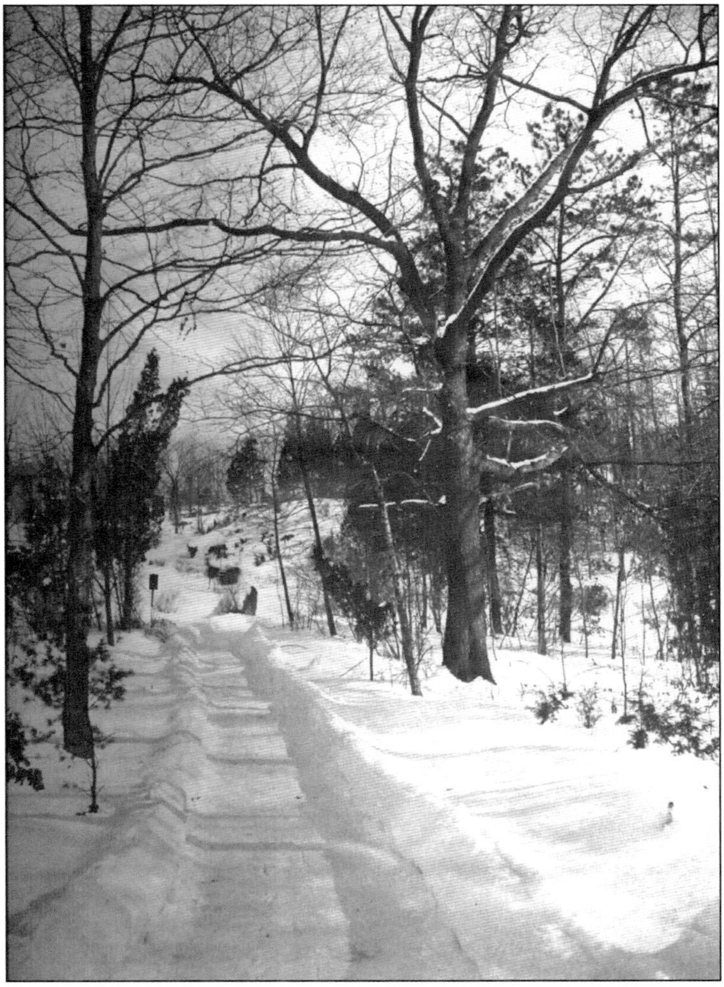

In the "General Plan of Franklin Park," the Wilderness was supposed "to provide opportunity for a form of recreation to be obtained only through the influence of pleasing natural scenery upon the sensibilities of those quietly contemplating it. . . . Nothing shall be built, nothing set up, nothing planted as a decorative feature, nothing for the gratification of curiosity, nothing for the advancement or popularization of science." (Courtesy of the National Park Service, Frederick Law Olmsted National Historic Site.)

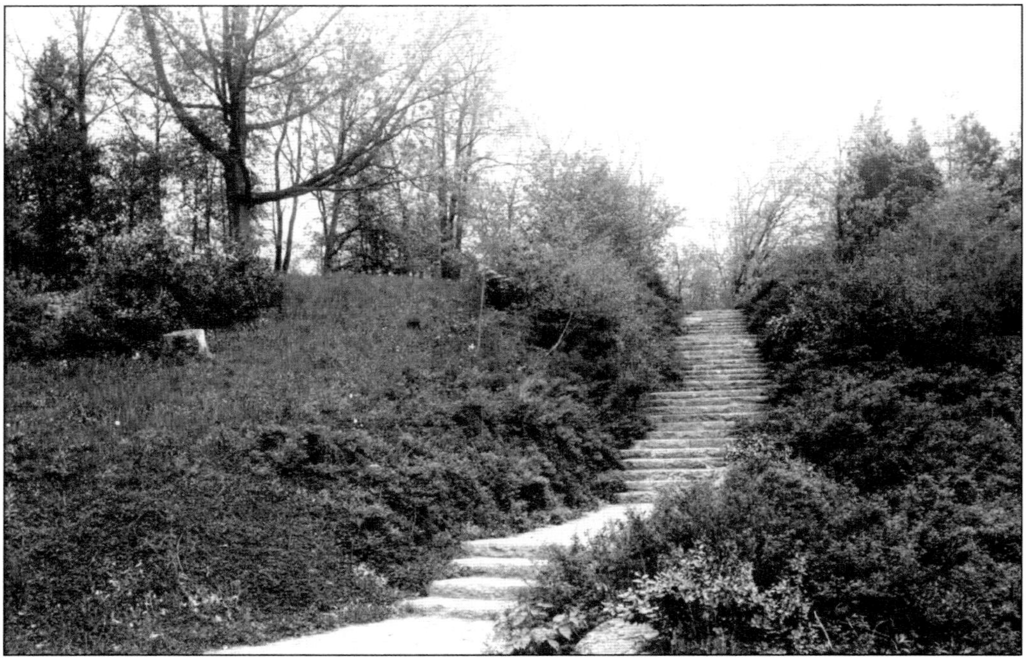

One hundred acres of the Country Park are encapsulated in the Wilderness, named for the "rocky wilderness area" on 18th-century maps of the Roxbury area. The area was rarely logged and never farmed and therefore offers an impression of how Roxbury may have been perceived in the 1630s. Frederick Law Olmsted used this land to create a typical New England forest and made few changes to the area other than enhancing existing plantings and pathways. After Olmsted's retirement, John Pettigrew removed many of Olmsted's "exotic" plantings and added thousands of trees and shrubs that were native to New England and would require little maintenance. (Above, courtesy of the National Park Service, Frederick Law Olmsted National Historic Site; below, courtesy of the Franklin Park Coalition.)

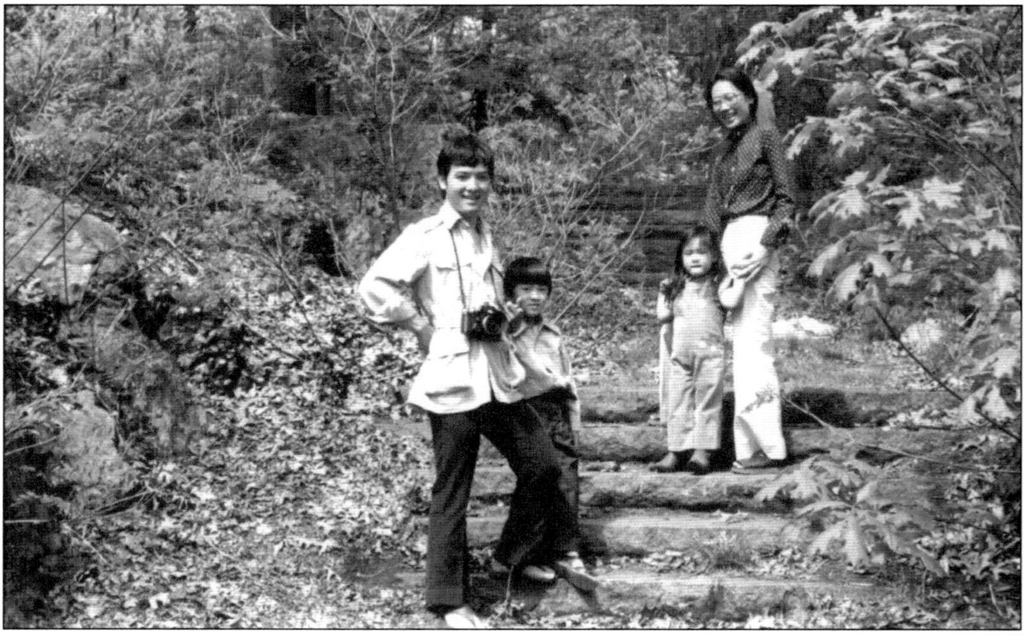

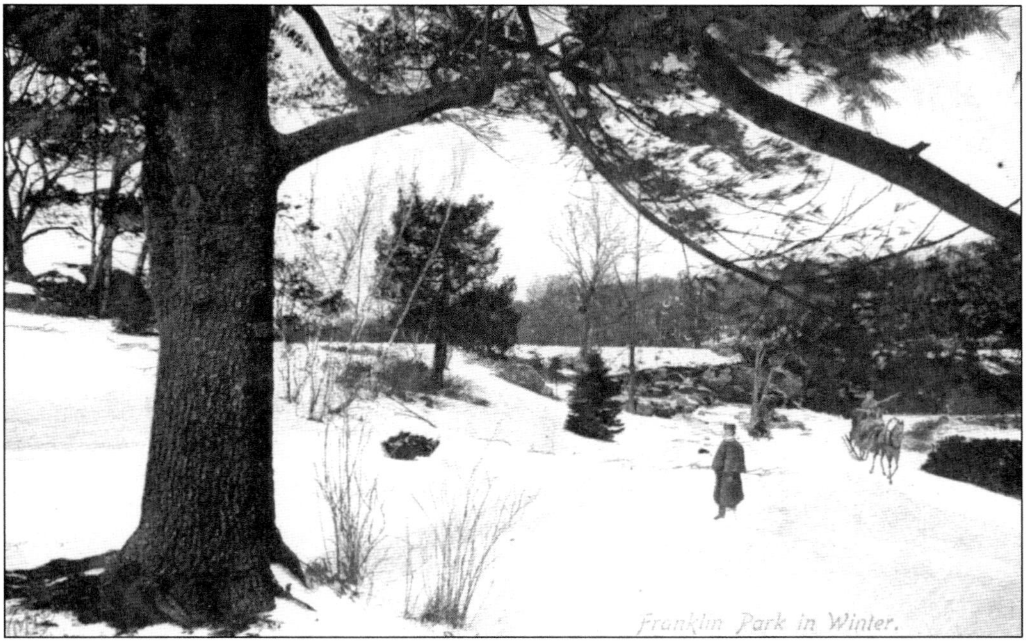

A sleigh ride captures the romance of winter. Frank Bonnelle's poem "The Winter Brook in Franklin Park," published in the *Boston Herald Traveler* in February 1899 reads, "Just now the snow lies deep within the woods; the fleecy flakes through branches downward shift; and all the stones and stumps wear caps and hoods; yet still the little brook its voice doth lift." (Courtesy of the National Park Service, Frederick Law Olmsted National Historic Site.)

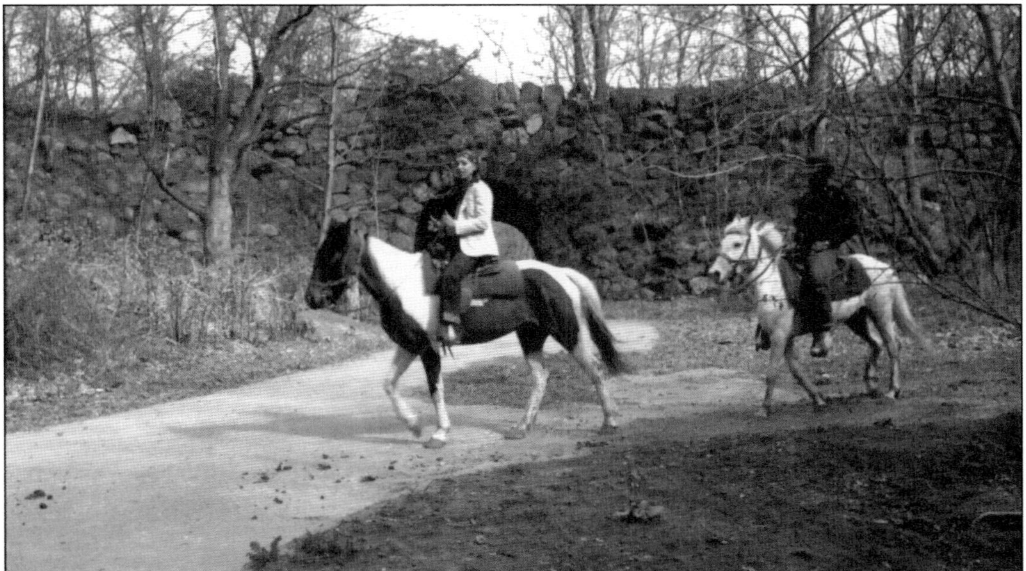
Olmsted envisioned a bridle path that would extend from the Back Bay into Franklin Park. He also planned for "a riding course in the Greeting . . . adjoining the carriage promenade" and a path through the Wilderness for riders. Stables, with horses and equipment available for nominal fees, were located in Jamaica Plain, just outside the park boundaries. (Courtesy of the Franklin Park Coalition.)

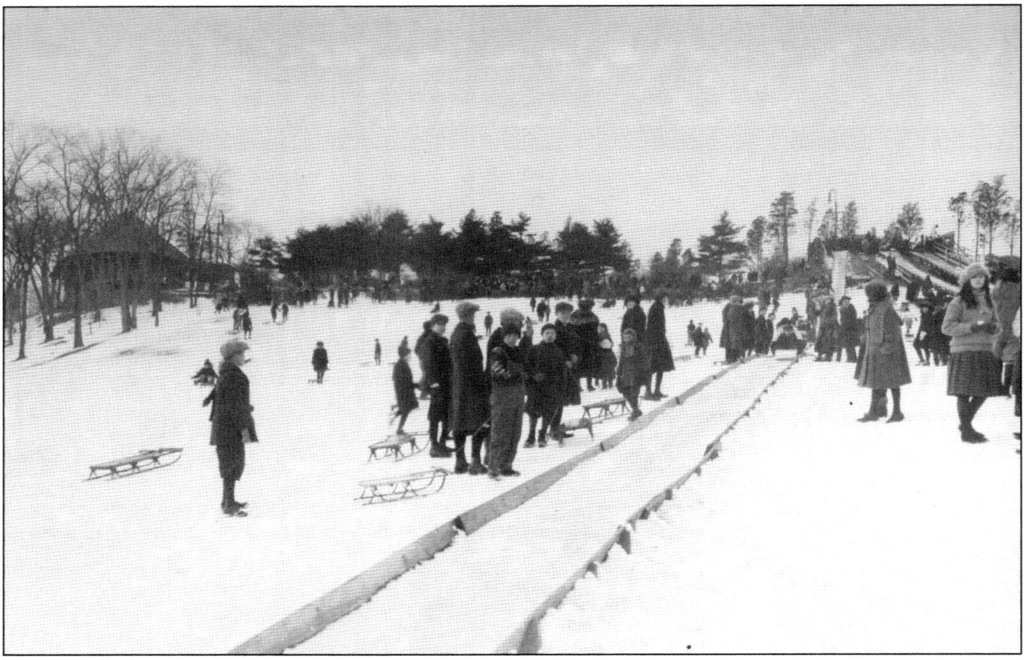

Franklin Park was a year-round recreation ground. In order to compete with an ice-skating rink in nearby Franklin Field, the Boston Park Department installed a toboggan run on Schoolmaster Hill in 1902. The runs were constructed of wood and featured stairs that made it easy to climb to the top of the hill. (Courtesy of the Boston Public Library Print Department.)

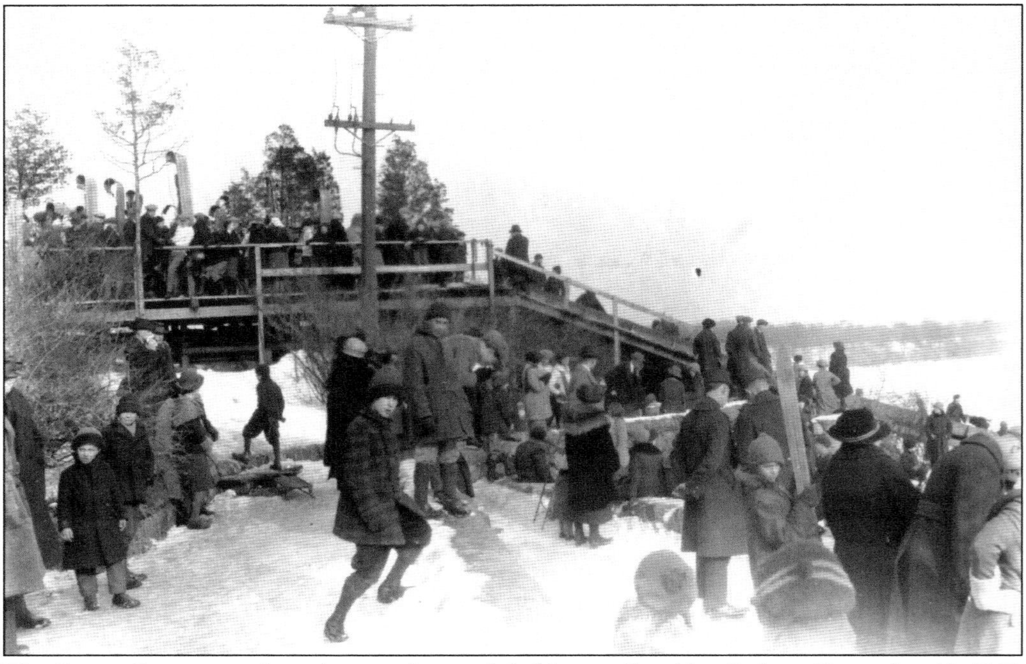

The *Boston Post* reported on the popularity of sledding in Franklin Park on December 18, 1917. "Tobogganing has been one of the most patronized sports at the park for years and the department is to make ample provision for the entertainment of the devotees of the sport." (Courtesy of the Boston Public Library Print Department.)

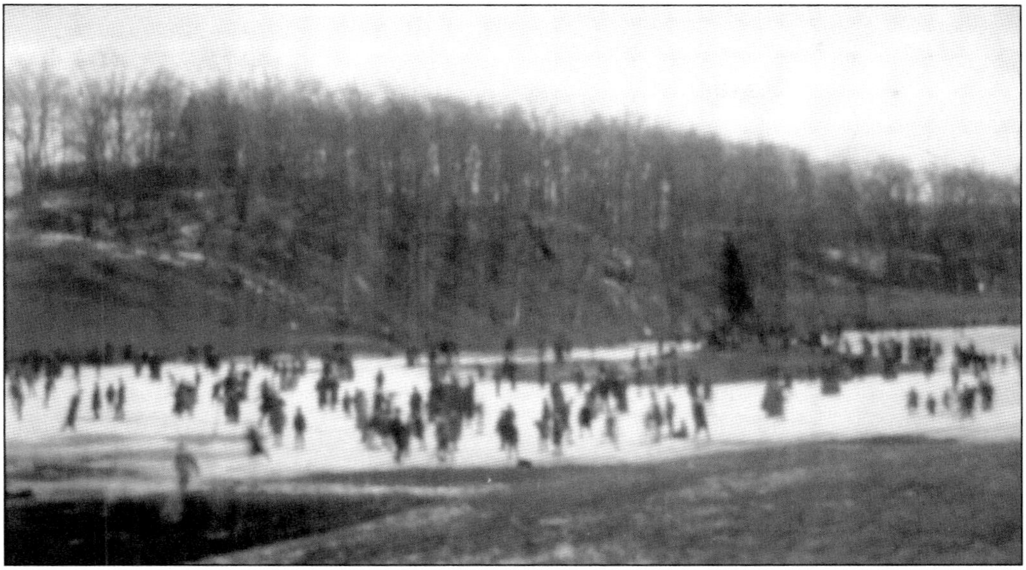

Before Franklin Field was constructed in 1894, ice sports were popular in Franklin Park. The area known as Nazingdale would naturally flood. Hundreds of skaters enjoyed the area on a daily basis. When Scarboro Pond was built, it was engineered to be filled with eight feet of water in the summer to accommodate boats and fishing. In the winter, the water was lowered to four feet to allow the water to freeze faster and make it safe for skaters. The water was regulated from an outlet near Morton Street. John Pettigrew ordered the removal of this pumping station, which rendered the Scarboro Pond system inoperable. Nonetheless, hockey, ice-skating, and curling remained popular among the gamut of recreational activities available in Franklin Park during the winter months. (Above, courtesy of the National Park Service, Frederick Law Olmsted National Historic Site; below, courtesy of the Franklin Park Coalition.)

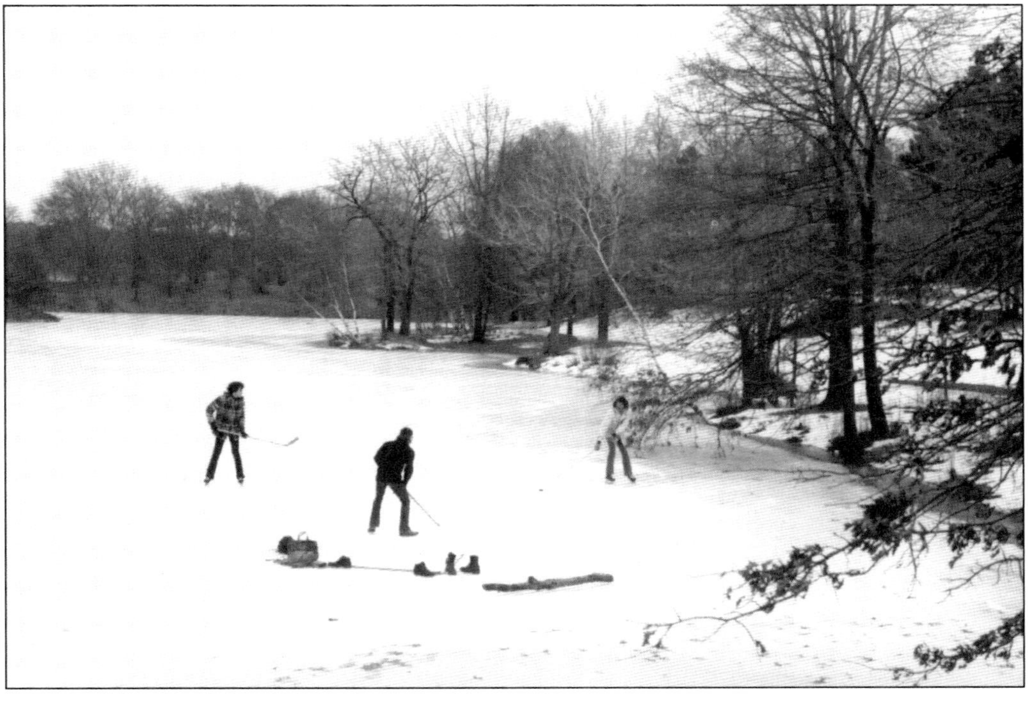

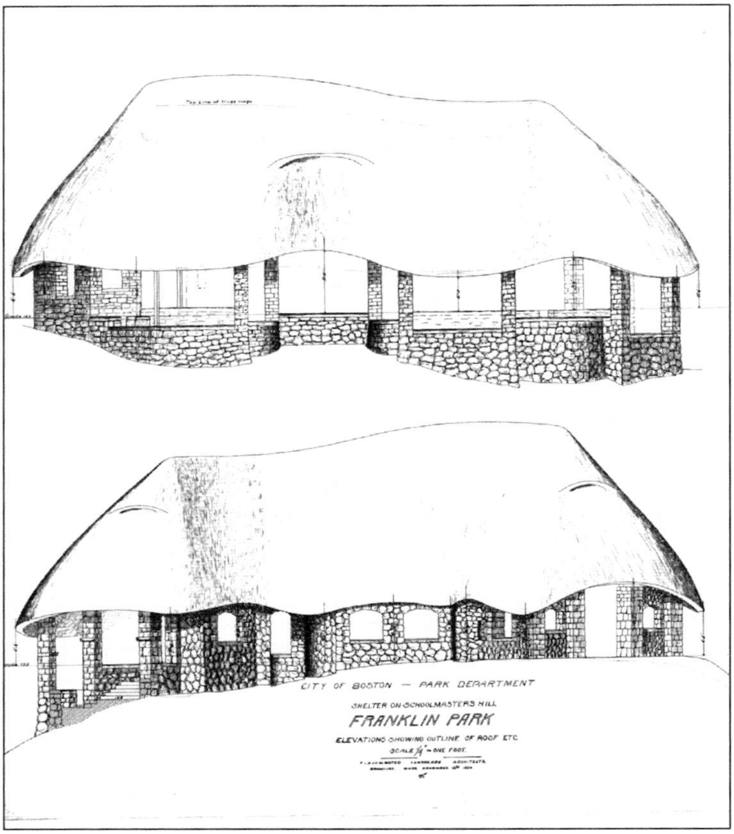

The Schoolmaster Hill terrace opened in 1892. It was "covered by vines on trellises, and furnished with tables and seats. . . . The arbors are intended especially for the use of family basket parties. A small house placed among them, to contain [a superintendent's] office . . ., a parcel room and closets, and at which, hot water for making tea can be had without charge." (Courtesy of the National Park Service, Frederick Law Olmsted National Historic Site.)

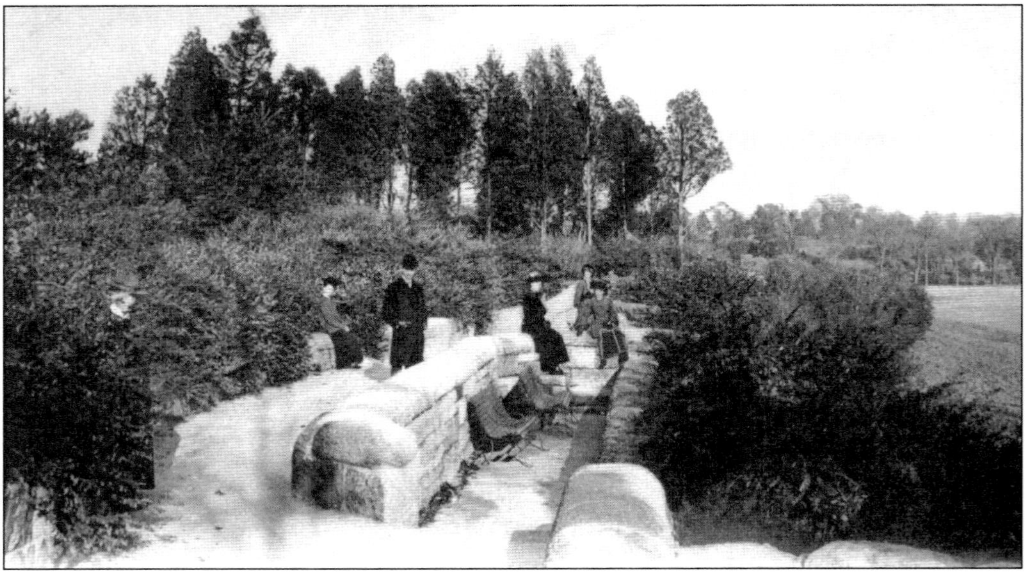

The terrace proved to be a fashionable promenade in the park. From here, people could enjoy views of the pastoral Country Park, scattered with sheep, or enjoy a picnic in one of the private nooks built into the hill. Red cedars were planted around Schoolmaster Hill in 1900, adding to the stunning landscape in the Country Park. (Courtesy of the National Park Service, Frederick Law Olmsted National Historic Site.)

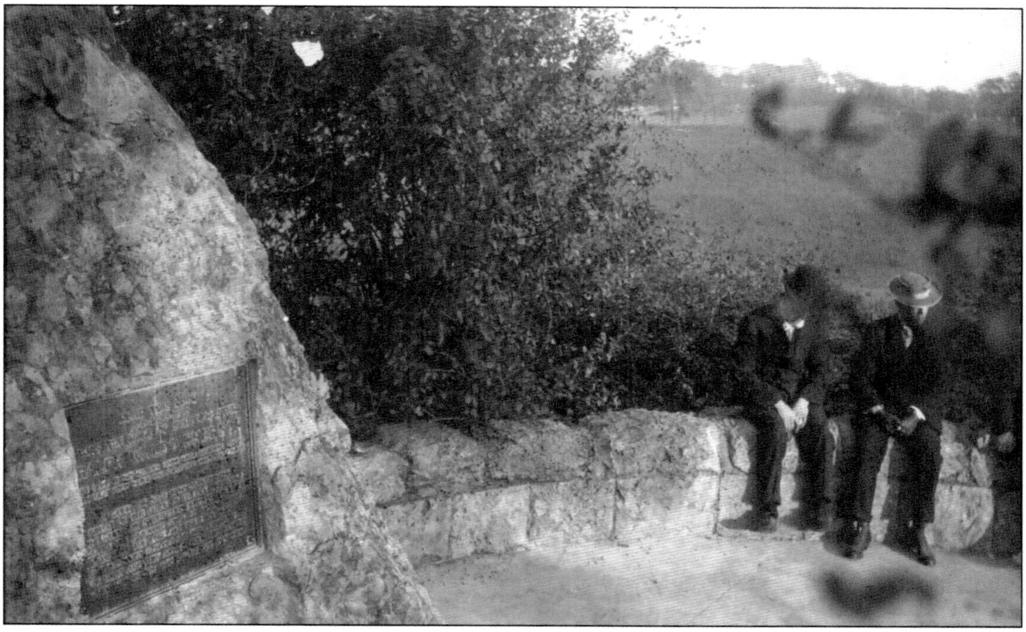

Ralph Waldo Emerson was a schoolmaster in Roxbury from 1823 to 1828. He rented property from Stedman Williams. Emerson wrote, "I stand beneath the same rocks, I touch the same greensward and my heart is exhilarated by the selfsame scenery by which the patriarch of the infant world pitched their tenets, or the herald angels unfolded their wings when they came down from heaven." The dedication plaque was set in 1896. (Courtesy of Historic New England.)

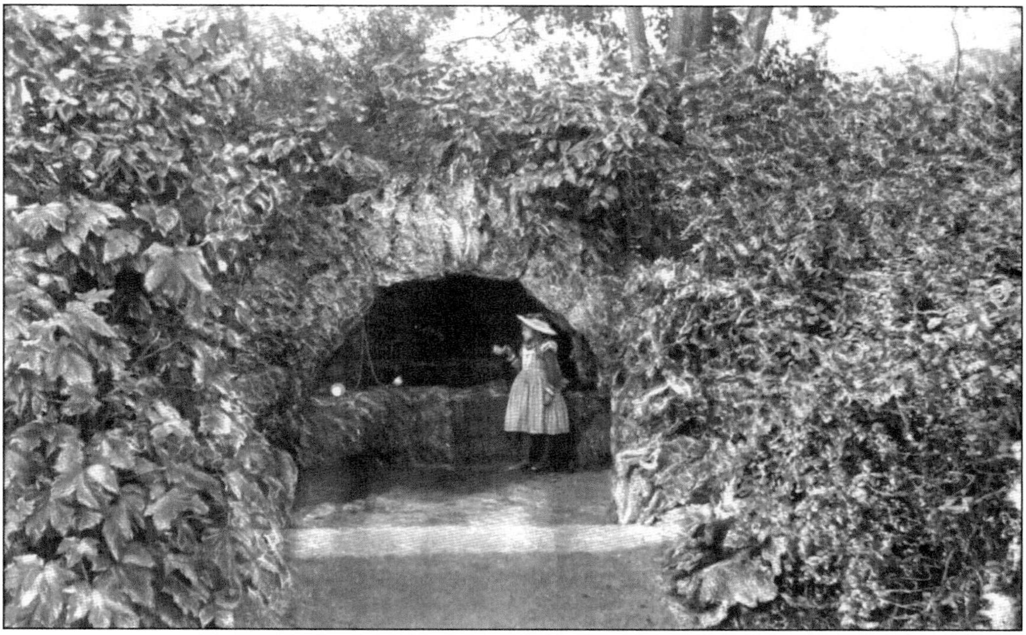

In the April 1898 issue of *American Architecture and Building News*, the drinking fountains in Franklin Park were rated as the "utilitarian equipment of the place, but like other features of that equipment, an artistic character is demanded. Interesting examples are . . . formed of rough stonework and adorned with climbing plants." (Courtesy of the National Park Service, Frederick Law Olmsted National Historic Site.)

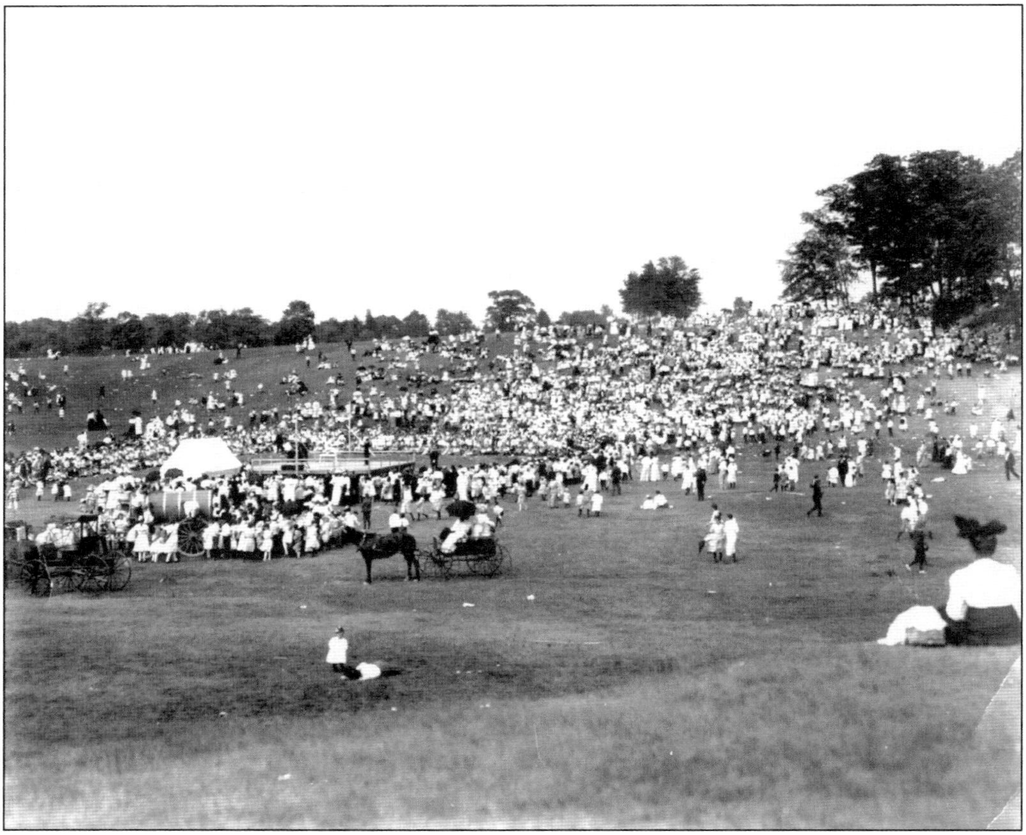

Franklin Park was the venue of choice for large festivals and picnics. Whether it was a large gathering of Irish Catholics from nearby Dorchester or a Mother's Day celebration orchestrated by Mayor James Michael Curley in 1903, the Country Park afforded its users unsurpassed beauty and space. Franklin Field was designed nearby to accommodate large public gatherings after they were banned without permits in 1891. These events are not banned today and draw tens of thousands to the park in the warm weather months and include rides, parades, games, music, and dance. (Above, courtesy of the National Park Service, Frederick Law Olmsted National Historic Site; below, courtesy of the Franklin Park Coalition.)

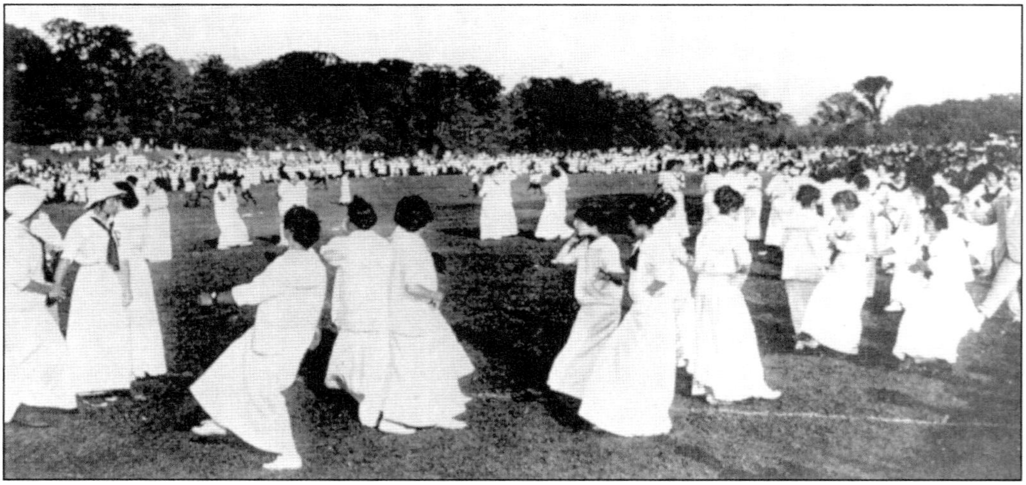

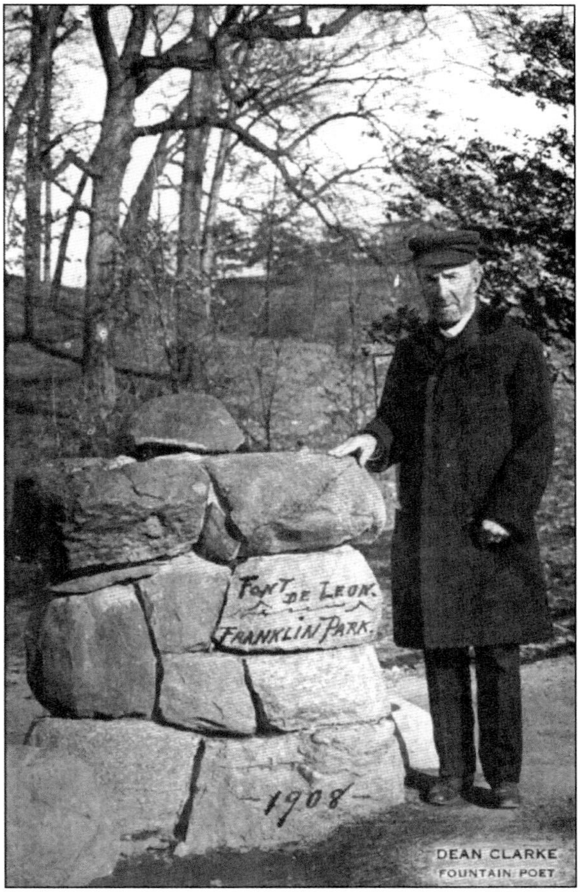

In 1906, this pudding stone fountain was installed at the site of a spring in Abbottswood. For years, the "healing spring" was believed to have special restorative qualities. For many neighbors who did not have running water in their homes, the spring and fountain were sources of water. After a dysentery outbreak in 1908, John Pettigrew blocked the fountain and ordered the spring to be rerouted into the ground. The Victorian name for this area is Mother's Rest. The area has recently been refurbished. The benches have been replaced, and weeds and trees that crowded the area were removed. (Below, courtesy of Jerry Burke.)

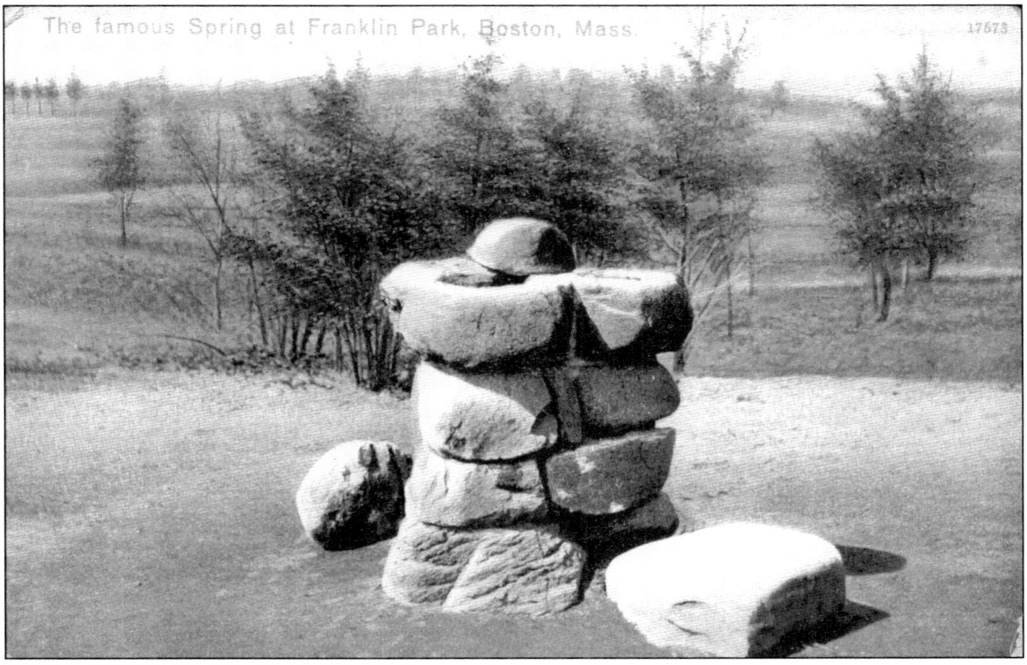

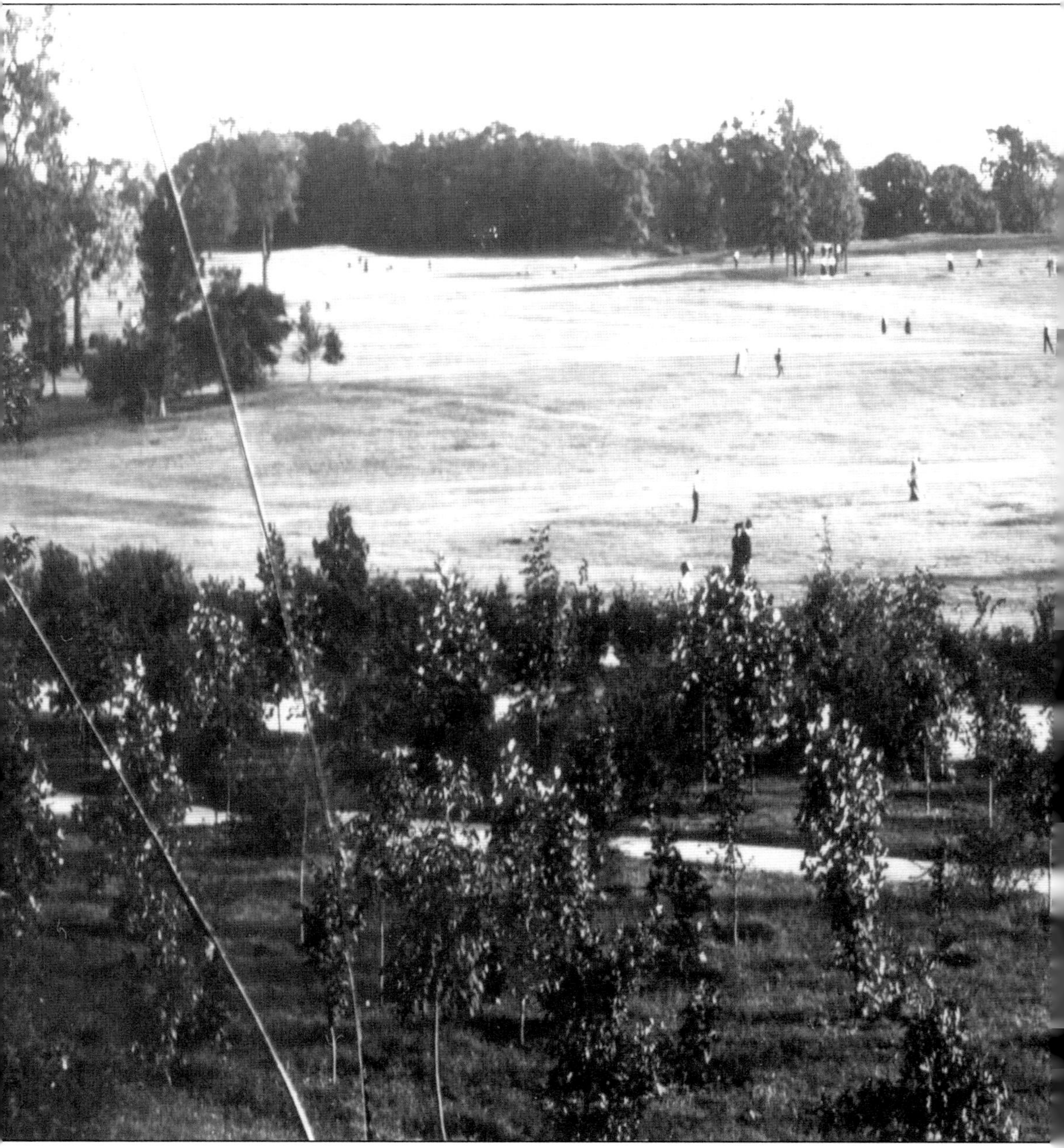

Around 1890, a mysterious set of balls and clubs arrived with cricket supplies at Wright and Ditson's Sporting Goods Store. George Wright, a former shortstop for the Cincinnati Red Stockings and co-owner of the shop, created a display with the items. A local Scotsman saw the display and inquired about the location of local links. Since Wright had no knowledge of the game, the man drew a picture of an ideal course and shared instructions for play. Wright received permission from the City of Boston to play his first round of golf on December 10, 1890,

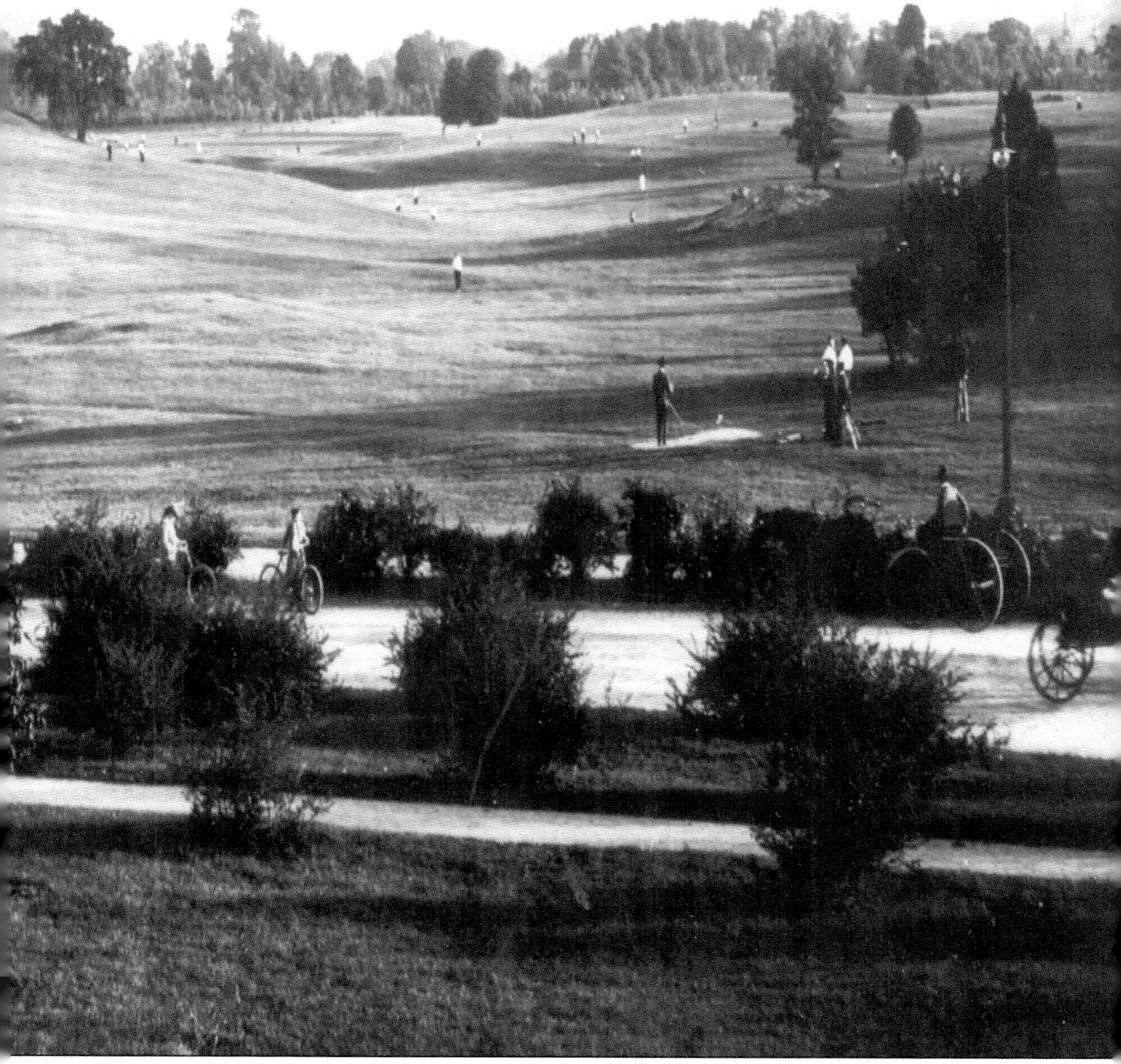

with Sam Donald, Fred Marshfield, and Temple Craig. J. B. Smith was the scorer. He made the holes in the frozen ground and put up red flannel flags. It is generally accepted that this is the first game of golf played in the United States, and definitely the first played in Boston. The first official course was laid out in 1896. By 1900, 40,000 played golf in Franklin Park. (Courtesy of the National Park Service, Frederick Law Olmsted National Historic Site.)

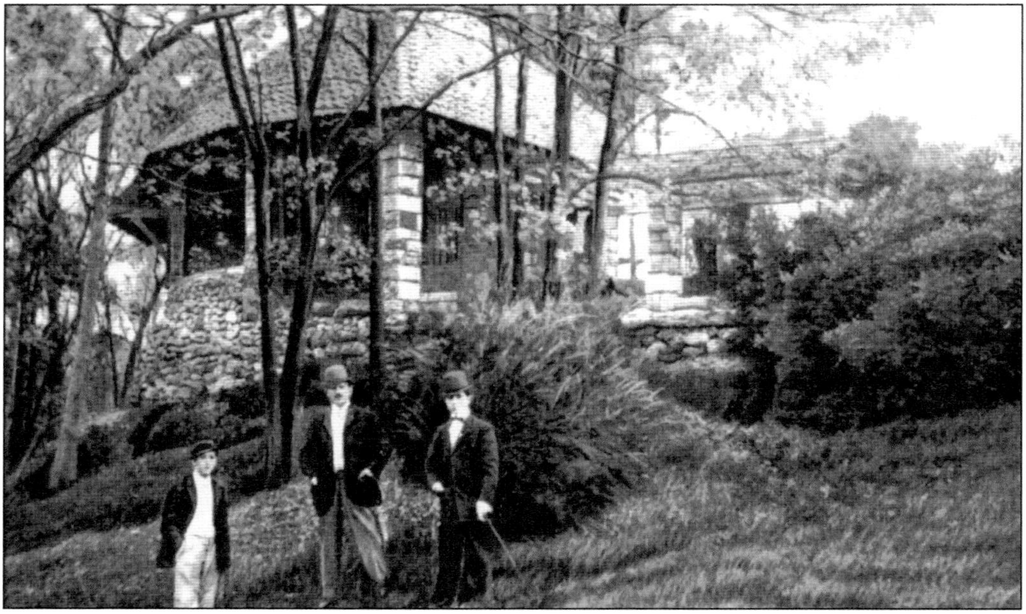

Willie Campbell was the first golf professional at Franklin Park and was responsible for the design of the first official course in 1901. His wife, Georgina, was the custodian of 450 lockers in the golf clubhouse, which opened on Schoolmaster Hill on July 14, 1901. She was also the first female golf professional. The Campbells began golfing at Franklin Park in 1896. (Courtesy of the Dorchester Historical Society.)

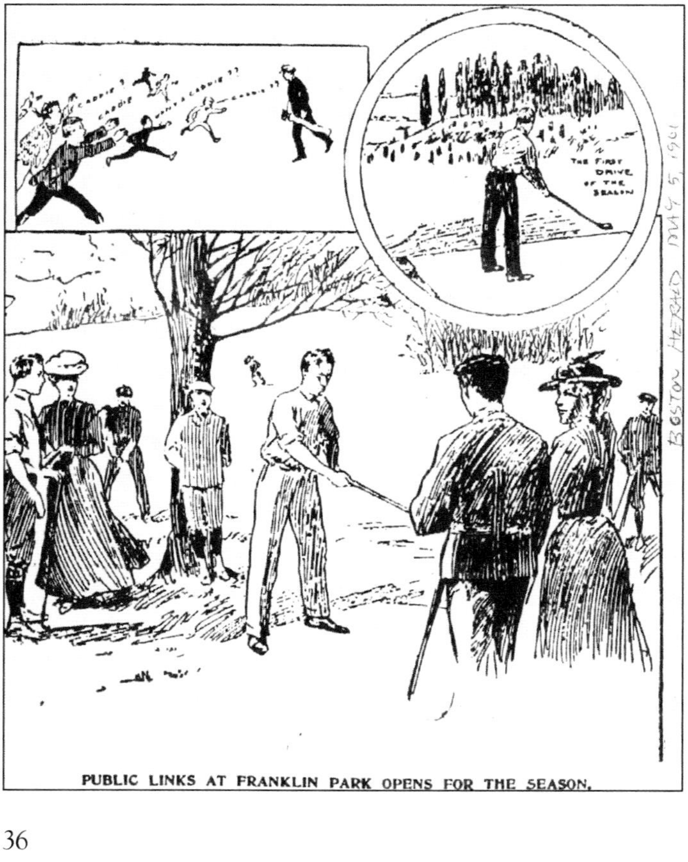

On May 3, 1901, the newly designed public links opened. The holes were named Harvard, Valley Gate, Schoolmaster, Pettigrew, Scarborough, Canterbury, Abbotts, Brooks, and Misery. The Franklin Park links progressed and regressed through the 20th century, including the stoppage of golf in 1917 for victory gardens, the filling of part of Scarboro Pond to enlarge the course in 1922, and the changes in clubhouses in 1949, 1979, 1989, and 1998.

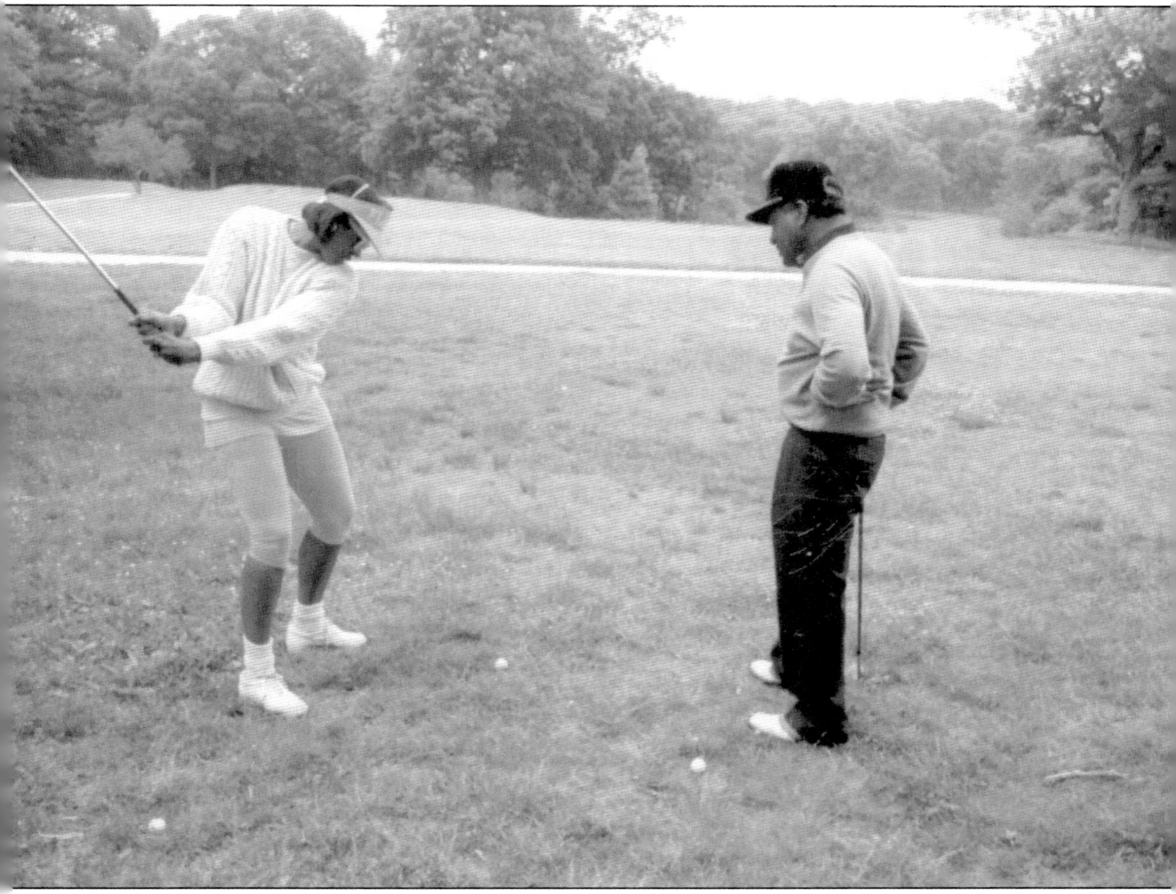

In 1905, John Charles Olmsted reported on the status of the design changes and construction in the Boston Park System. He was troubled by the Franklin Park course and noted that "the nerves of the visitor are still further irritated by the anxiety as to being hit by the hard and swiftly driven balls. It seems too bad that a few scores of people should be allowed practically to monopolize a hundred acre, or perhaps two hundred acres, of the most beautiful park pastures, excluding, or at any rate causing discomfort to, thousands of other visitors." Nonetheless, a day on the links was a social event. The newspapers reported, "Golfers of both sexes played in the afternoons. The women wore bright colored sweaters and jackets." The Franklin Park course was known to be one of the finest public courses in the country. Famous golfers to hit the links include Bobby Jones, founder of the Masters Tournament, and Tiger Woods. (Courtesy of the Franklin Park Coalition.)

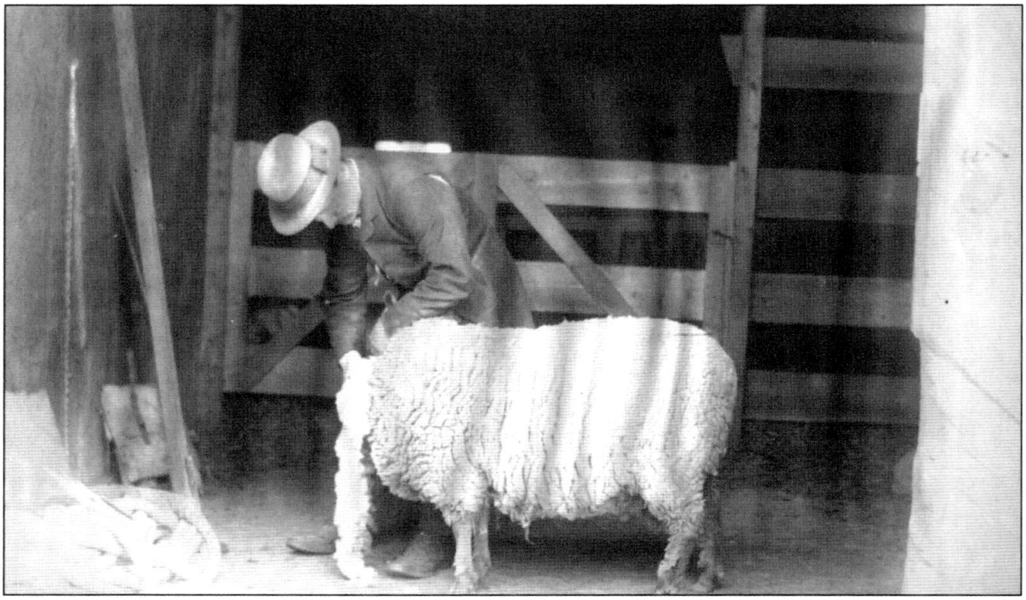

Although provisions were made to sell wool on an annual basis, the income of a few hundred dollars was not enough to support the famous Franklin Park sheep. They were moved to nearby Franklin Field in 1896. The Galvin House and Barn, where the shepherd and sheep were housed, respectively, was razed shortly after. The public outcry lasted for years after their removal. Even though the park commissioners viewed the "land more valuable for vegetables and crops and cold weather required indoor housing of sheep which is expensive," the public's desire for the return of the sheep lasted through the 1920s. (Courtesy of the National Park Service, Frederick Law Olmsted National Historic Site.)

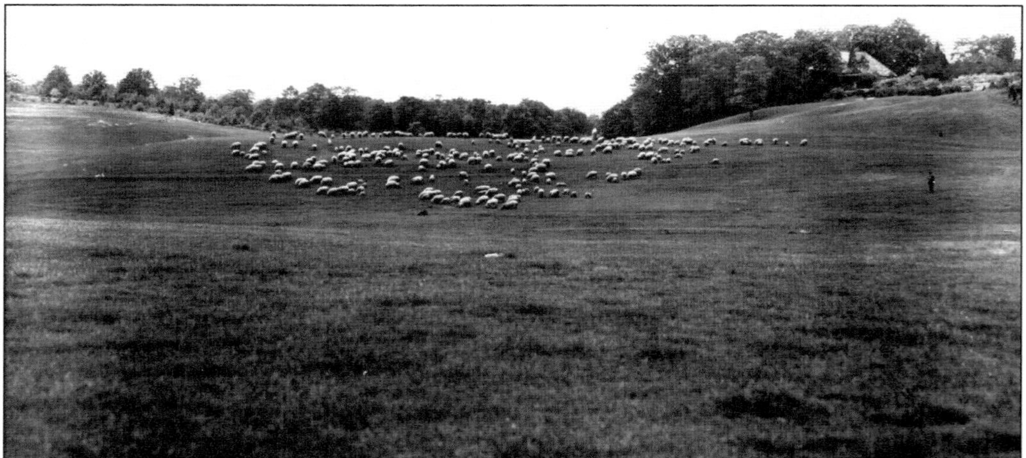

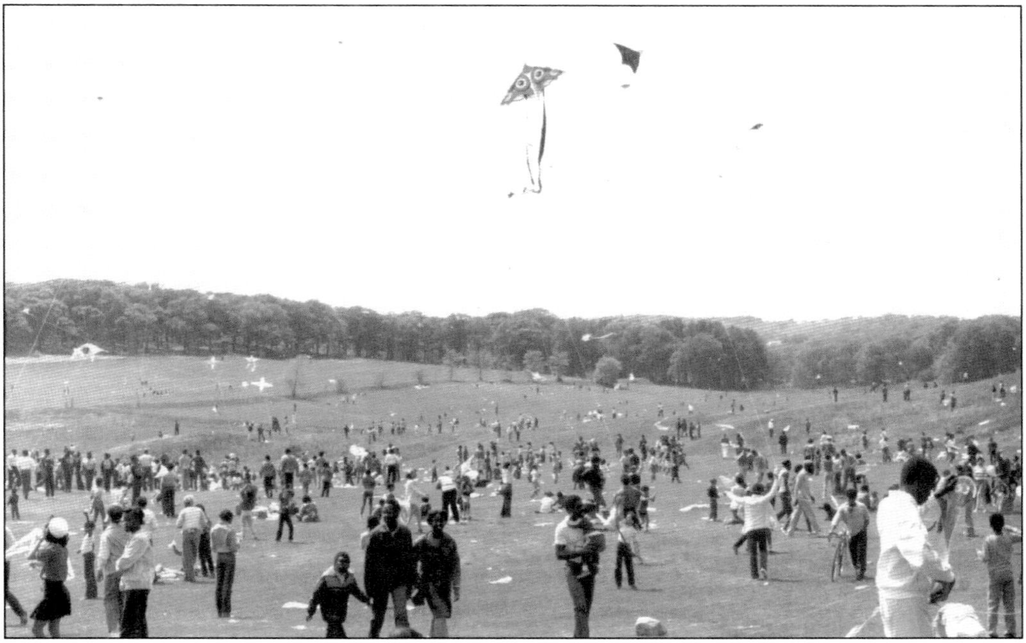

The kite festival is a Franklin Park tradition. In 1975, the Committee for the Better Use of Air sponsored it. Fifteen thousand people participated in the festival, which included judging in categories such as the highest kite flown by the smallest person, the kite that looks most like its owner, and the loveliest kite. (Courtesy of the Franklin Park Coalition.)

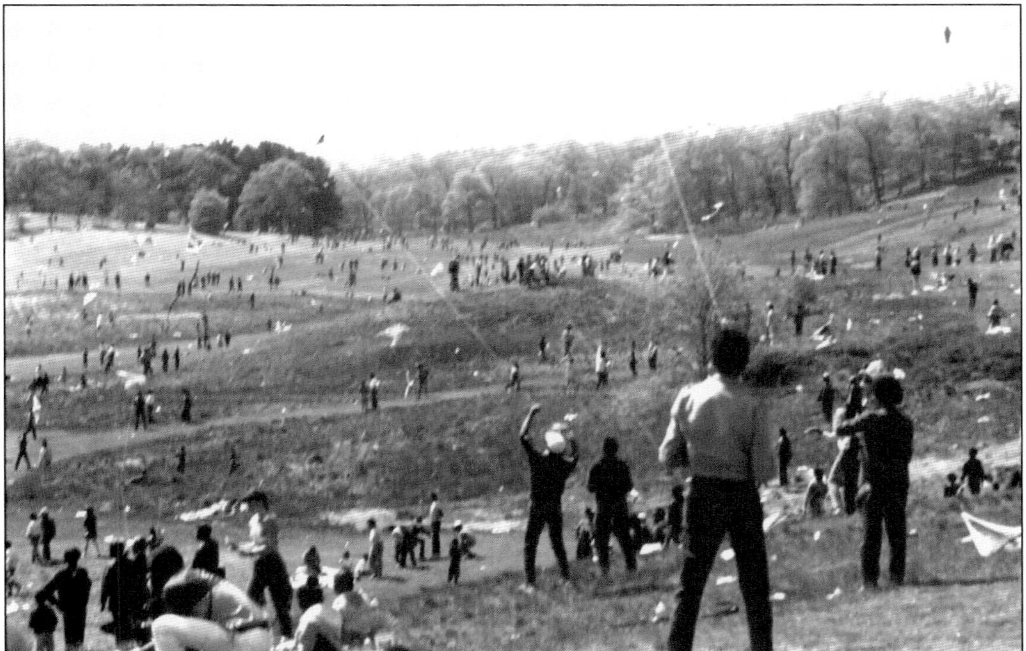

Kites are not the only popular flying objects in the area. On November 6, 1909, the *Boston Herald Traveler* reported that a biplane took off from the high grounds opposite Schoolmaster Hill. Shep Wolsky recalls standing behind the bear dens on Seaver Street and watching the *Hindenburg* hover above the neighborhood in the 1930s. (Courtesy of the Franklin Park Coalition.)

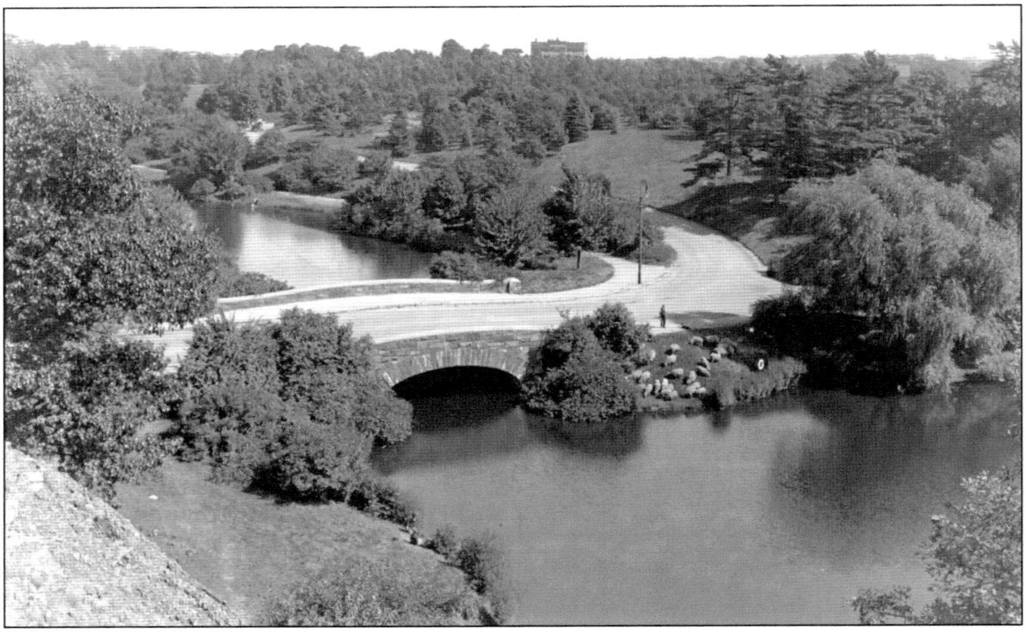

John Scarborough was the original owner of the seven acres of land that became Scarboro Pond in 1893. Many Bostonians agreed that Franklin Park needed a body of water. Sixty signed an official petition. According to the 1890 annual report, the "landscape architect set about a revision of the plan which should provide for such a moderate water basin as could very likely be maintained." (Courtesy of the Boston Public Library Print Department.)

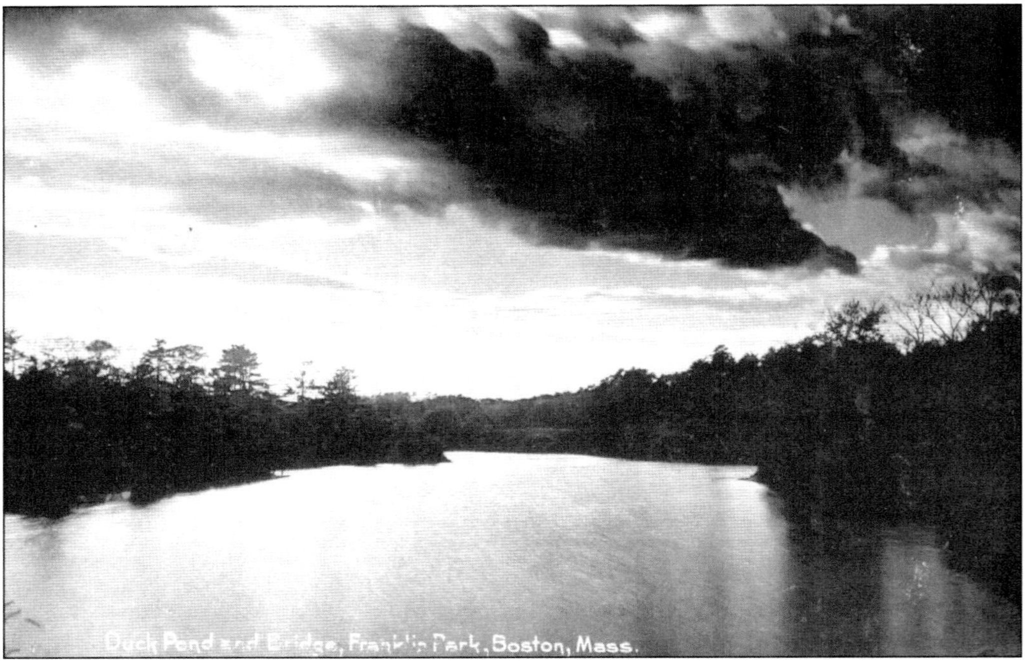

Excavation of Scarboro Pond began in June 1892. The pond was designed with islands for waterfowl habitats. Water in the pond was meant to come from natural sources within the park and the 851,000-gallon Hagbourne Hill Reservoir, completed in 1896. The total cost for construction of the pond was $24,067.

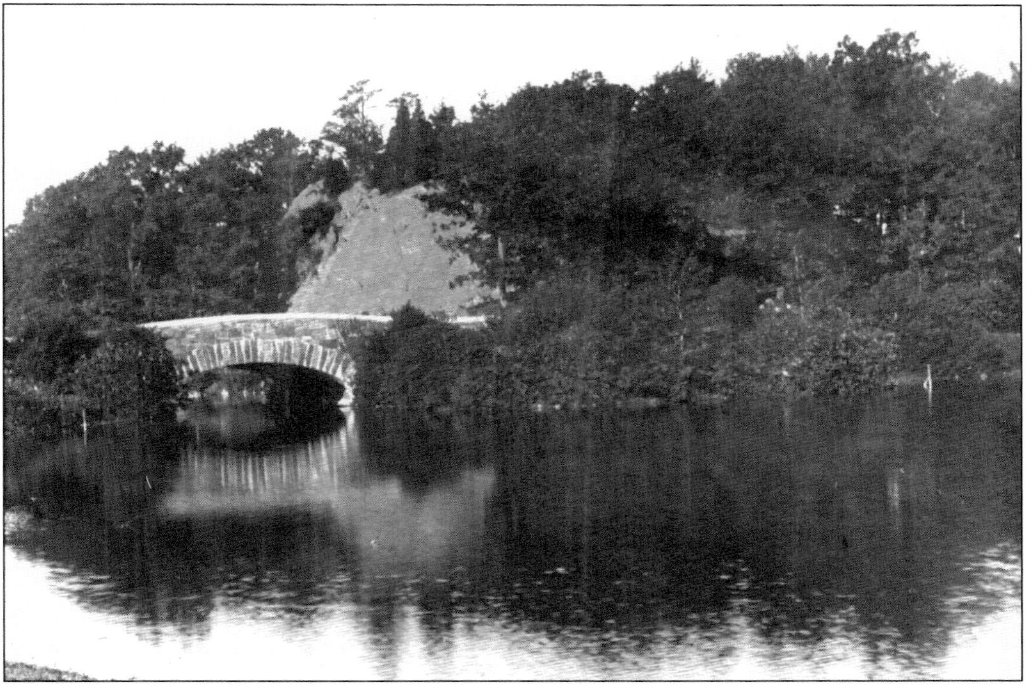

The carriage bridge and footbridge over the pond were completed in the fall of 1893. They were designed by Shepley, Ruttan, and Coolidge and constructed of red granite. The carriage bridge was 40 feet across to accommodate traffic and horses, while the footbridge was smaller in scale for the sole use of pedestrians. (Courtesy of the National Park Service, Frederick Law Olmsted National Historic Site.)

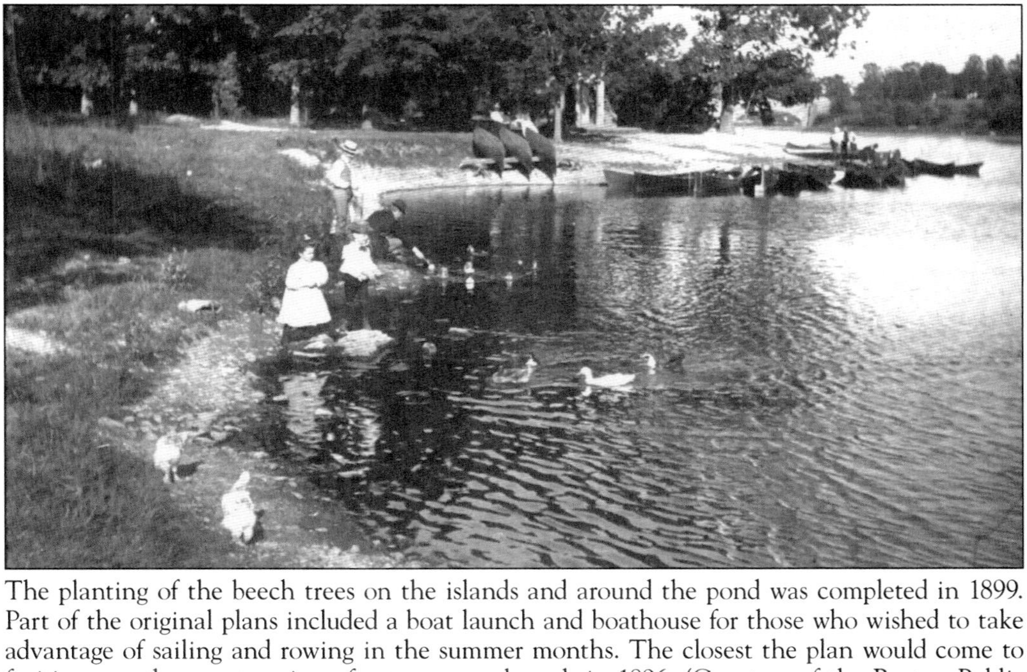

The planting of the beech trees on the islands and around the pond was completed in 1899. Part of the original plans included a boat launch and boathouse for those who wished to take advantage of sailing and rowing in the summer months. The closest the plan would come to fruition was the construction of a temporary launch in 1896. (Courtesy of the Boston Public Library Print Department.)

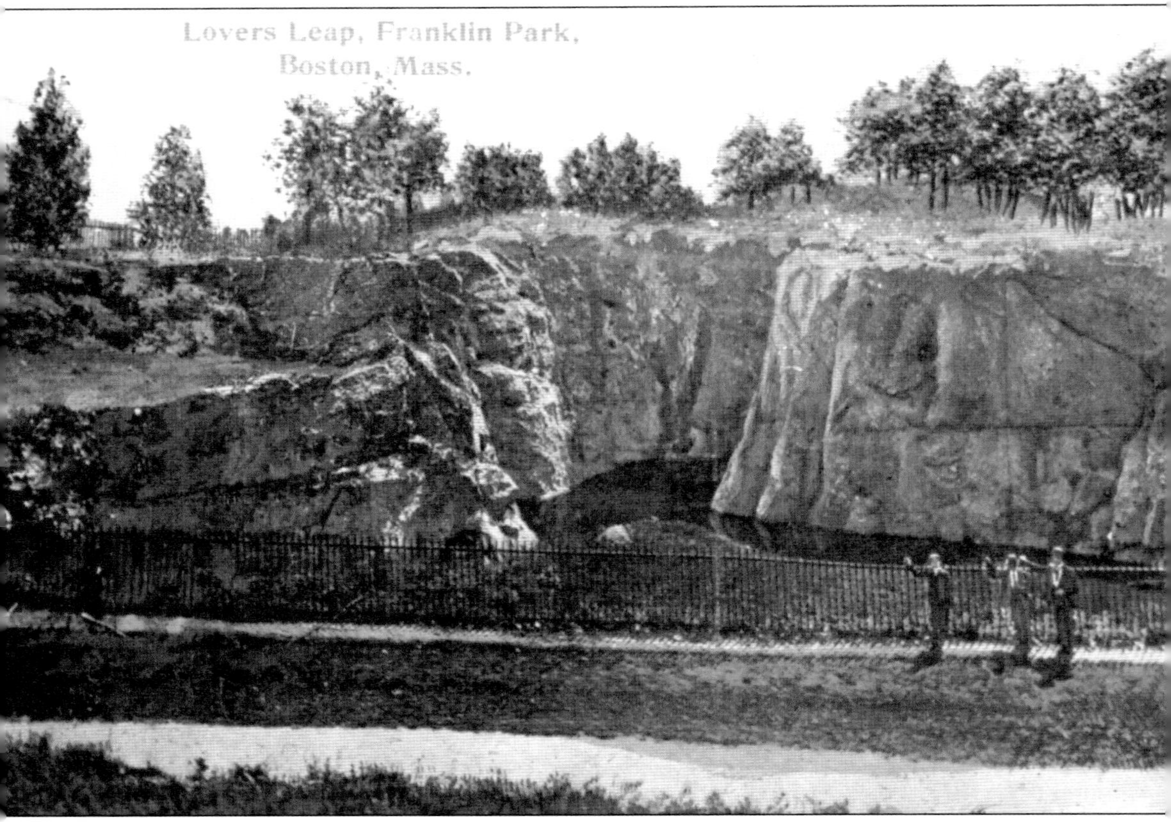

Lover's Leap was a local, romanticized name given to the area Frederick Law Olmsted called Rock Morton. The area was named as such for a rock ledge that was on the Morton Street side of Franklin Park. Rock Milton, located on the opposite side of Scarboro Pond from Rock Morton, is a similar ledge. It was named for its location, facing Milton and the Blue Hills. Balanced Rock is located near the Wilderness and Hagbourne Hill. Table Rock, known by various locals for various reasons, is located in the Wilderness near Heathfield. Finally, Giants Chair is located between the Long Crouch Woods and Glen Road. This pudding stone boulder has been a favorite landmark for generations of children that grew up near the park.

Three

The Playstead

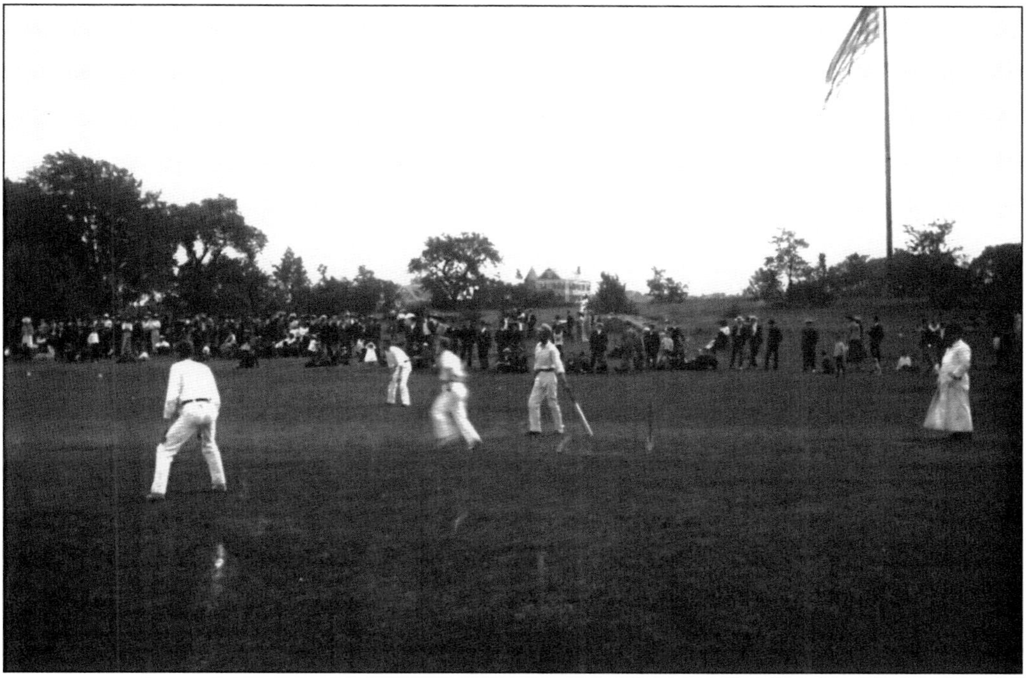

The "General Plan of Franklin Park" describes the Playstead as "a field of turf thirty acres in extent to be used for athletic recreation and education of the city's school boys, and for occasional civic ceremonies and exhibitions. The Overlook . . . is an elevated platform for spectators. It is eight hundred feet long, covering a barren ledge that would otherwise be disagreeably prominent." (Courtesy of the Dorchester Historical Society.)

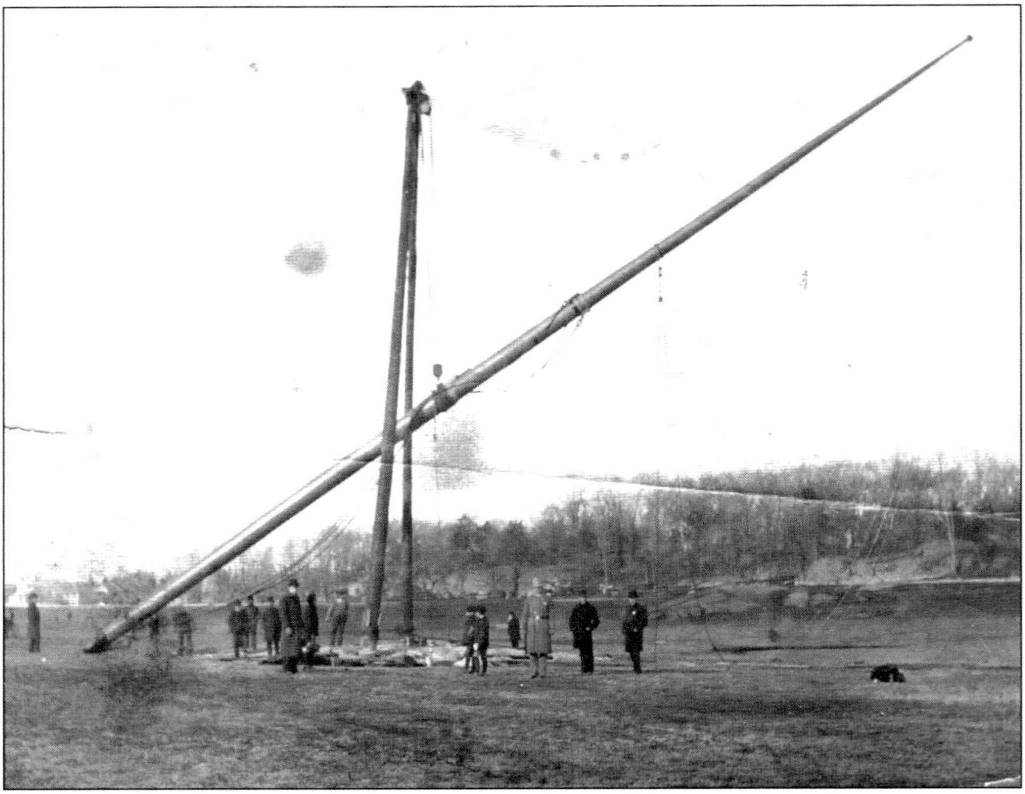

Construction commenced on the "nearly flat ground on the property, little broken by rock" in April 1886. It included the removal of boulders, grading of the turf and drives, installation of a drainage system, and building of five carriage entrances. The construction of the Playstead took approximately three years, much to the dismay of those who anticipated using the lands immediately. The 1887 annual report detailed the laying of turf and preparing the grounds. The 1888 annual report noted, "A flagstaff, consisting of a single stick 105 feet in length, has been erected. It stands . . . in about the centre of the green."

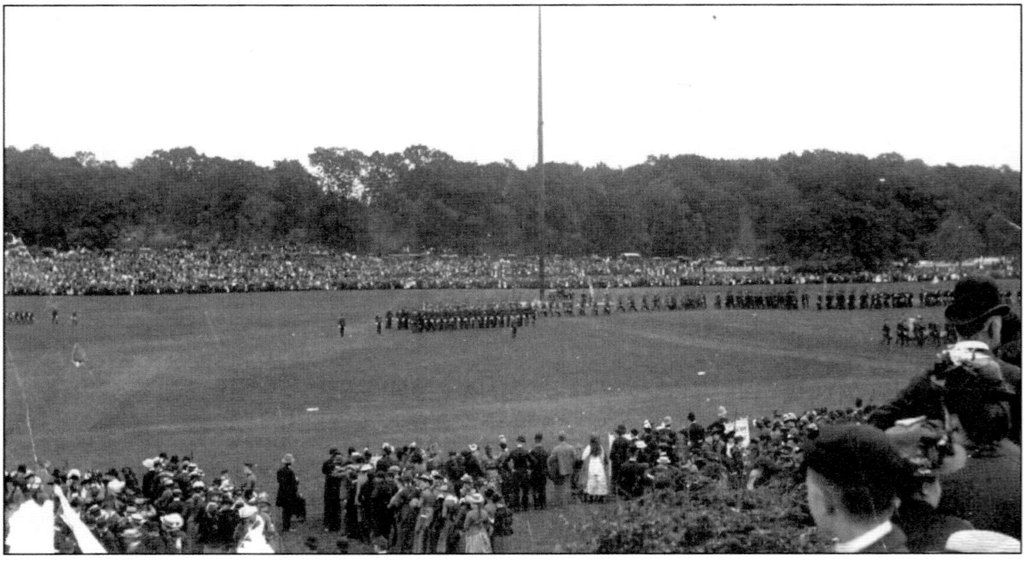

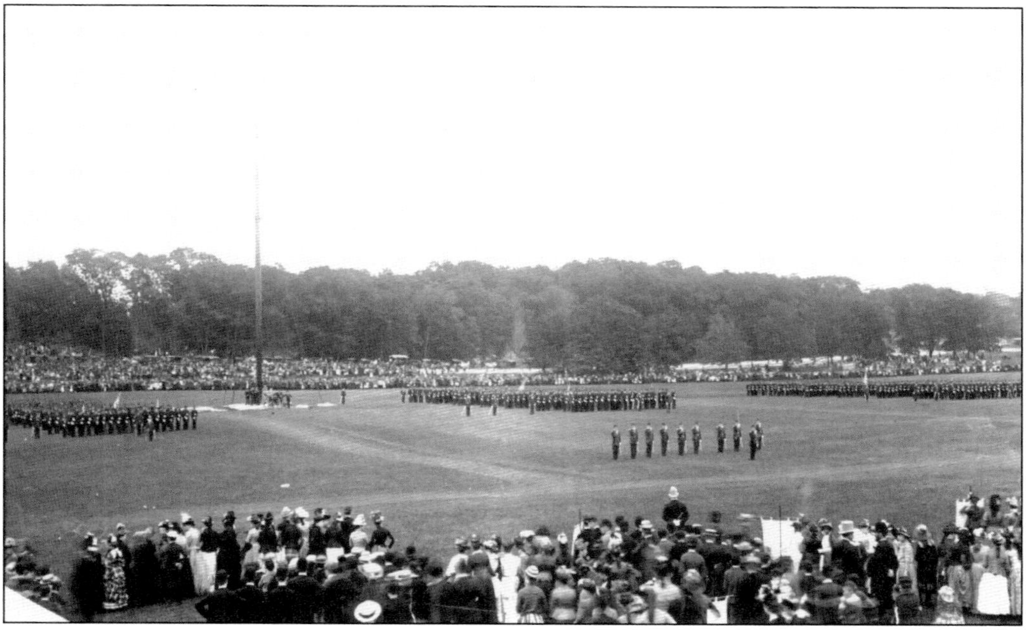

The Playstead dedication was a major event held on June 12, 1889. Afternoon sessions of public school were cancelled so that thousands of parents and children could attend the opening ceremonies. H. M. Whitney, the proprietor of the West End Street Railway Company, donated transportation to the event as well as a marching band. Sailors from the Charlestown Navy Yard raised the flag to the band's rendition of "The Star-Spangled Banner." Schoolchildren marched in detachments and carried banners depicting their respective schools. Other officials included the governor, the mayor, and city council members. The *Boston Herald Traveler* review stated that the Playstead was the "finest playground ever set apart for children's exclusive use in this country."

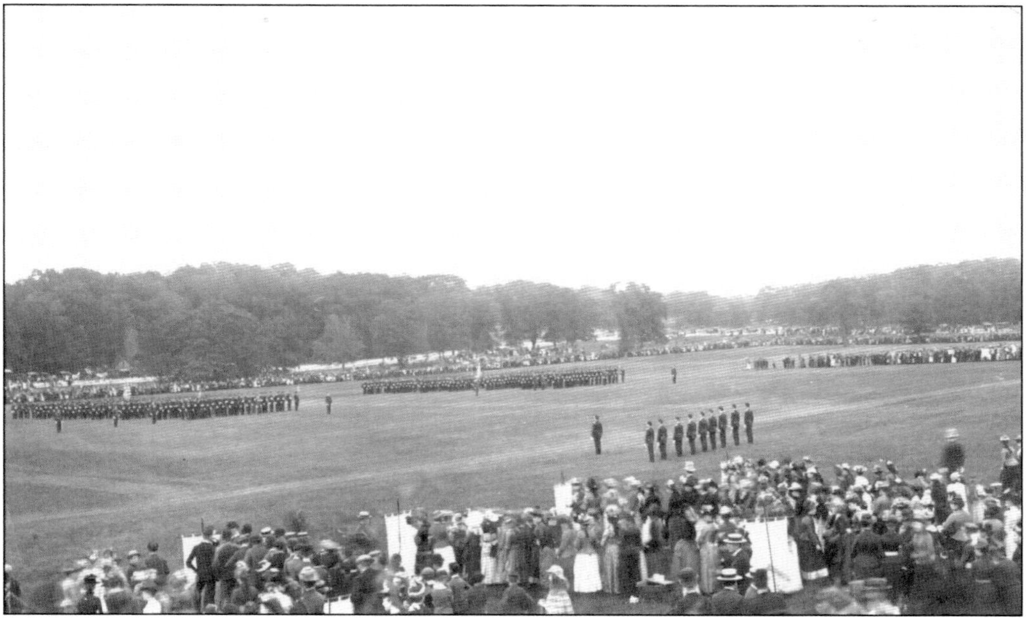

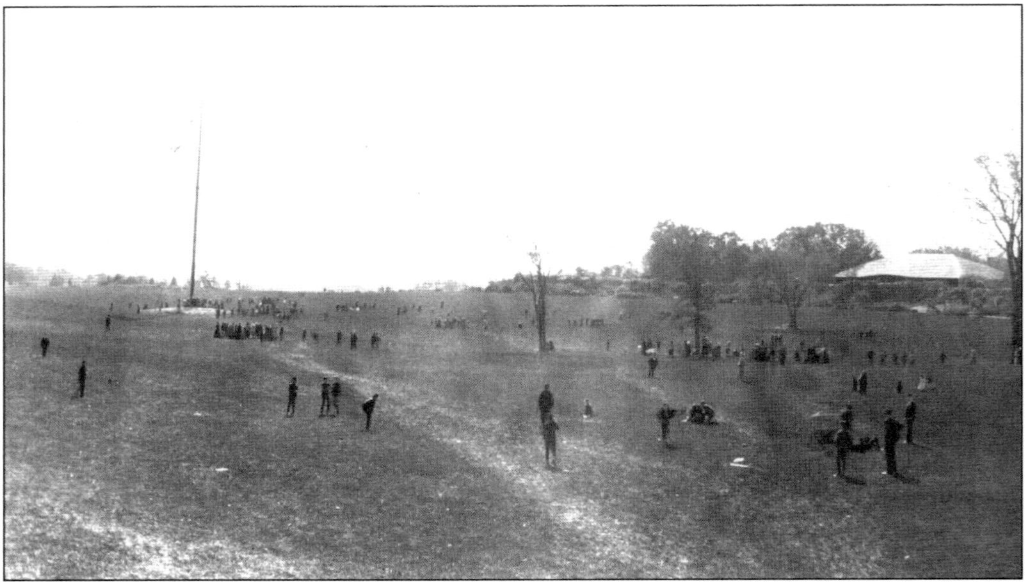

In April 1945, the Playstead was plowed and turned into victory gardens. In 1947, gardeners and those who wanted the landscape restored came to blows in the "Beanstalks and Baseballs" debate. The players won the battle, and in 1947, four baseball diamonds were constructed in the area of the victory garden. (Courtesy of the National Park Service, Frederick Law Olmsted National Historic Site.)

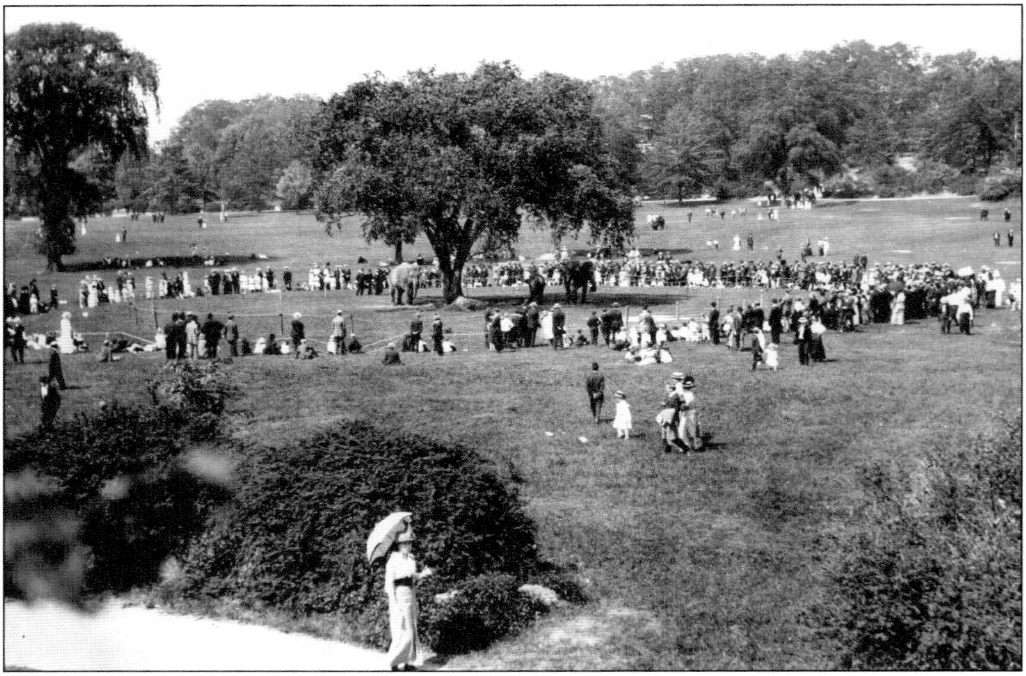

The elephants were presented to the Franklin Park Zoo from the schoolchildren of Boston in a ceremony that took place at Fenway Park on June 6, 1916. Fifty thousand people crammed into the park for the dedication, and a parade followed that brought the elephants to the park. The elephants performed on the Playstead until their home was completed in the zoo. (Courtesy of the Boston Public Library Print Department.)

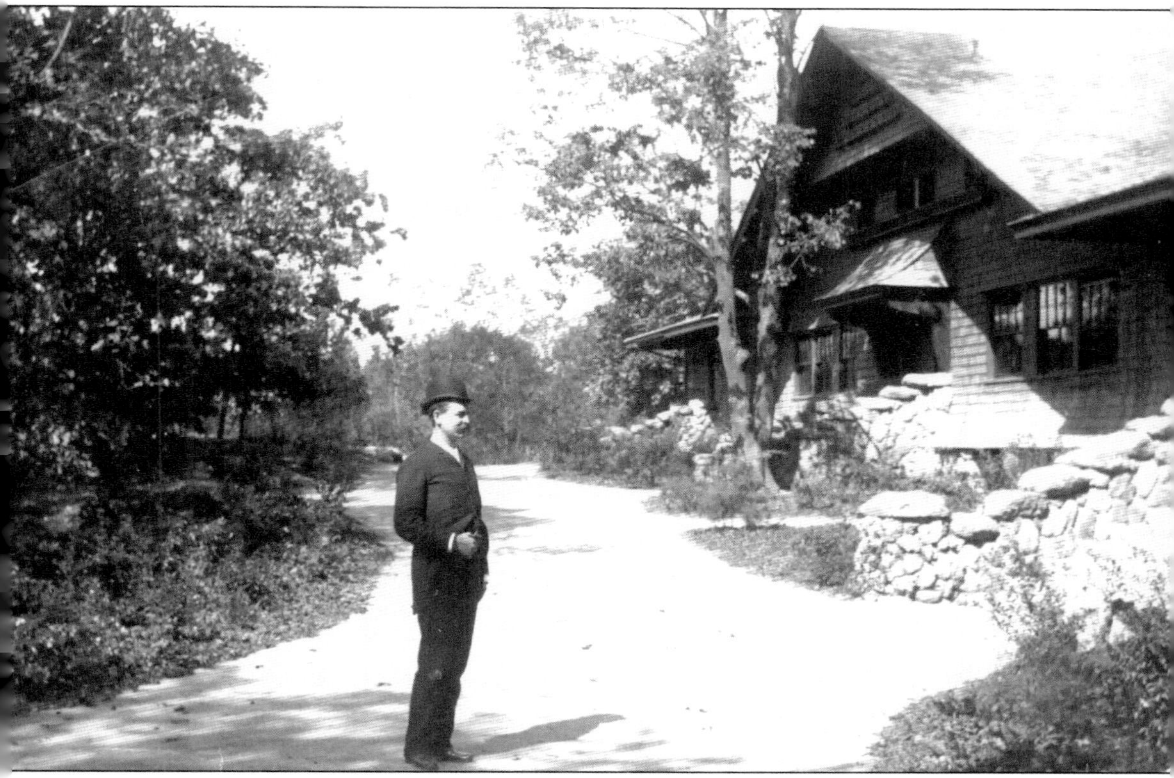

Frederick Law Olmsted called the 800-foot pudding stone ledge that rose above the Playstead the overlook. The ledge was considered too expensive to destroy and, therefore, would be used as an ideal location to view sporting events and other active recreation on the Playstead. A shelter that included lockers, equipment storage and rental, lavatories, and a base for the park police was a pivotal part of the plan for this area of the park. The shelter was designed by Olmsted and C. Howard Walker to blend into the landscape. It featured a low, hipped roof, red cypress shingles, and plantings native to Massachusetts, including wild roses, ferns, and shrubs. The rhododendrons were the most dramatic plantings and were reviewed positively in many articles about the overlook. A promenade with seats built into the stone allowed for a place to spectate and relax. An arch was built into the ledge that connected the playing fields with the basement-level lockers and lavatories for easy access.

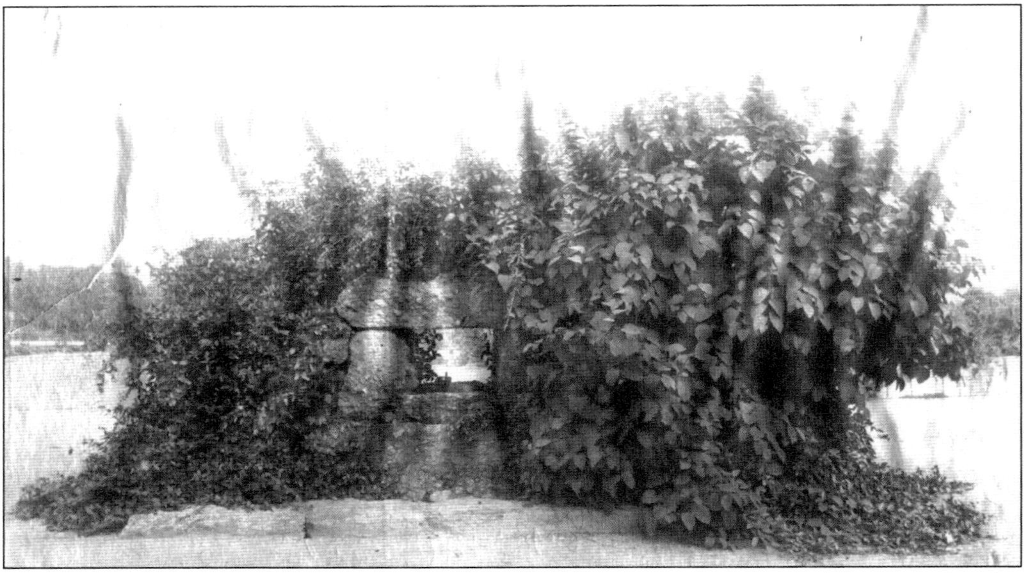

Frederick Law Olmsted was a firm believer in providing resources for refreshments within his park designs. Three pudding stone fountains were built around the overlook shelter in the year 1886. In September 1889, J. A. Hendrie and Brothers Caterers were granted a contract to sell ice cream, soda, and candy from the overlook shelter. (Courtesy of the National Park Service, Frederick Law Olmsted National Historic Site.)

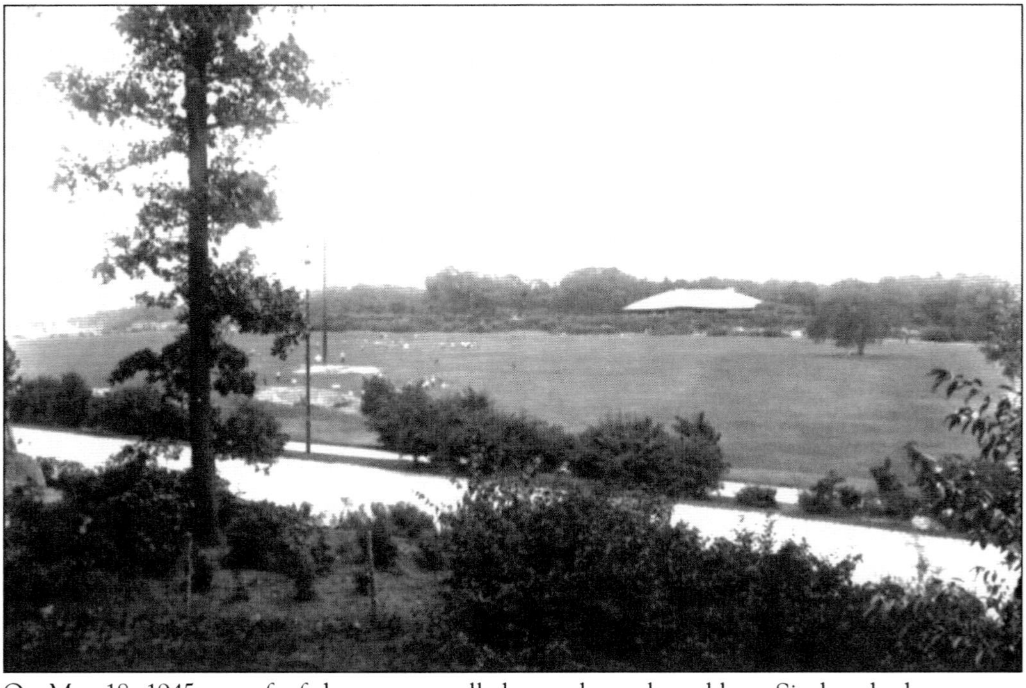

On May 18, 1945, area firefighters were called to a three-alarm blaze. Six hundred were sent to the Boston City Hospital with minor and serious injuries as a result. The overlook shelter was destroyed and would never be rebuilt. In the 1960s, the area would be revived as the site of Elma Lewis's Playhouse in the Park stage. (Courtesy of the National Park Service, Frederick Law Olmsted National Historic Site.)

Olmsted designed the Playstead as a place for the active recreation of young boys under the age of 16. In 1907, the age limit for boys rose to 19 and attendance increased "especially on Sundays and holidays." Women and girls, in 19th-century fashion, were expected to partake in passive recreation in the Country Park. (Courtesy of Shep Wolsky.)

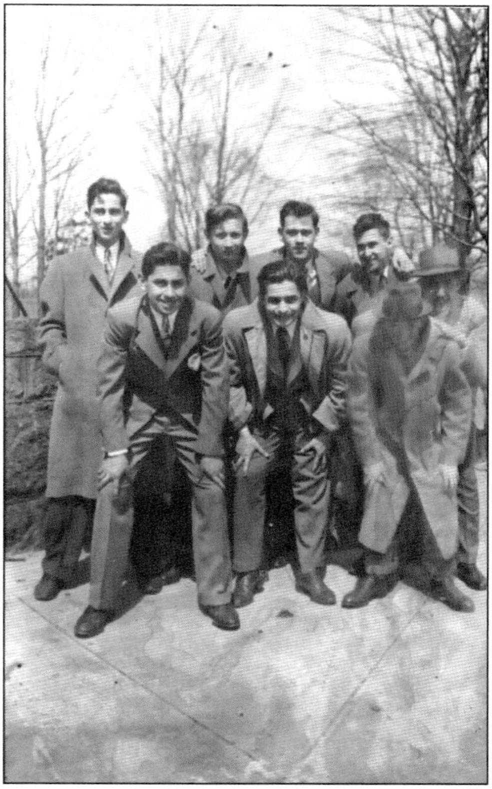

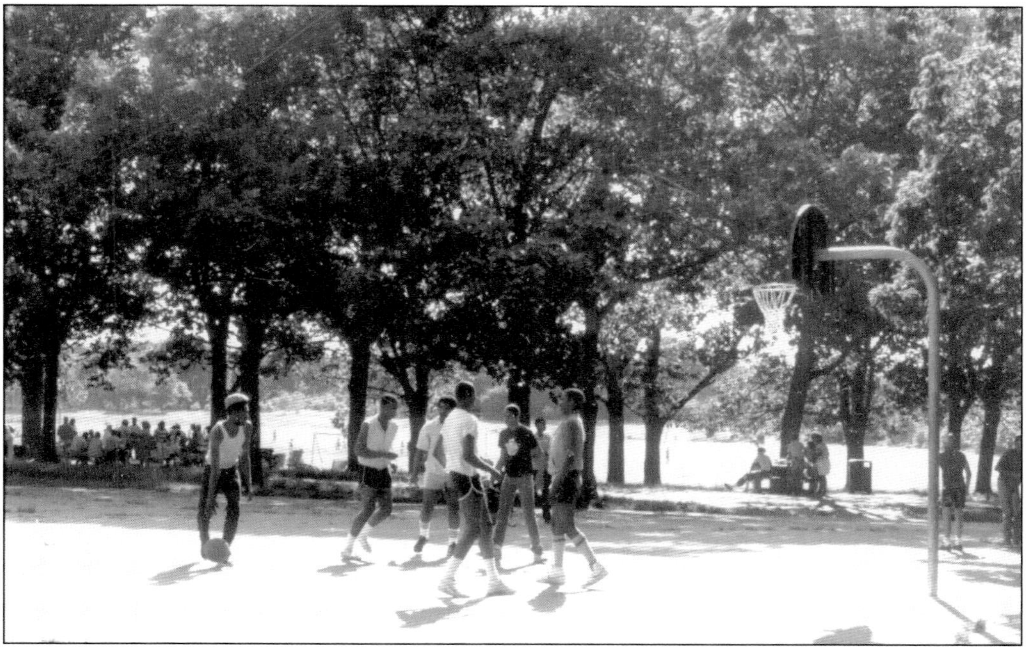

In 1888, Olmsted lamented that baseball was ruining the fresh turf on the Playstead. His thoughts and plans defined active recreation with examples such as tennis or croquet. Through the years, the Playstead has hosted a variety of sporting events, including running, cricket, rugby, Gaelic football, and basketball. (Courtesy of the Franklin Park Coalition.)

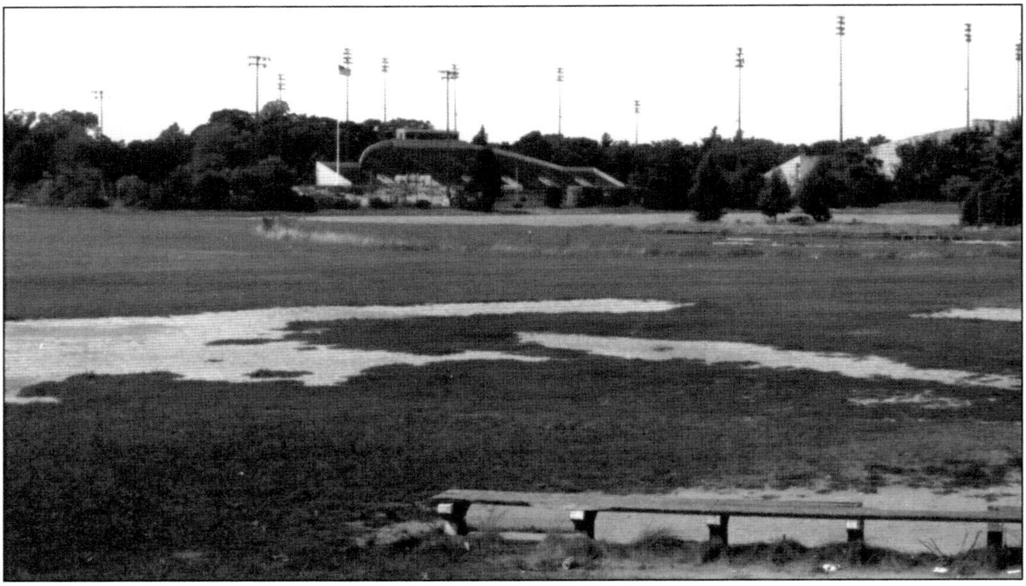

Schoolboy Stadium was the recreational facility that came to fruition out of a variety of proposals. The parks department requested $2 million from the George Robert White Fund. The stadium was designed and constructed by the architectural firm Desmond and Lord. The process proved to be a source of turmoil between the mayors that were involved in the planning and completion of the project. (Courtesy of the Franklin Park Coalition.)

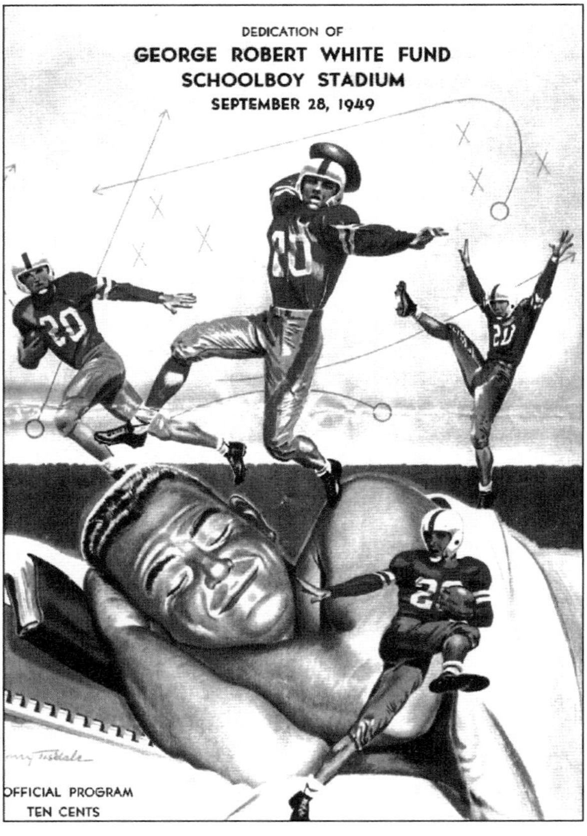

Schoolboy Stadium opened on September 28, 1949, with a capacity crowd of 10,000. The first football game took place between Roxbury Memorial and Boston Latin High Schools. The stadium was built with the idea that children should be kept off the streets, but it was a source of controversy concerning the use of Frederick Law Olmsted's planned landscape and the costs that it entailed. (Courtesy of Jerry Burke.)

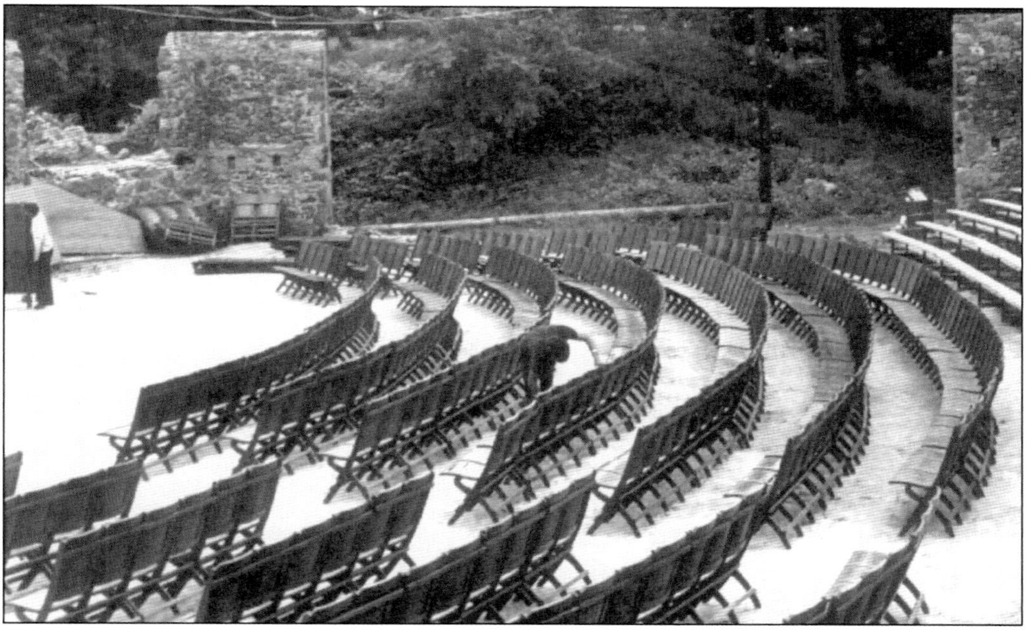

Olmsted planned the Music Court to be a "sylvan amphitheatre adapted to concerts." This vision was finally realized in 1966 when Elma Lewis began the Playhouse in the Park series. Two hundred students from the Elma Lewis School of Fine Arts performed *A Midsummer Night's Dream* around the park. The school was granted permission to build a stage near the former overlook shelter. (Courtesy of the National Center of Afro-American Artists.)

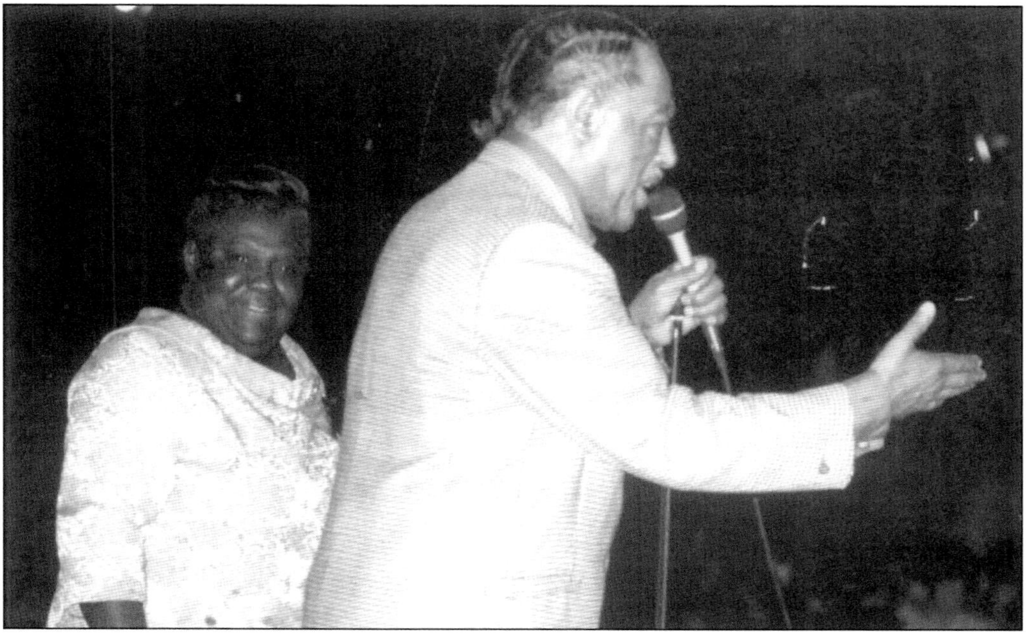

The first season of the Playhouse in the Park attracted 100,000 visitors. Performers through the years include Duke Ellington, the Commodores, Odetta, and the Boston Pops. Students from the Elma Lewis School of Fine Arts and the National Center of Afro-American Artists performed jazz, ballet, and ethnic dance routines. White Stadium was also used for the Uptown in the Park series held from 1973 to 1976. (Courtesy of the National Center of Afro-American Artists.)

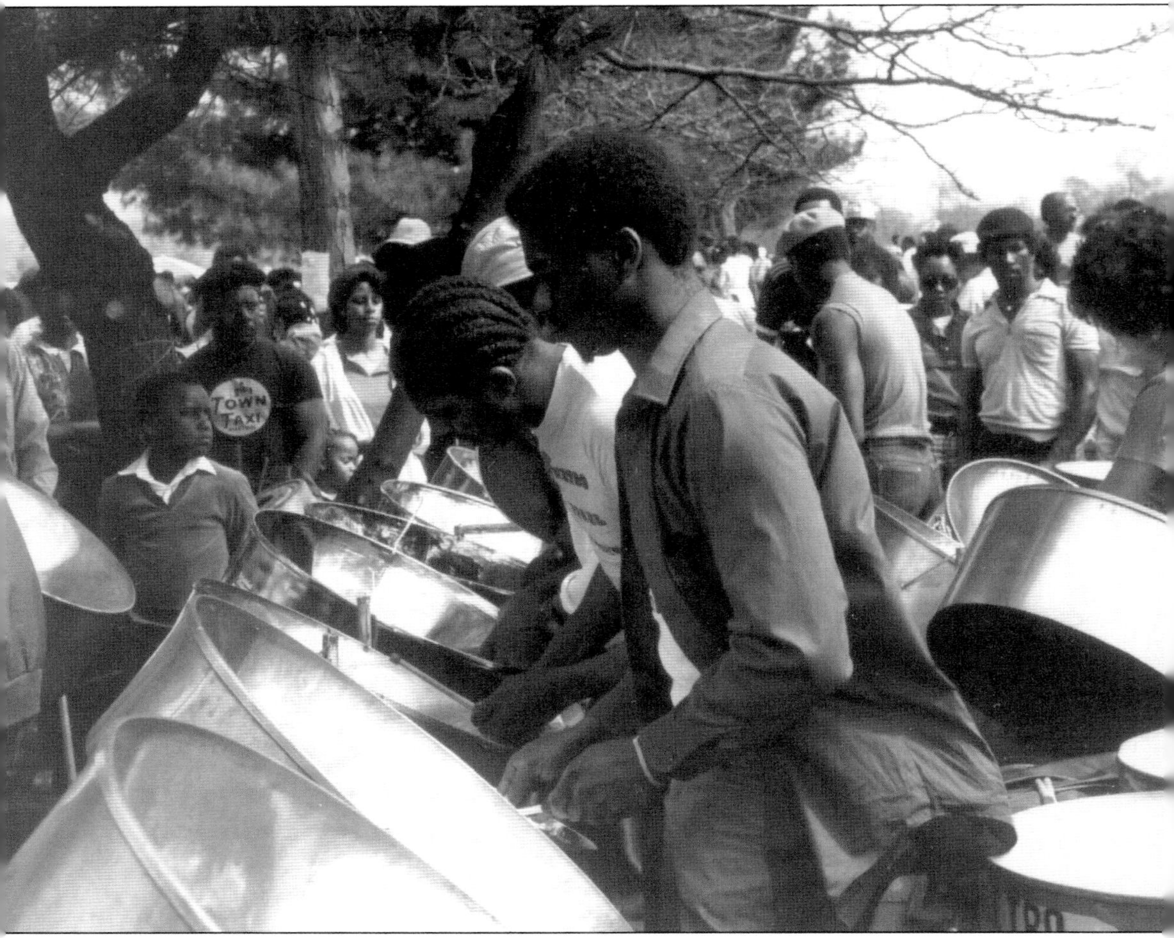

The establishment of Playhouse in the Park spurred a variety of ethnic festivals and performances that reflected the diverse demographics surrounding Franklin Park. In a typical summer, the Roxbury Homecoming, also known as Juneteenth, is held. This celebration remembers the emancipation of Texas slaves by Abraham Lincoln. The Puerto Rican Festival, held in July, started in 1967. While Franklin Park is at the center of the celebration, events that recognize Puerto Rican heritage are held all over Boston. The Caribbean American Association sponsors the West Indian Festival, which has been held in the park since 1973. The commonality of all the festivals is the opportunity to remember and celebrate the array of customs, arts, and foods that define the park neighbors. In 1984, a park user was quoted in the *Franklin Park Bulletin*, stating the park "holds a great significance to the neighborhoods around it. It's always been a place where the people could get together. Things like Unity Day and the Kite Festival would not be the same if held anywhere else." (Courtesy of the Franklin Park Coalition.)

Four

The Ante Park

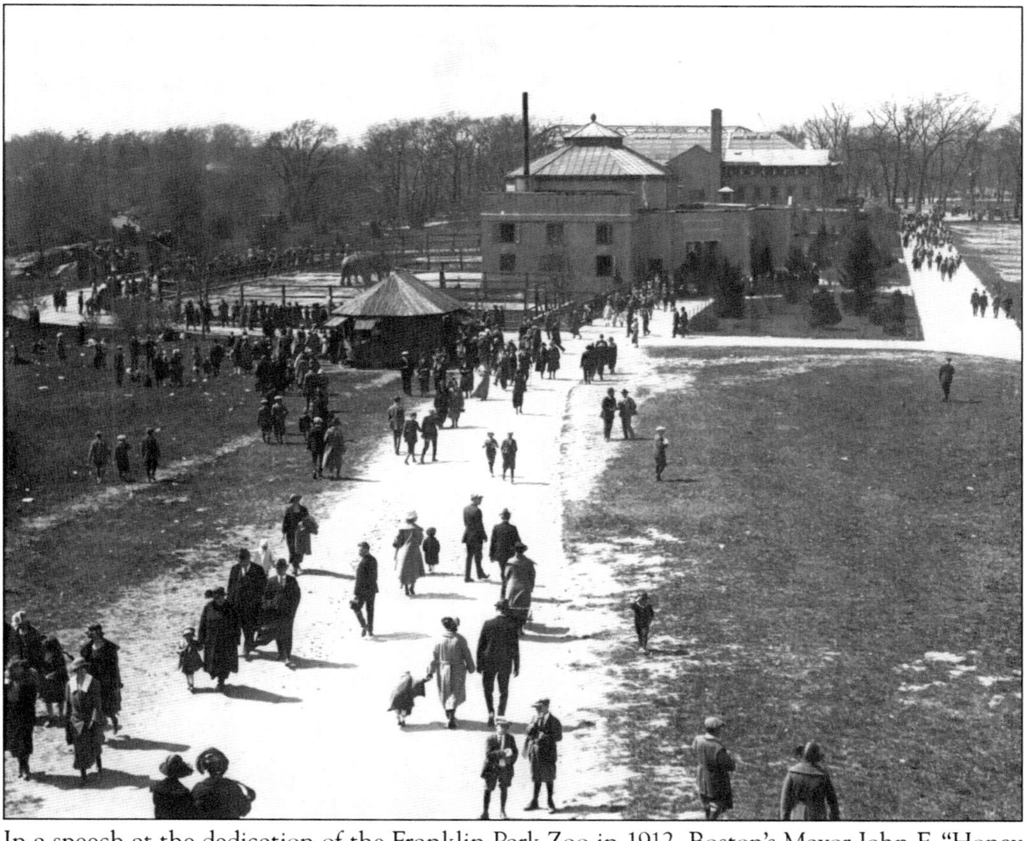

In a speech at the dedication of the Franklin Park Zoo in 1912, Boston's Mayor John F. "Honey Fitz" Fitzgerald stated, "4 years ago it appeared to me that our park system was somewhat desolate and forbidding especially on Sundays and holidays and I thought that something of the human and appealing should be introduced for the recreation and education of our citizens." (Courtesy of the Boston Public Library Print Department.)

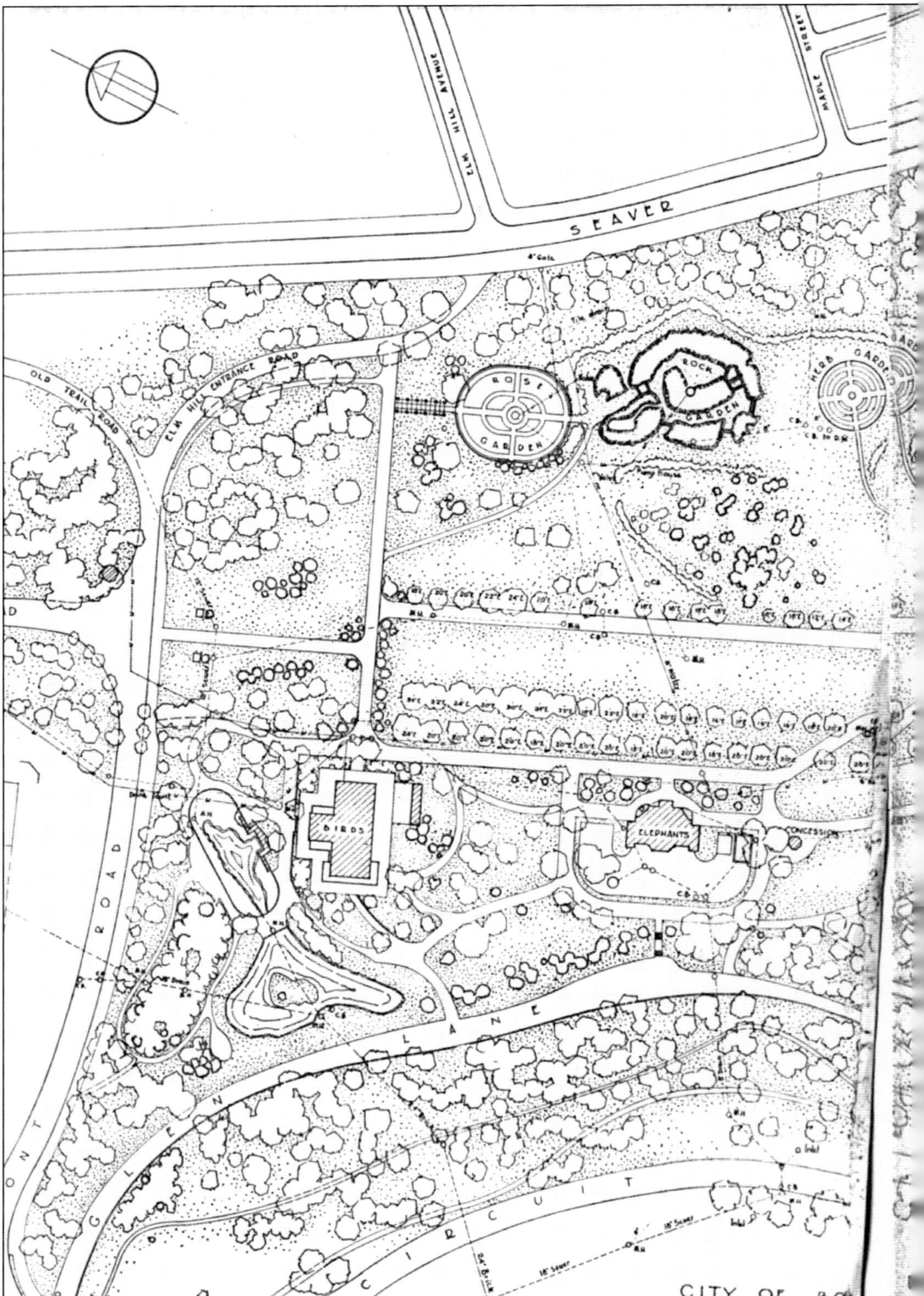
SEAVER
ELM HILL AVENUE
MAPLE STREET
OLD TRAIL ROAD
ELM HILL ENTRANCE ROAD
ROSE GARDEN
ROCK GARDEN
HERB GARDEN
BIRDS
ELEPHANTS
CONCESSION
GLEN LANE
FRONT ROAD
CIRCUIT
CITY OF BO
PAR

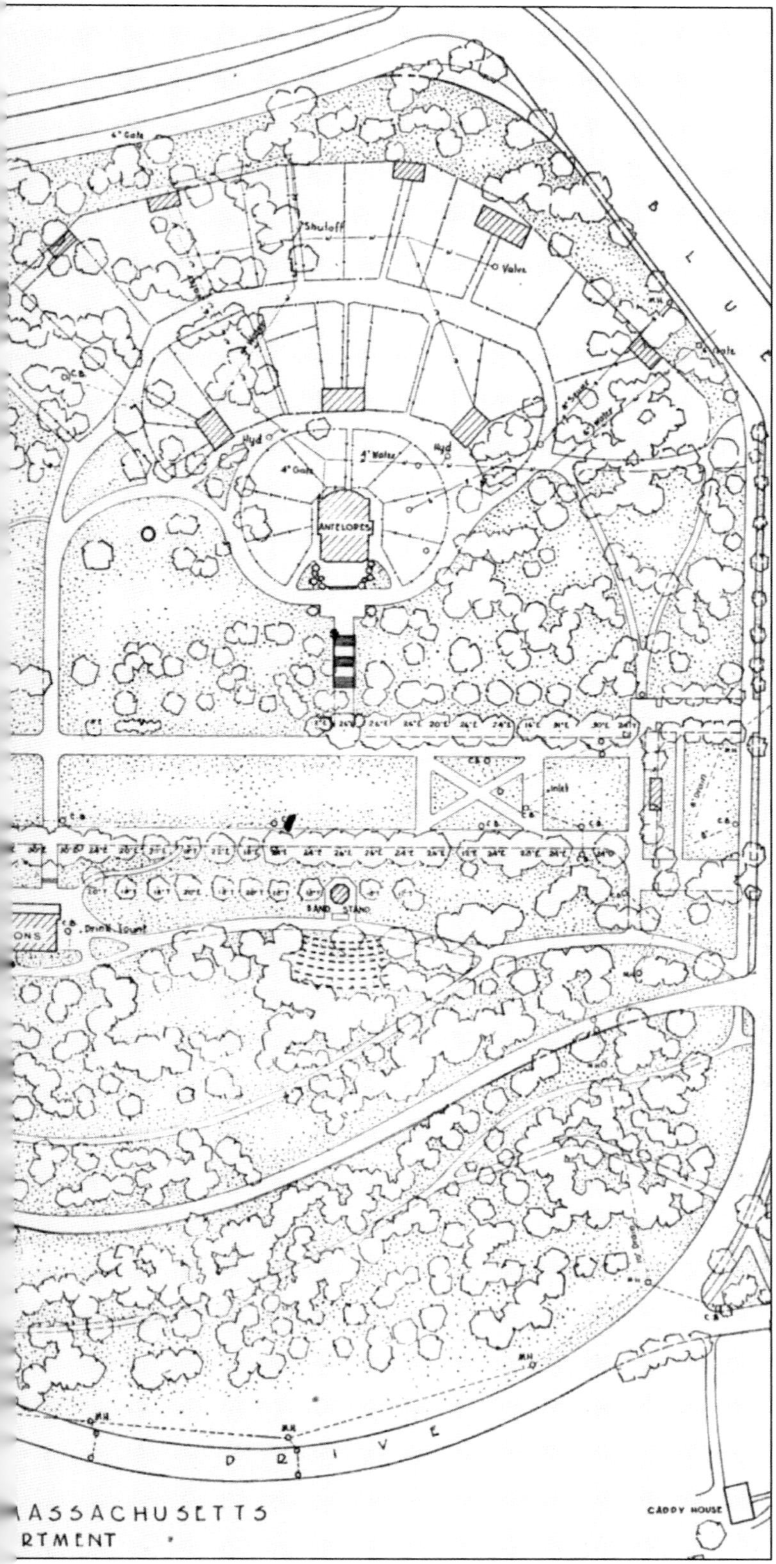

The urge to place a zoo within the confines of Franklin Park was an idea almost from the onset of park construction. Frederick Law Olmsted believed that animals could enhance the landscape in the proper setting and included plans for a deer park and bears in the Little Folks Fair, although he did not necessarily believe in zoos. In 1910, the Boston Society of Natural History stated that "considerable land within easy distance of the thickly inhabited parts of the city" was available. Faltering attendance in the early years of the 20th century pushed Boston closer to realizing a place to satisfy the curiosity of the masses. In May 1910, Mayor James Michael Curley approved the use of the Parkman Fund for obtaining estimates for zoological gardens. In a report to the Boston park commissioners, Arthur Shurtleff, hired in 1910 as the landscape architect for the zoo, agreed that "great country parks require secondary amusements of just that kind of zoological gardens to enable to hold their places in competition with seashore reservations, bathing beaches, and the modern highly developed playground." (Courtesy of Jerry Burke.)

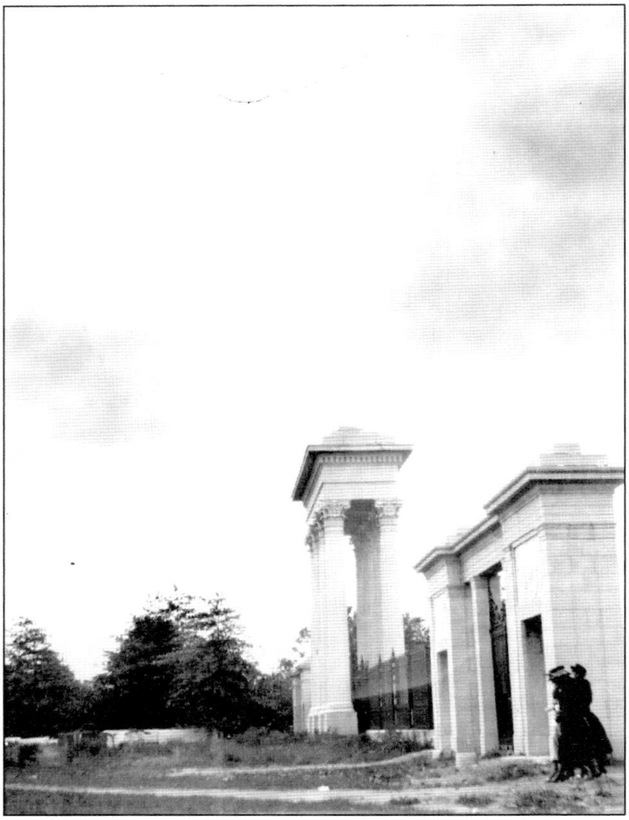

According to the "General Plan of Franklin Park," "The Greeting is to be wholly occupied by a series of parallel and contiguous drives, rides, and walks, a double length of each, under rows of trees forming a Promenade or Meeting Ground, half a mile in length." Frederick Law Olmsted's designs were never completed. In 1897, John Pettigrew altered the design to be "simple in design . . . not of costly character." (Courtesy of the Boston Public Library Print Department.)

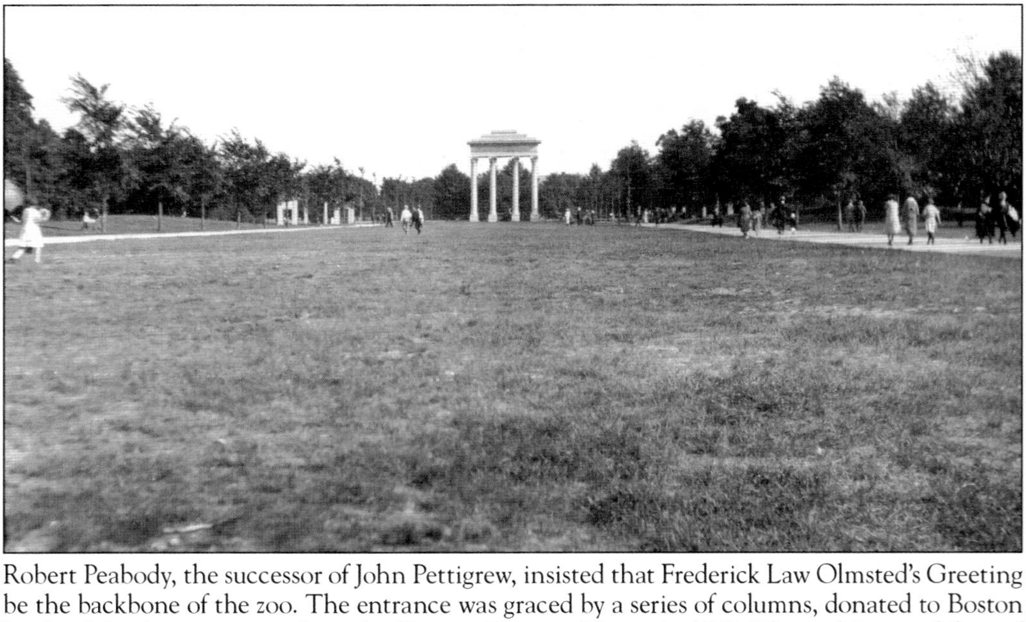

Robert Peabody, the successor of John Pettigrew, insisted that Frederick Law Olmsted's Greeting be the backbone of the zoo. The entrance was graced by a series of columns, donated to Boston by the federal government from the Boston Customs House in 1913. The architectural firm of Fisher, Ripley, and Le Boutillier completed the design for their use in April 1918. The columns were removed in February 2007. (Courtesy of the National Park Service, Frederick Law Olmsted National Historic Site.)

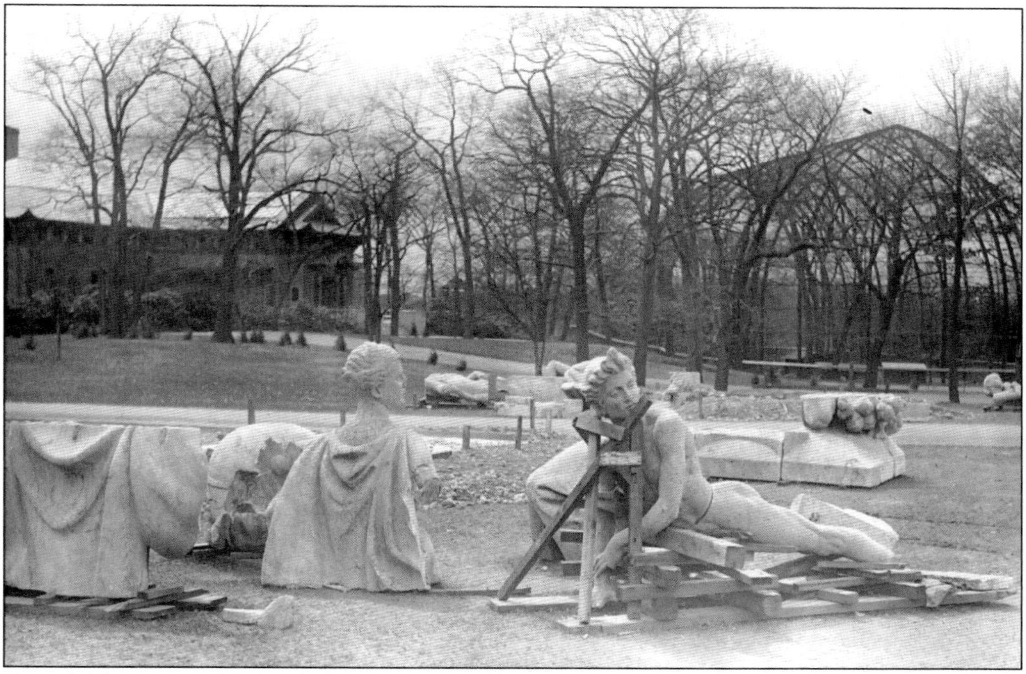

Daniel Chester French carved *Science* and *Industry* for the post office and subtreasury building in downtown Boston in 1885. French is most famous for the statue of Abraham Lincoln at the Lincoln Memorial, the design of the Pulitzer Prize medal, and locally for the John Boyle O'Reilly statue in the Back Bay Fens. (Courtesy of the Boston Public Library Print Department.)

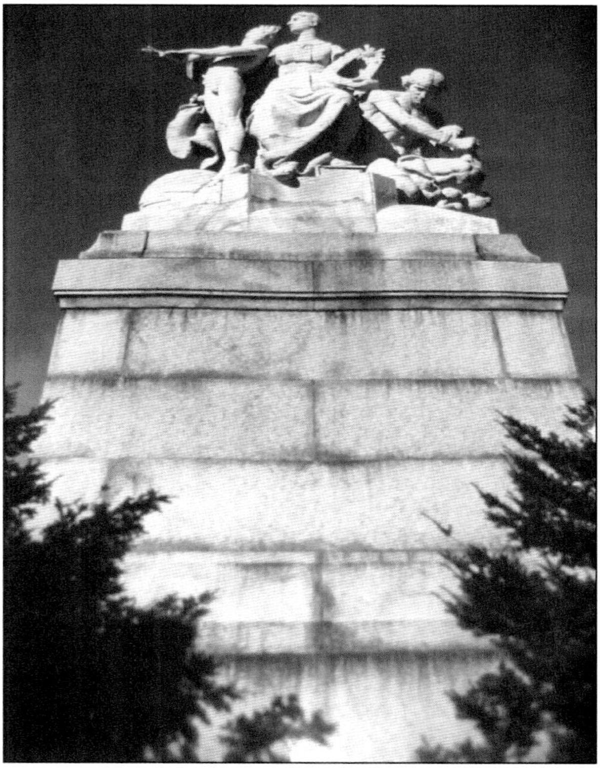

Frederick Law Olmsted did not approve of statuary in his designs. Before the Greeting columns, there were no monuments in Franklin Park. *Science* and *Industry* marked the second major installation. The statues were removed from Post Office Square and donated to the parks and recreation department. They were installed at the rear of the zoo in 1934. (Courtesy of the Boston Public Library Print Department.)

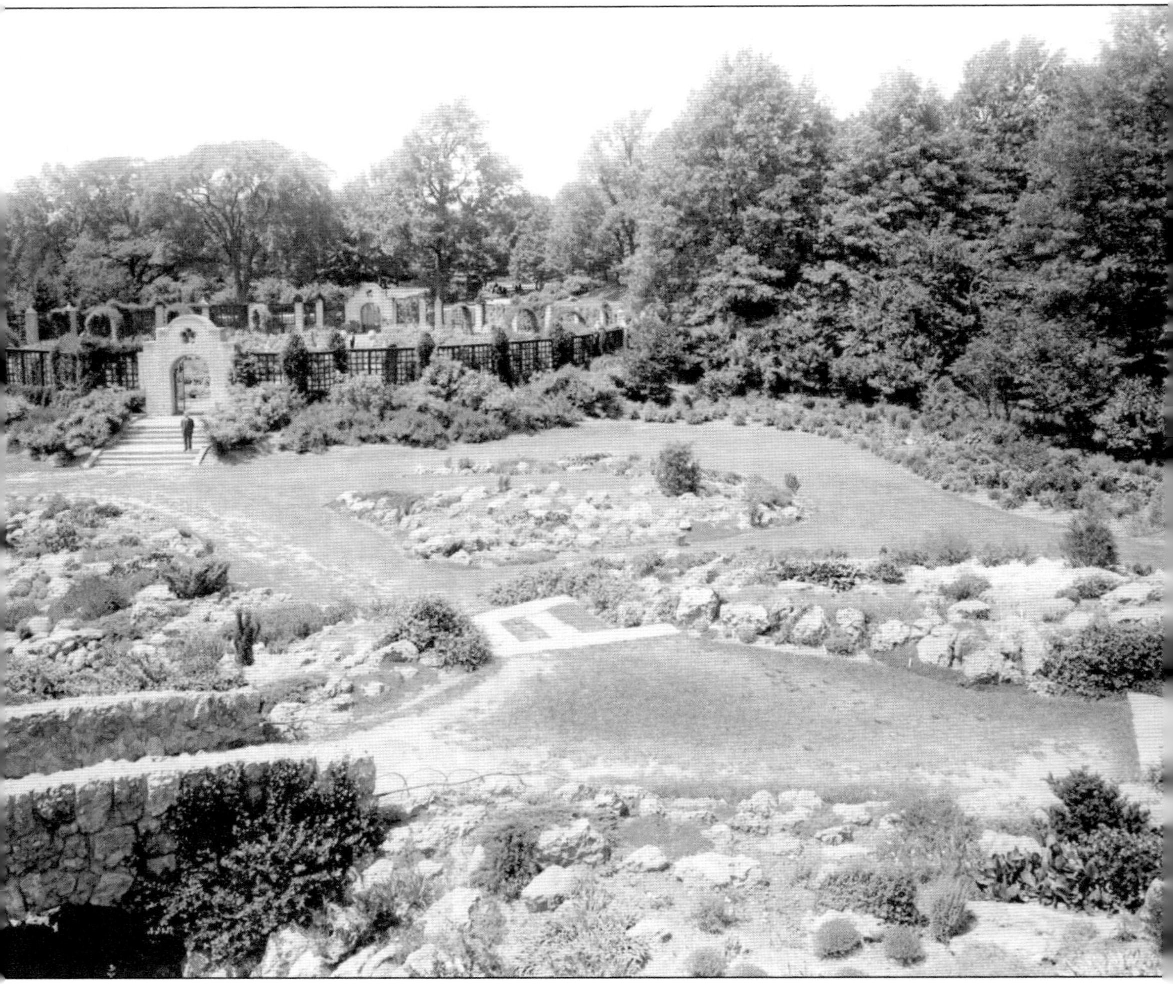

Frederick Law Olmsted described Sargent's Field as a "ground being comparatively free from rock, and to be easily brought to a nearly level surface of good turf, tennis courts and a small ball ground may be provided in it; the object being to save players coming from the east from walking further to reach a playing ground." The area was named for Lucius Manlius Sargent, whose land was purchased by the Boston Park Department in 1883. Arthur Shurtleff designed three gardens—rock, herbaceous, and rose—in the area. While the herbaceous garden featured naturalistic trees and shrubs, the rose garden featured 400 varieties of roses in a specially designed oval garden. The cost to design and construct the rose garden was estimated to be $100,000. (Courtesy of the Boston Public Library Print Department.)

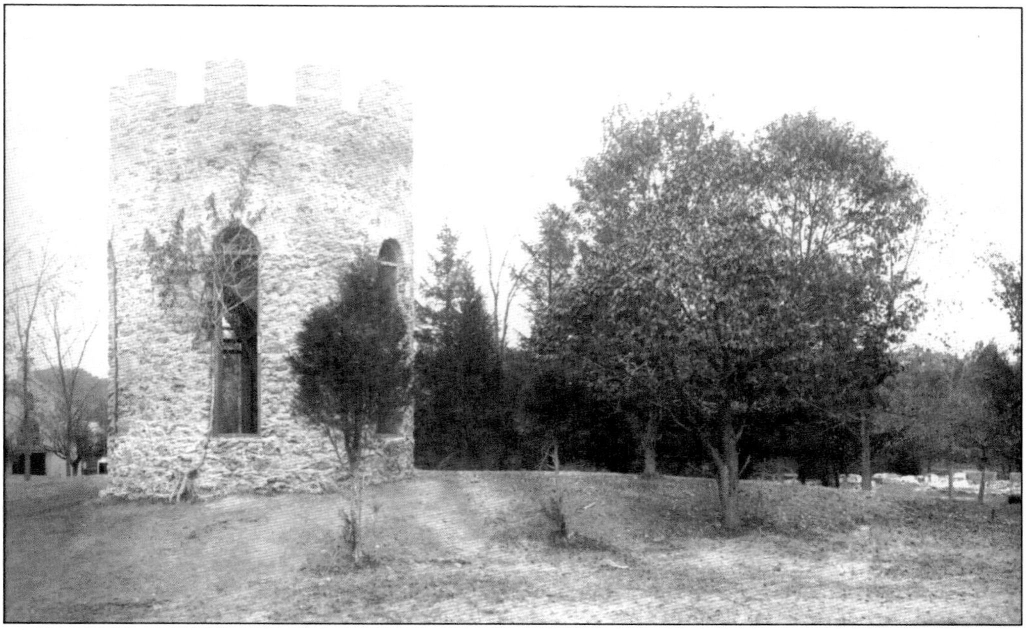

The two towers that stand within the zoo were part of the estate of Lucius Manlius Sargent, a Boston temperance advocate and writer, and are the only remaining prepark structures that exist. One of the towers was built for astronomical observation, and the other was a folly—a decorative structure added to a landscape. (Courtesy of the National Park Service, Frederick Law Olmsted National Historic Site.)

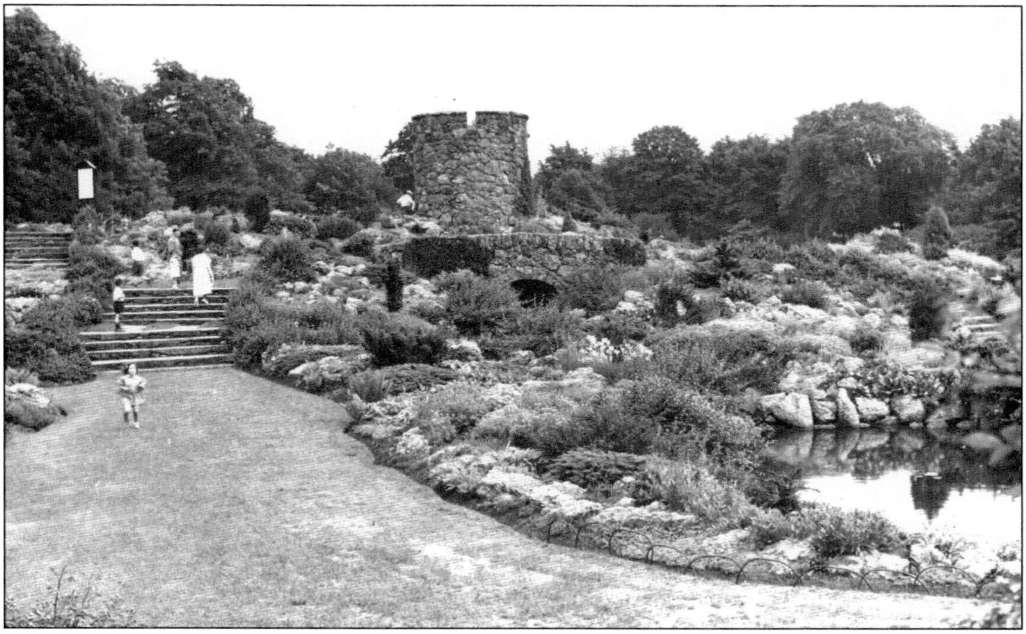

The rock garden was located at the highest point in Sargent's Field at 196 feet above sea level. The 1884 annual report described the view from the tower as a "fine view panorama stretching from Milton and Brookline on the south and west to the harbor and bay on the north and east, and including the city and adjacent country." (Courtesy of the Boston Public Library Print Department.)

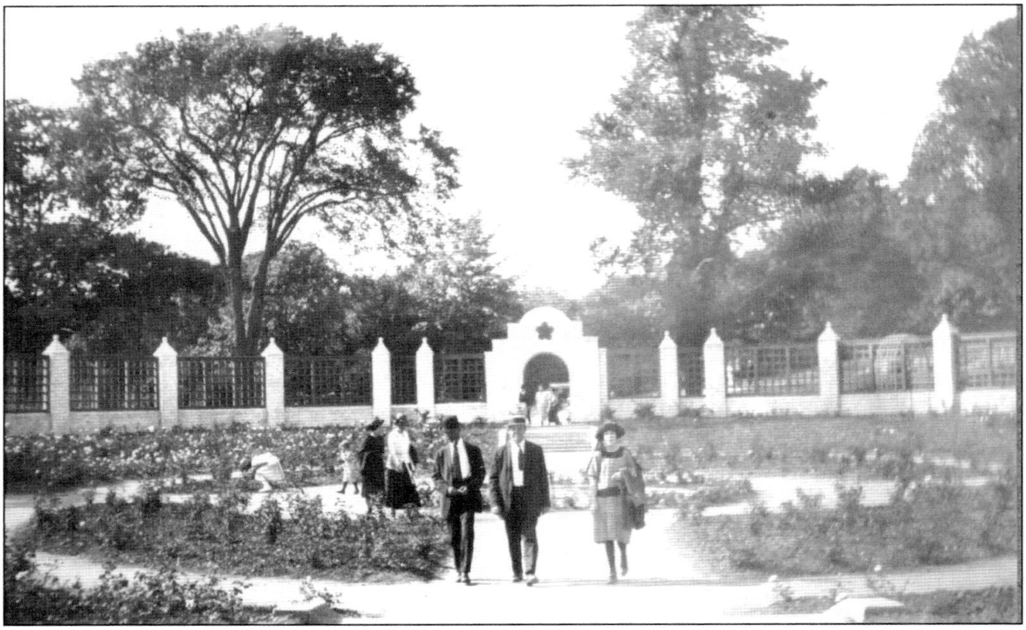

Mayor James Michael Curley insisted on a formal rose garden as part of Franklin Park. The first installations were made in 1923, and the area was dedicated in 1927. Tens of thousands of visitors strolled through the gardens on an annual basis. (Courtesy of the National Park Service, Frederick Law Olmsted National Historic Site.)

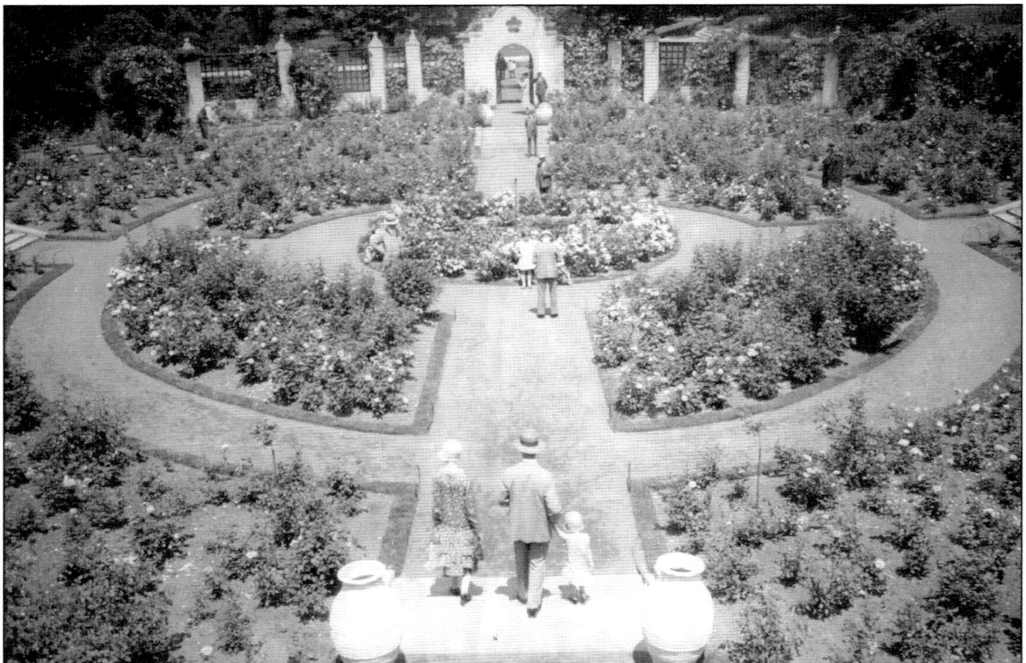

Constant maintenance of the gardens was a necessity. World War II brought more than the "Beanstalks and Baseballs" debate into the park culture. People who lived around the park in the 1940s recall hearing stories about and seeing Italian prisoners of war tending to the gardens. (Courtesy of the Boston Public Library Print Department.)

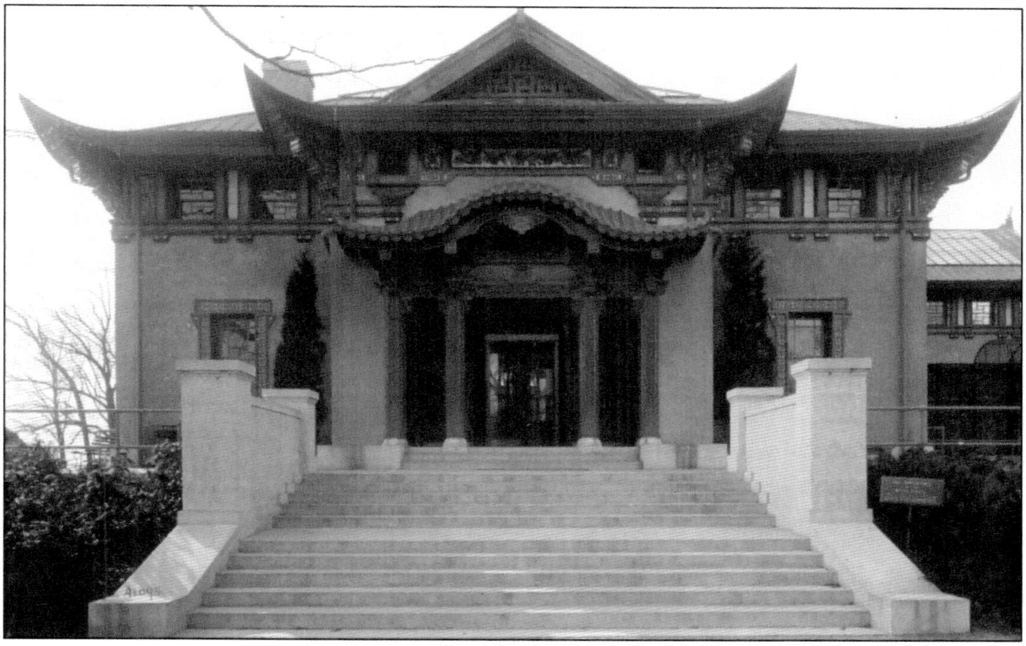

The first zoo exhibits included the bear dens, the aviary, and the birdhouse. These were constructed between 1910 and 1912. Each opening ceremony attracted thousands. Through the first half of the 20th century, the zoo had its fair share of successes and criticisms. The parks and recreation department operated it until 1957, when management was transferred from Boston to the Metropolitan District Commission (MDC). (Courtesy of the Boston Public Library Print Department.)

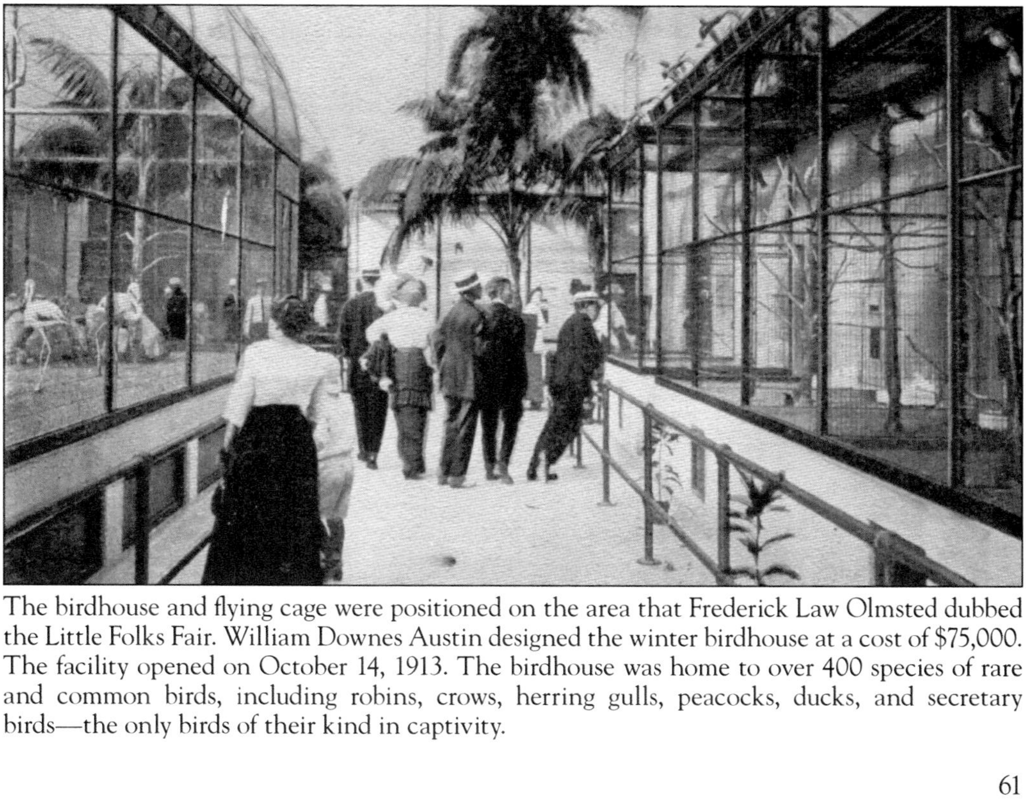

The birdhouse and flying cage were positioned on the area that Frederick Law Olmsted dubbed the Little Folks Fair. William Downes Austin designed the winter birdhouse at a cost of $75,000. The facility opened on October 14, 1913. The birdhouse was home to over 400 species of rare and common birds, including robins, crows, herring gulls, peacocks, ducks, and secretary birds—the only birds of their kind in captivity.

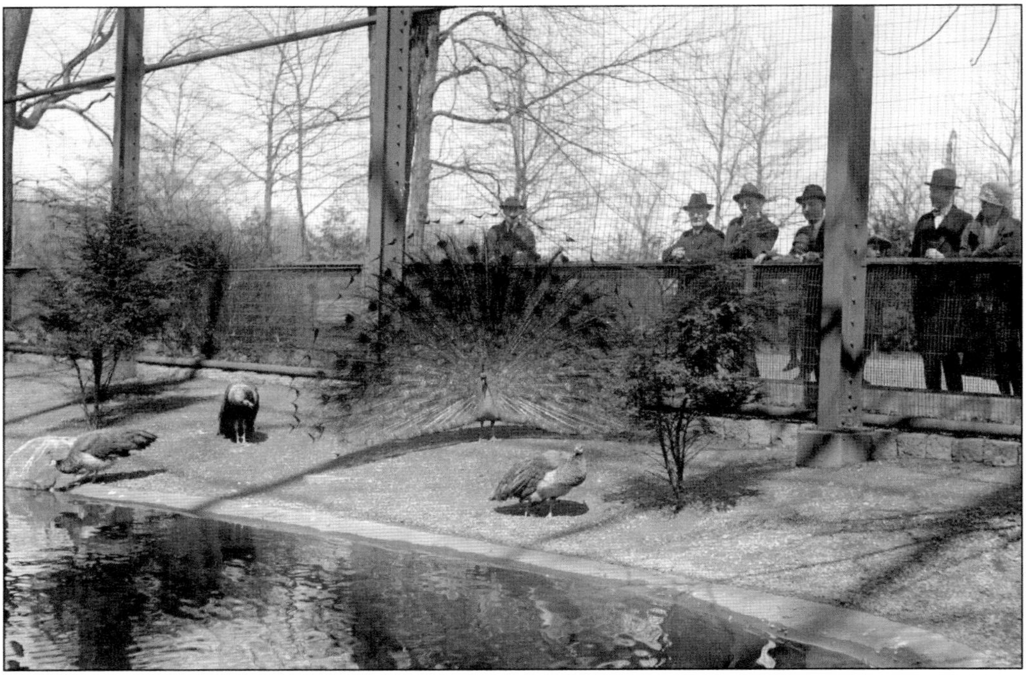

The New England Structural Company constructed the flying cage, which measured 190 feet in length and 60 feet in width and height. A *Boston Post* reporter described the 1912 opening, saying it was "a pleasure to watch them flying in the big cage in the middle of the day when they are taking their baths, a whole crowd, splashing like boys." (Courtesy of the Boston Public Library Print Department.)

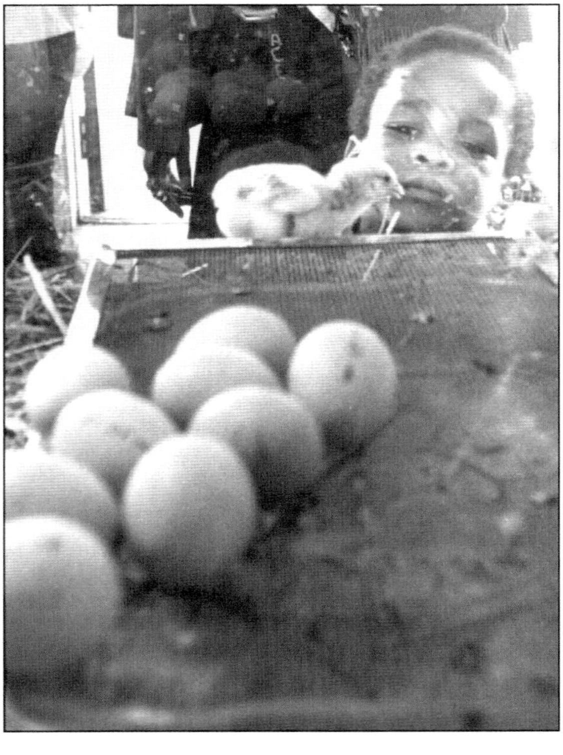

On July 26, 1912, the *Boston Post* reported from the opening of the aviary and birdhouse, "A crowd of several hundred children surrounding the big cage cheered as each small cage was opened and occupants released." In the children's zoo, a hatchery added to the wonderment of the study of nature. (Courtesy of the Boston Public Library Print Department.)

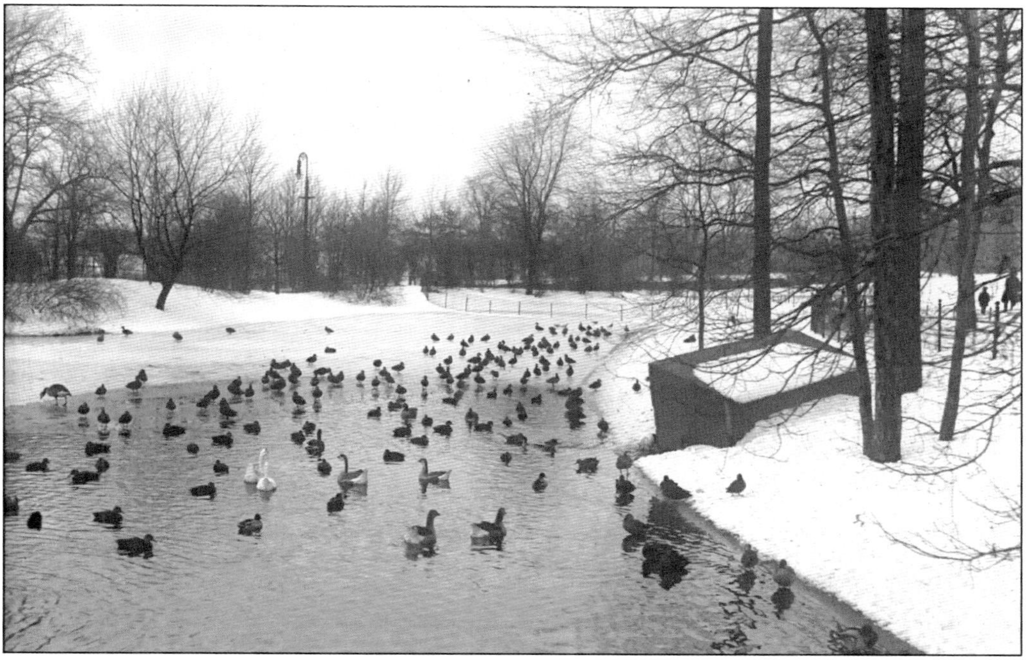

The first pigeons and peafowl were brought into Franklin Park in 1890. In 1903, native fowl were introduced to Scarboro Pond. The success of Scarboro Pond inspired the waterfowl pool, which opened in the flying cage in 1912. King and Queen were the named swans added to the flock in December 1912. A dovecote was added in May 1915. (Courtesy of the Boston Public Library Print Department.)

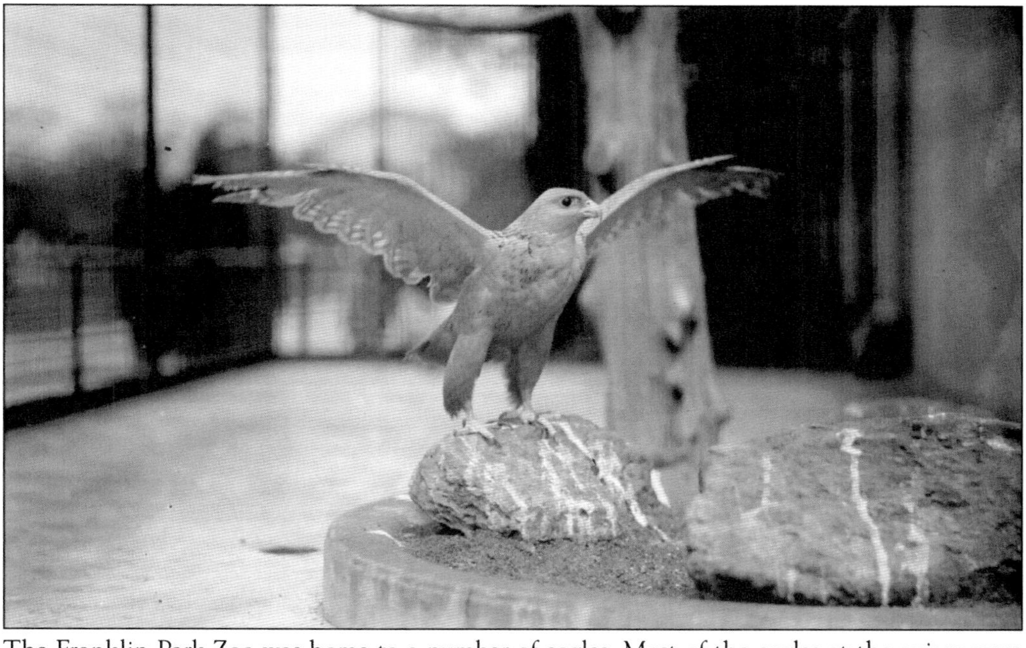

The Franklin Park Zoo was home to a number of eagles. Most of the eagles at the aviary were rescued from migratory situations. Others were donated. One of the famous residents was Margo, the Boston College mascot, from 1961 to 1966. Margo was named by combining the school's colors—maroon and gold. (Courtesy of the Boston Public Library Print Department.)

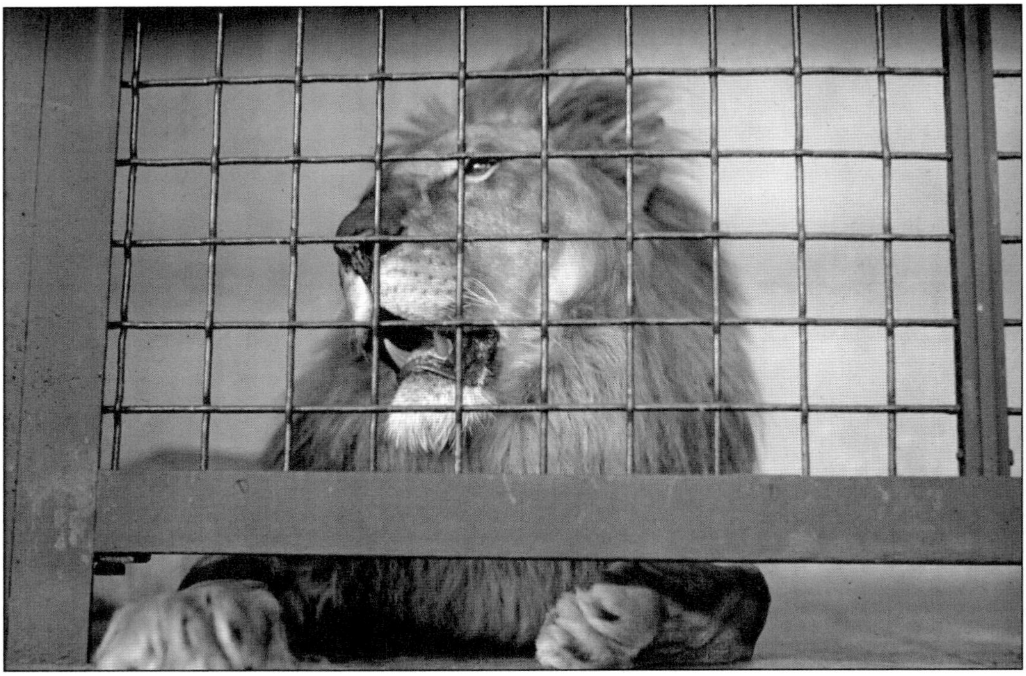

William Downes Austin also designed the feline house. The facility opened in 1920 and housed lions, tigers, panthers, cougars, and leopards. In *Marie Visits the Zoo*, a children's book written in 1953 about a day at the Franklin Park Zoo, Marie declares, "They walked down the lane to the big cat's lair; there were lions and tigers and jaguars there." (Courtesy of the Boston Public Library Print Department.)

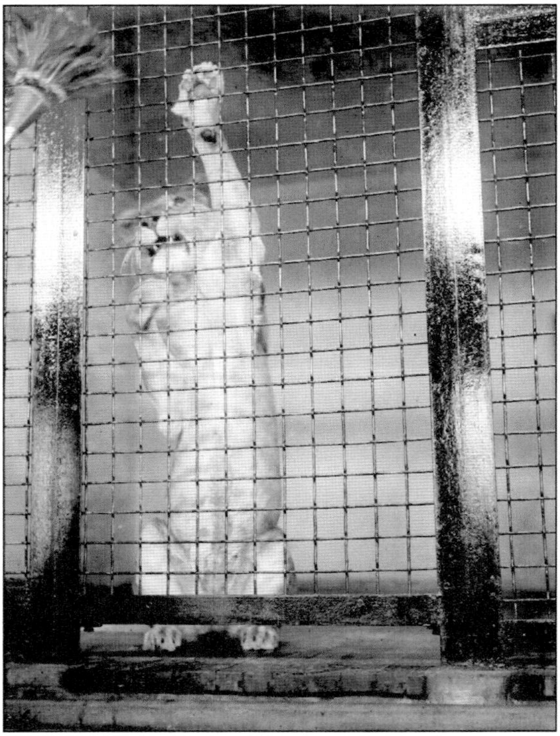

Although Jim the lion and the other felines were a source of entertainment, the management of the feline house was a source of controversy. A shipment of unhealthy animals, due to be displayed in the facility, was rejected by zoo officials in May 1926. The costs to properly feed animals sometimes were too much. The facility was razed in 1978. (Courtesy of the Boston Public Library Print Department.)

The elephant house was designed by G. Henri Desmond and featured a relief of Tony, the baby elephant, over the entrance. The gray cement building was opened to the public on January 5, 1915. The facility was one of the quickest ones to be constructed. It featured three pens for Molly, Waddy, and Tony and "realistic scenery and shrubbery of the jungle wilds." (Courtesy of the Franklin Park Coalition.)

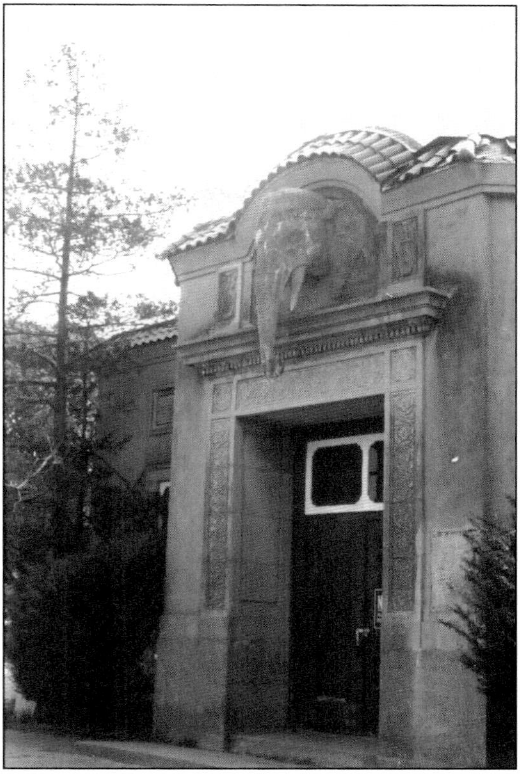

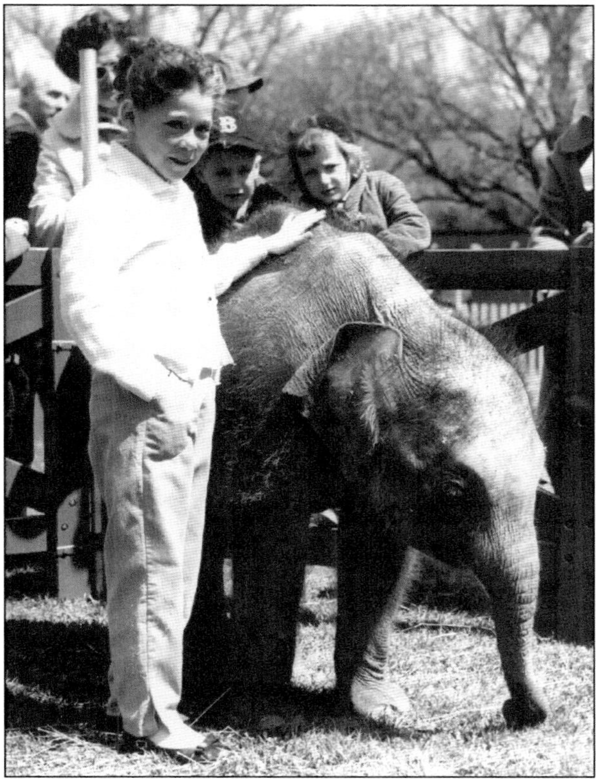

Molly, Waddy, and Tony were purchased with pennies and nickels by over 70,000 Boston schoolchildren in 1914. The *Boston Post* sponsored the collection. On opening day of the elephant house, the newspaper stated, "The children of Boston must be considered smart by the children of other cities." The performing elephants were one of the most popular additions to the free zoo. (Courtesy of the Boston Public Library Print Department.)

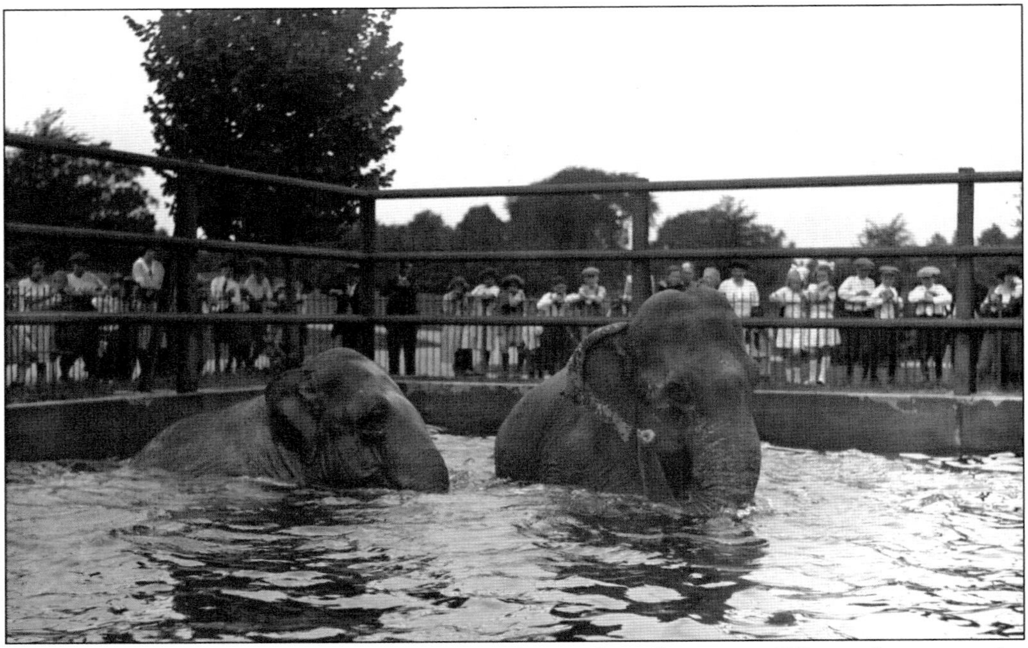

The bathing pool for the elephant house was designed to allow up to 500 people to view the "ever-sportive" Tony or the others at play and hurling "huge sprays of water from their trunks." A concession stand was located just outside the bathing pools where visitors could purchase popcorn, peanuts, and Cracker Jacks. (Courtesy of the Boston Public Library Print Department.)

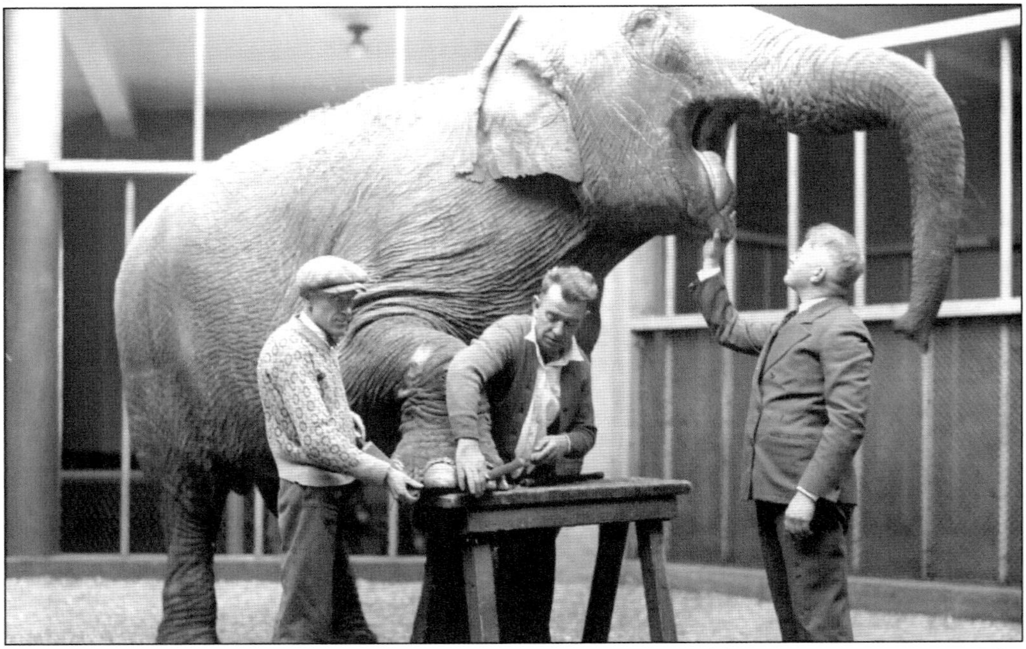

It was a treat to watch Molly, Waddy, or Tony go through the weeklong grooming process. The elephants were soaped down with 150 pounds of soap, dried, sandpapered, and rubbed with pure Indian oils. The total cost for grooming was approximately $300. Grooming could be dangerous for the keepers, and there were reports of injuries and attacks. (Courtesy of the Boston Public Library Print Department.)

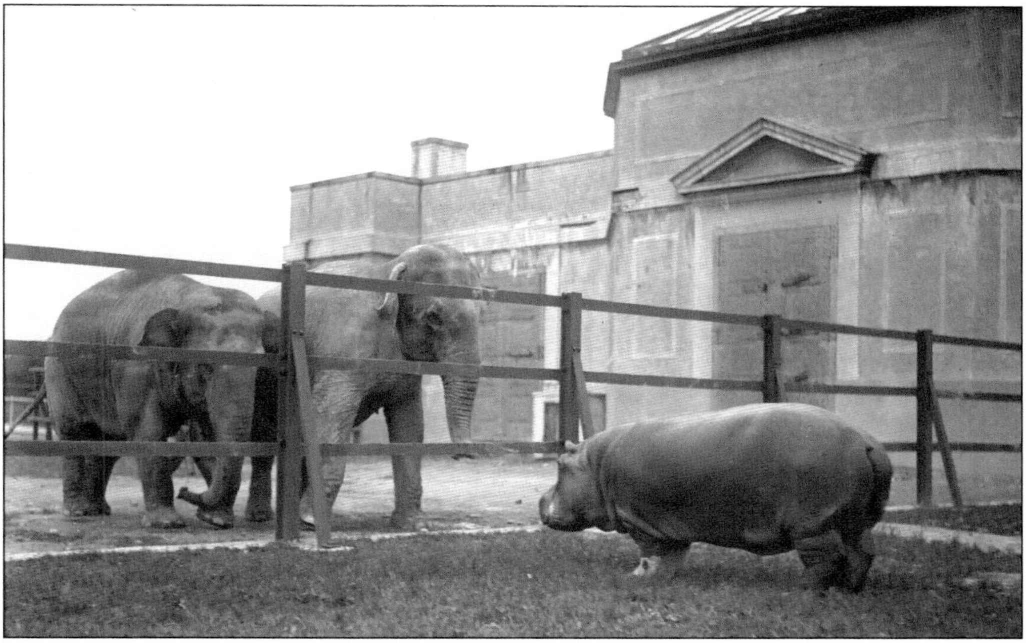

Happy the hippopotamus was born in Philadelphia in 1918. He was brought to Boston in 1922. Happy received his name from a contest in the *Boston Post*. For 29 years, Happy and the elephants were neighbors and visitors delighted in their play. When Happy died in 1951, the *Boston Herald Traveler* reported that Happy would be "sorely missed by his neighbors at the elephant house." (Courtesy of the Boston Public Library Print Department.)

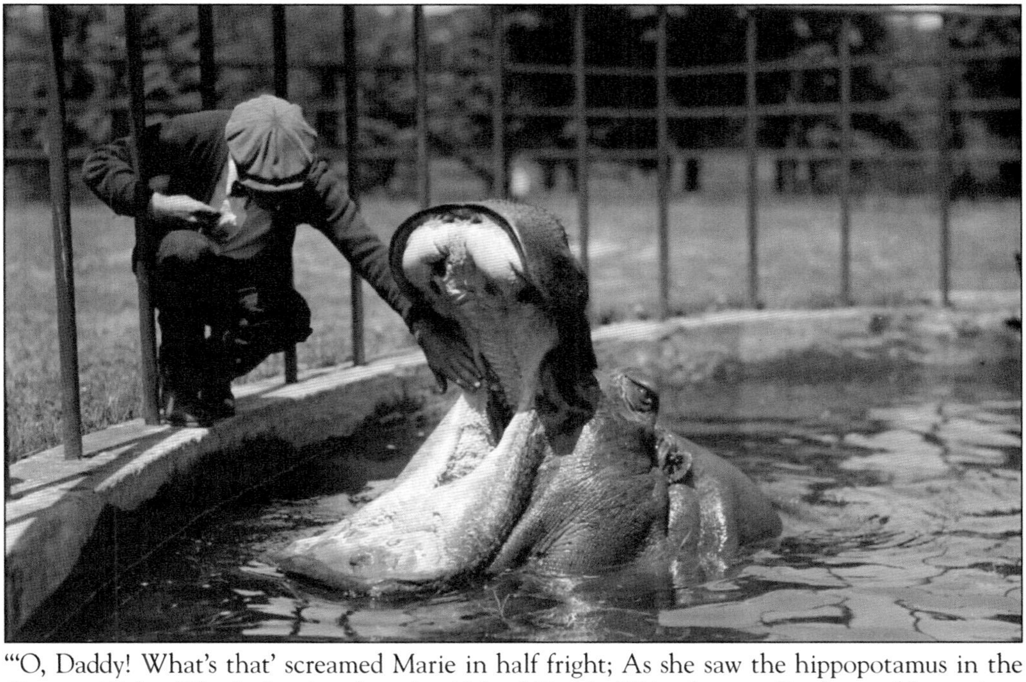

"'O, Daddy! What's that' screamed Marie in half fright; As she saw the hippopotamus in the dim semi-light; 'That's the river horse' said fond Daddy, lifting her up; So she could peer into the pool, round as a cup," reads *Marie Visits the Zoo*. Watching the animals get a checkup by curator Dan Harkins was a treat. (Courtesy of the Boston Public Library Print Department.)

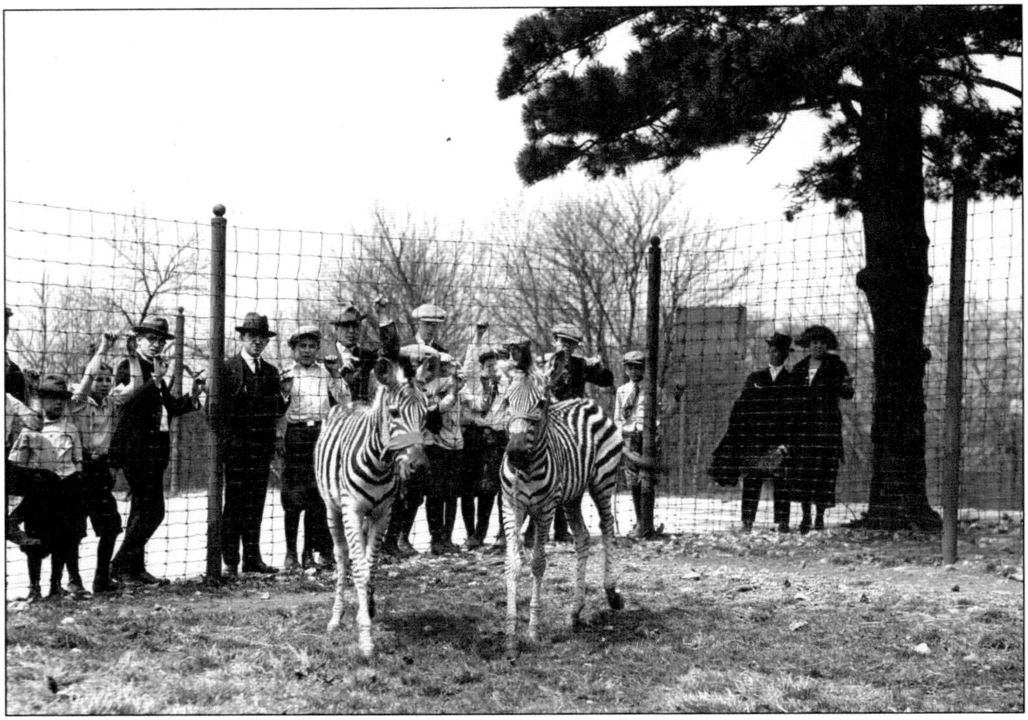

Zebras were introduced to the curious crowds at the Franklin Park Zoo in April 1923. The zebras shared range space and shelter in the Round House or outdoor sheds with the other hooved animals in the confines of the zoo. (Courtesy of the Boston Public Library Print Department.)

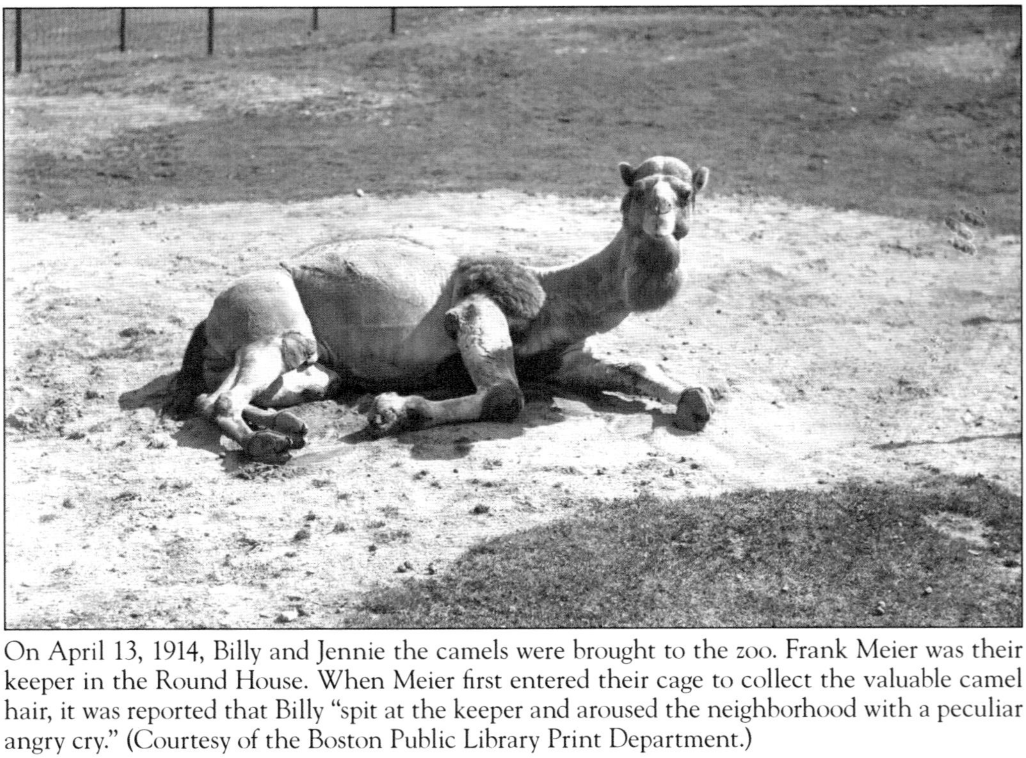

On April 13, 1914, Billy and Jennie the camels were brought to the zoo. Frank Meier was their keeper in the Round House. When Meier first entered their cage to collect the valuable camel hair, it was reported that Billy "spit at the keeper and aroused the neighborhood with a peculiar angry cry." (Courtesy of the Boston Public Library Print Department.)

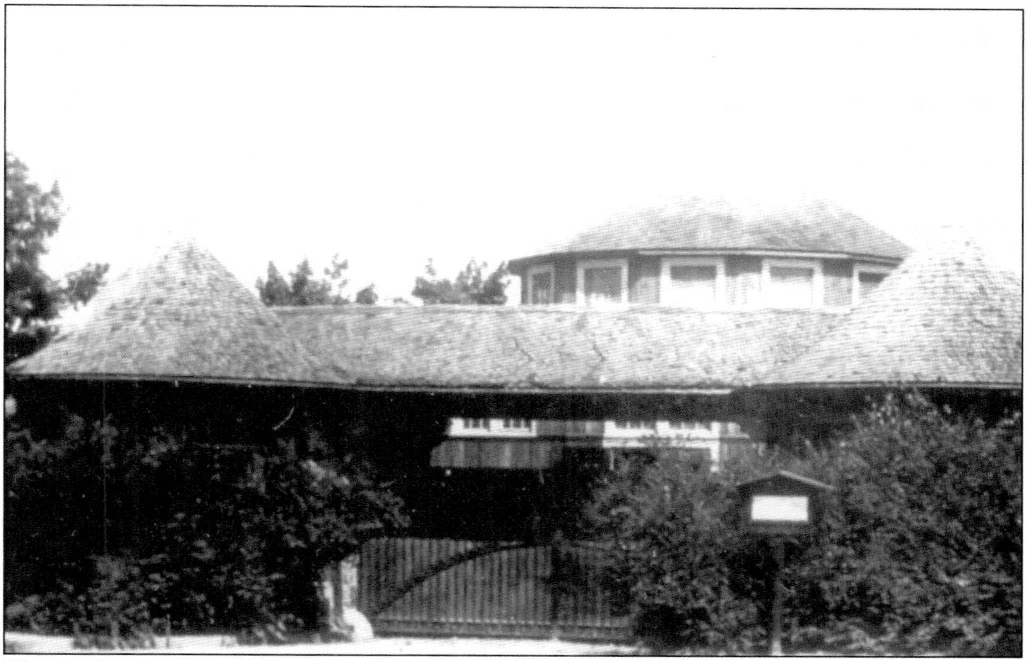

The facility known as the Round House was originally built as the carriage house for the Refectory building. It was converted to homes for various animals, including monkeys, baboons, porcupines, and Siberian dogs. The Round House was the winter home for some of the range animals as well. By critics, it was described as unsuitable and a "second-rate circus." (Courtesy of the Boston Public Library Print Department.)

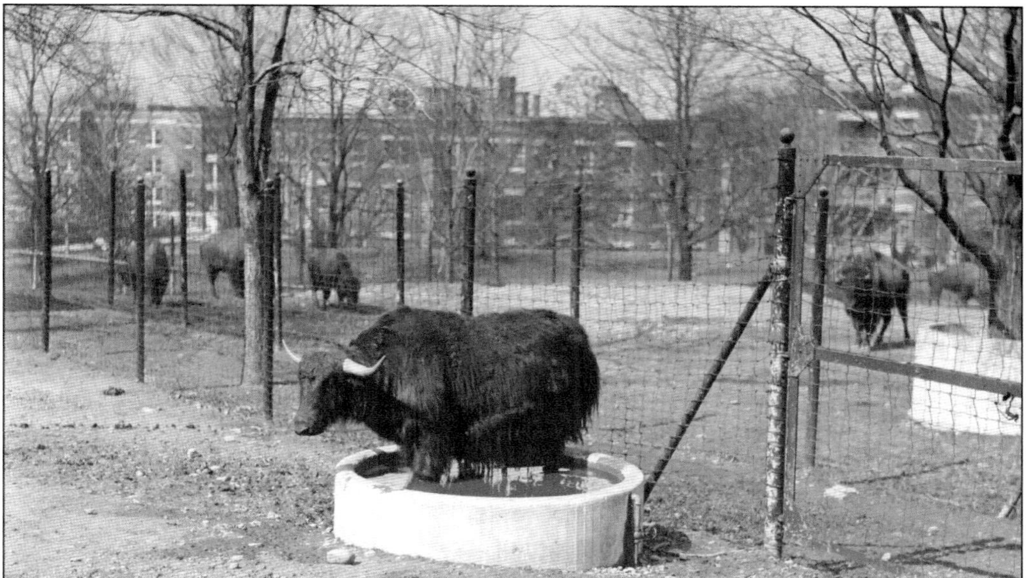

Frederick Law Olmsted planned for an area called the deer park in his original plans. The area was to "supply a range for a small herd to be seen from the Greeting." The idea of the deer park was realized in the plans for the Franklin Park Zoo but housed a variety of animals, including giraffes, buffalo, moose, deer, and yaks, over the years. (Courtesy of the Boston Public Library Print Department.)

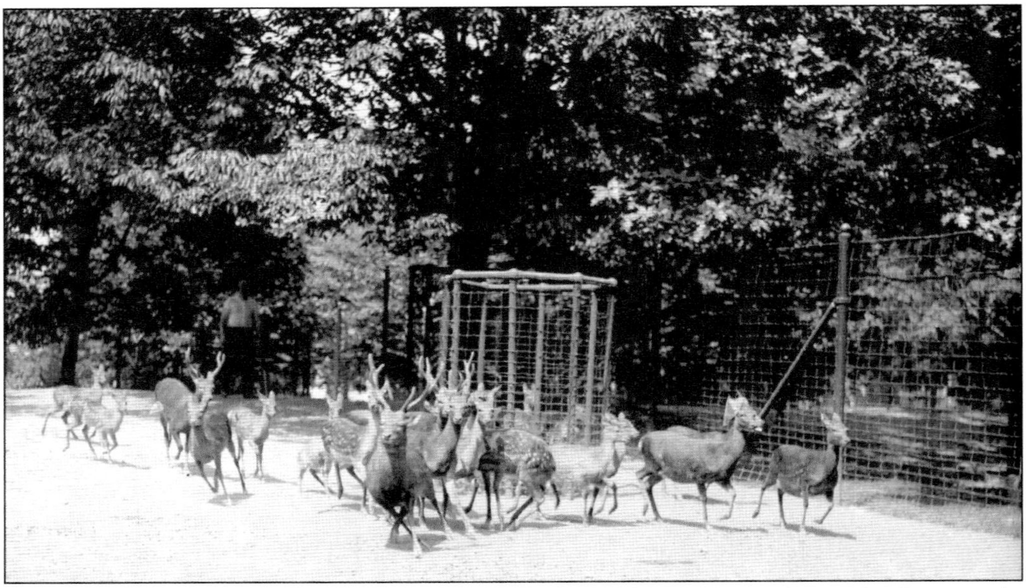

Since the Round House and sheds in the deer park were inadequate winter homes for the animals, an antelope house was constructed in 1931, using New Deal Works Progress Administration funds. It was an octagonal building with eight corrals that featured a specialized heating system and fireproofing. The building cost $68,000 and improved the "value of the tropical hooved animals by 100%." (Courtesy of the Boston Public Library Print Department.)

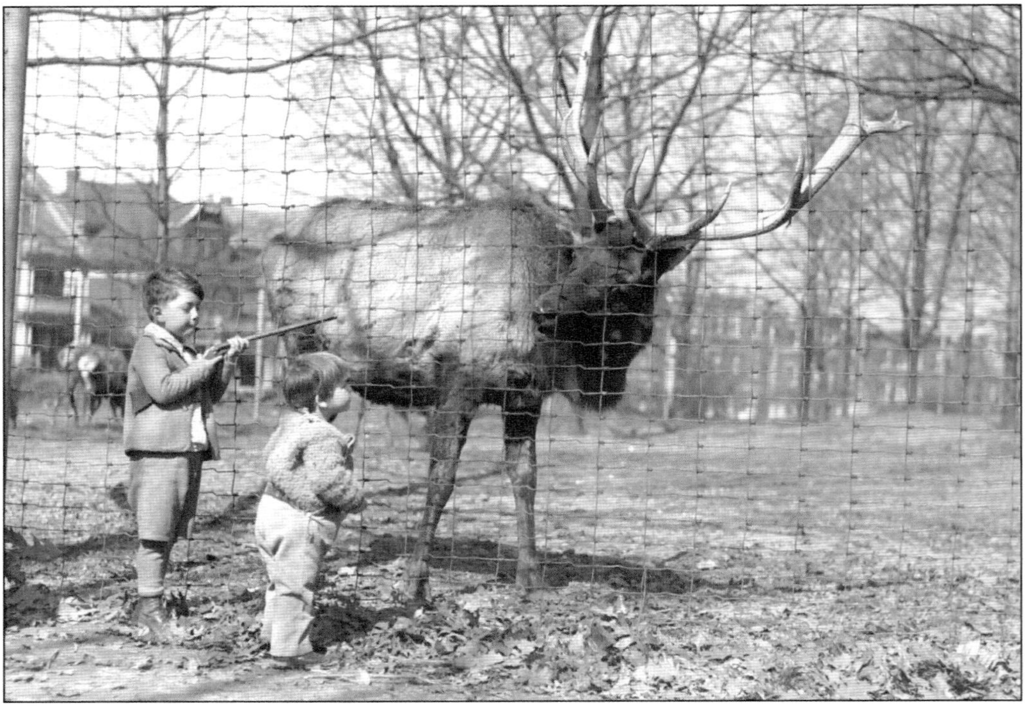

Leslie Jones, a photographer for the *Boston Herald Traveler*, captured life in Boston over his 40-year career. Many pictures in his collection contain humorous captions to describe the actions. "Animal by gosh! Shoot to kill!" is noted on the back of this picture of two small boys and a moose in the Franklin Park Zoo. (Courtesy of the Boston Public Library Print Department.)

There were opportunities in the zoo for children to fulfill their curiosity. In some cases, mischief and injuries occurred. Four boys climbed over the outer fence of the bear dens in 1933. Lillian the brown bear snatched the smallest. One of the older boys squeezed through the cage and whacked Lillian in the nose until she released the boy. A keeper rescued both boys. (Courtesy of the Boston Public Library Print Department.)

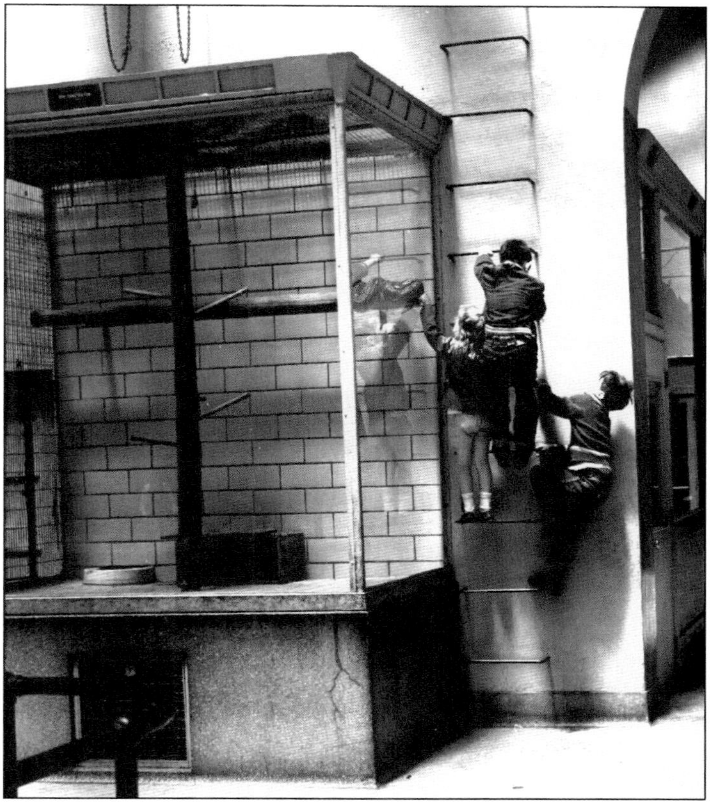

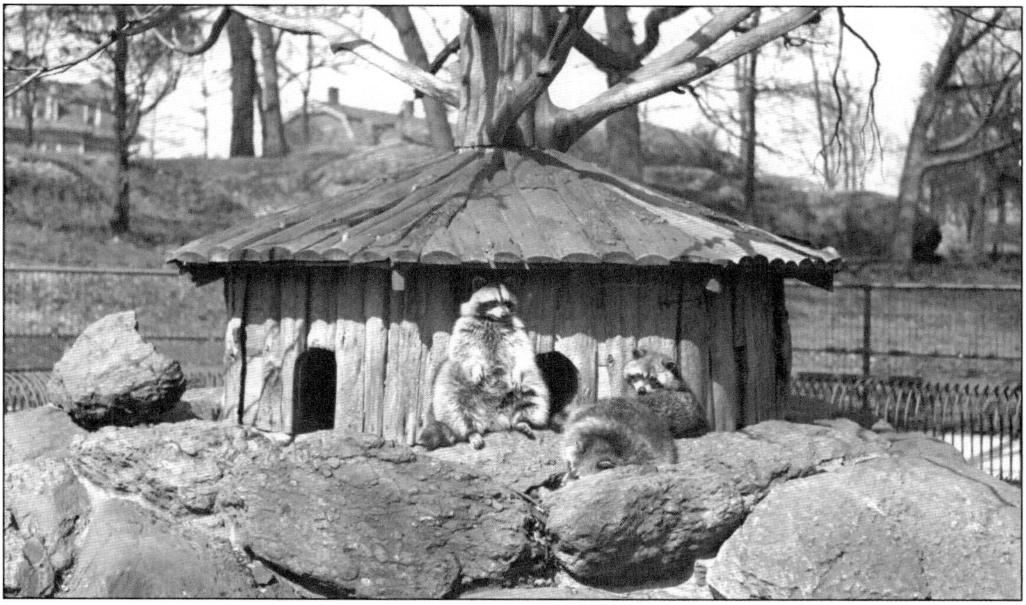

Raccoons were not the most exotic of animals. They were included in the original plan because they could endure New England weather. The 1954 Shurcliff and Shurcliff feasibility study reported, "Vandals repeatedly entered the area at night and stoned the animals to death." The study suggested moving the raccoons to the main zoo. (Courtesy of the Boston Public Library Print Department.)

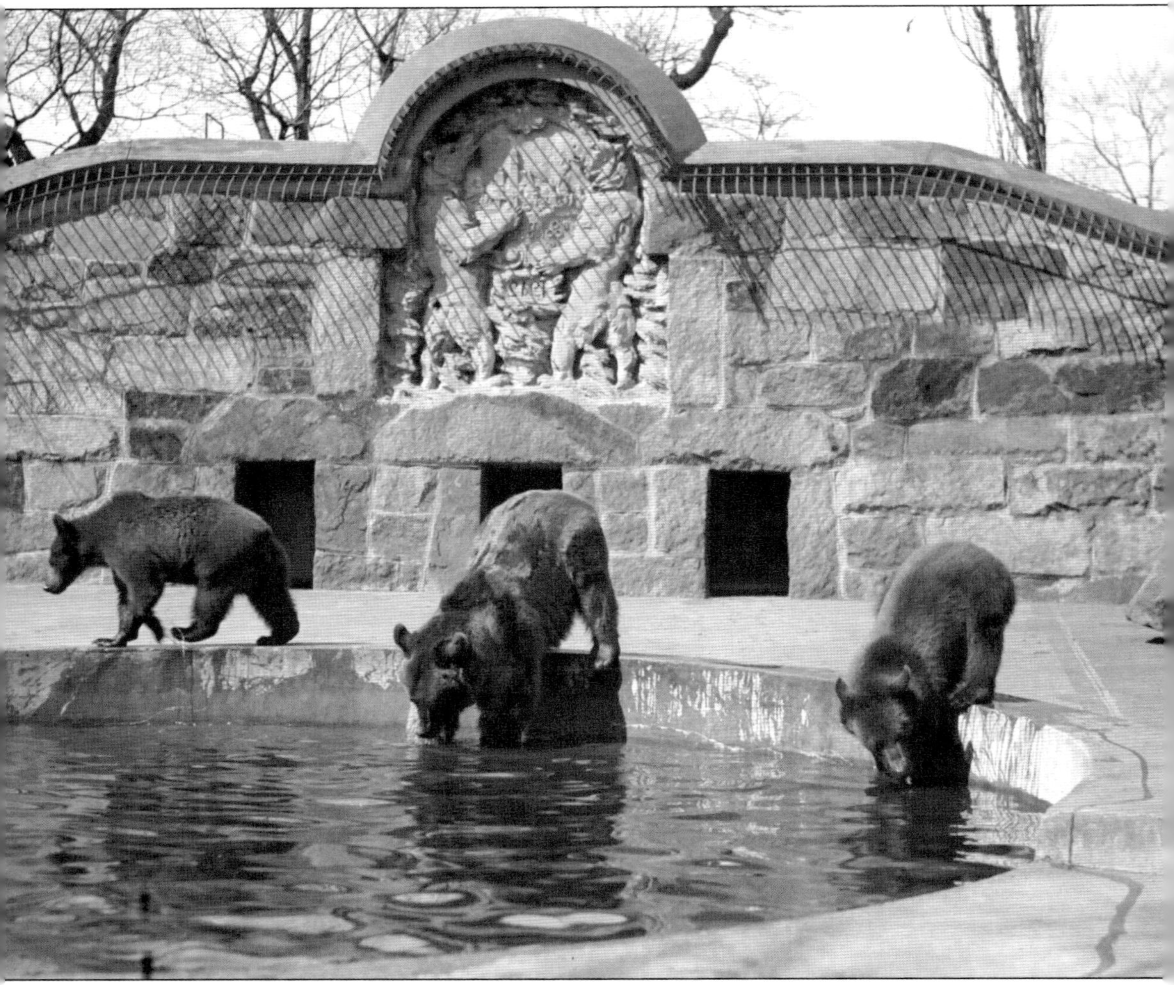

Arthur Shurtleff's first plans for the bear dens were submitted to the Boston Parks and Recreation Department in March 1911. The design showed four bear dens in the Long Crouch Woods area of Franklin Park. The woods were described in Frederick Law Olmsted's "General Plan of Franklin Park" as "a rambling ground, with sheltered southwestern slopes, to be held subject to lease to a suitable organization or zoological garden." Bears were purchased from Germany and Yellowstone National Park to be included in the first exhibitions. The dens were described as "an imposing character. The walls are completed and the ironworks and flagging of the yards are well underway. Each yard contains a small commodious pool. Beeches and oaks have been planted in openings among the old trees to provide shade for the concourse in front." The $100,000 bear dens opened to a crowd of 10,000 people on October 3, 1912. The bear dens were the first official exhibit to be opened in the Franklin Park Zoo. (Courtesy of the Boston Public Library Print Department.)

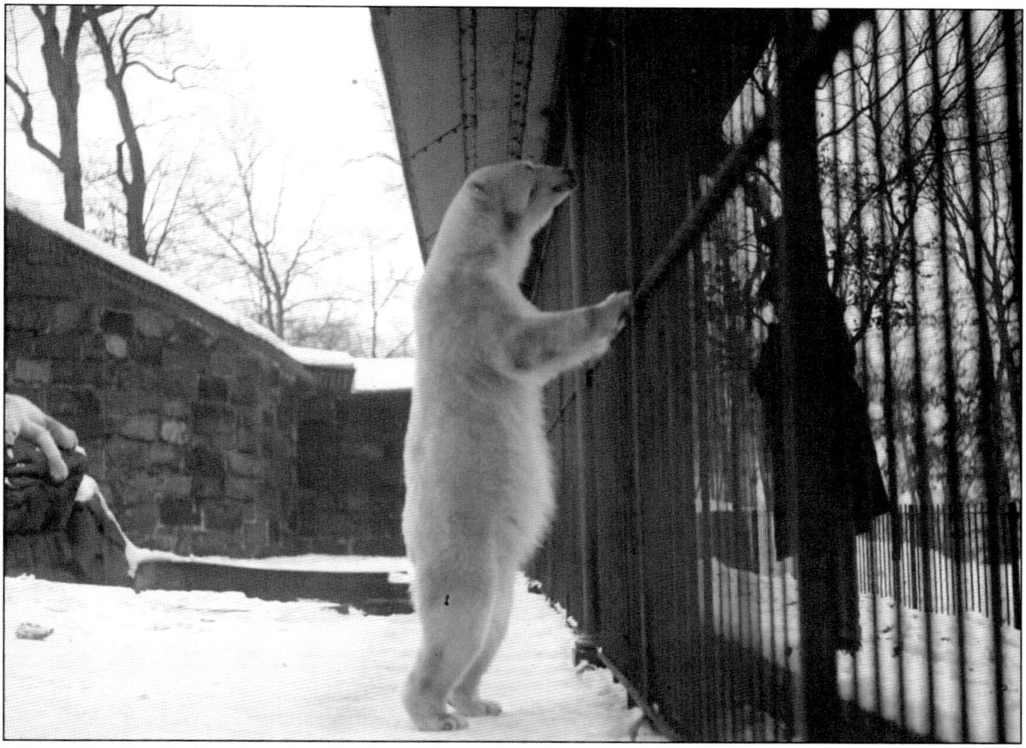

The 1954 Shurcliff and Shurcliff study suggested the closing of the bear dens due to the distance from the zoo, the safety of bears and visitors in the area, and the unacceptable nature of the exhibit in comparison to existing bear exhibits around the country at that time. Two polar bears were transferred to the Stone Zoo in July 1966. The other bears were sold to various zoos around the country. The last black bears were shipped to Clifty Acres in Indiana between July 30, 1966, and December 3, 1970. The last polar bear was included with the final trade to Clifty Acres. (Courtesy of the Boston Public Library Print Department.)

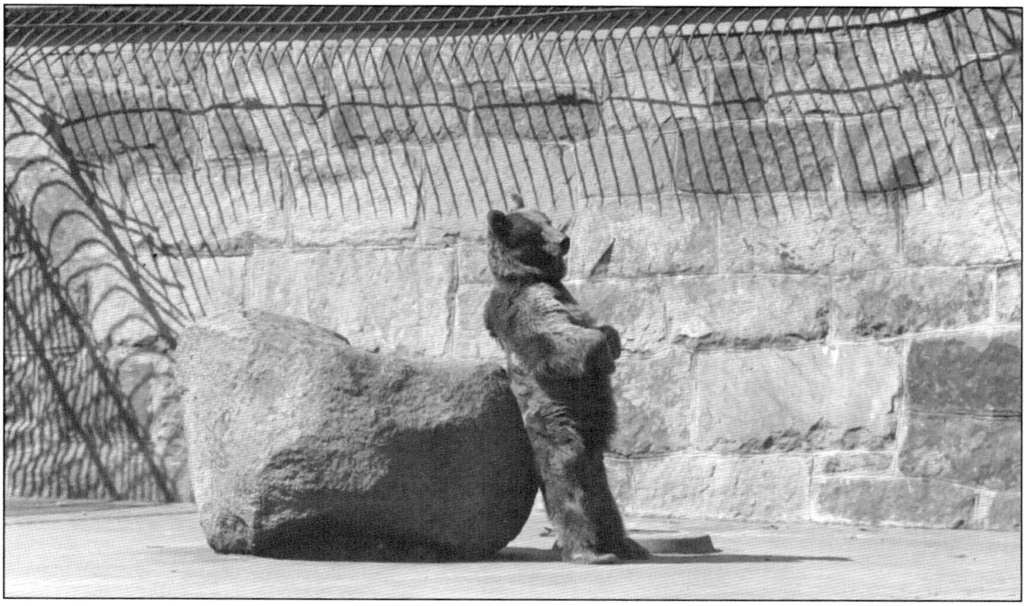

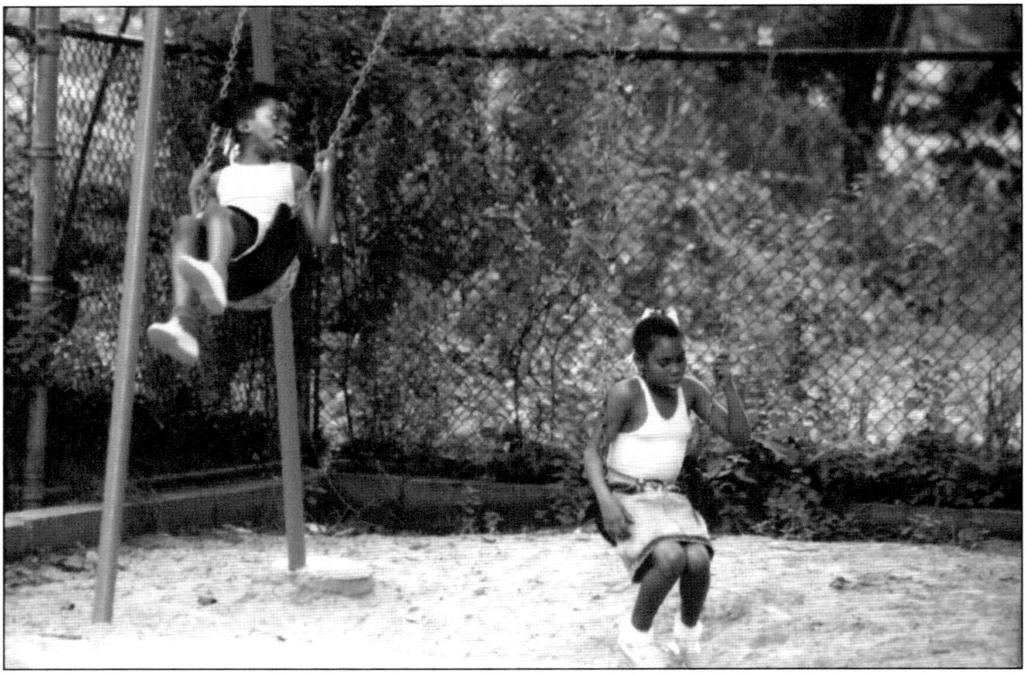

Frederick Law Olmsted's Little Folks Fair was described as "a division for childish entertainments, to be furnished, with Swings, Scups, and Seesaws, sand courts, Flying Horses, Toy Booths, Marionettes, Goat Carriages, Donkey Courses, Bear Pits, and other amusing exercises and exhibitions, mostly to be provided by lessees and purveyors, to be licensed for the purpose." (Courtesy of the Franklin Park Coalition.)

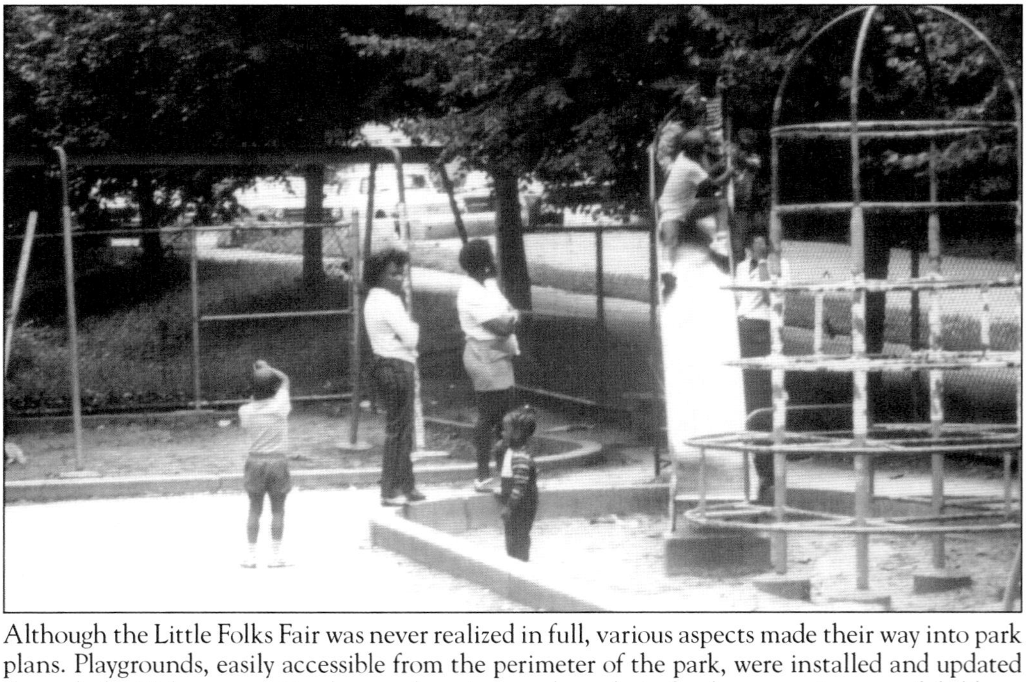

Although the Little Folks Fair was never realized in full, various aspects made their way into park plans. Playgrounds, easily accessible from the perimeter of the park, were installed and updated through the 20th century. Donkeys and ponies were brought in for the entertainment of children. Bear pits were included in the plans for the zoo. (Courtesy of the Franklin Park Coalition.)

Five

Refectory Hill

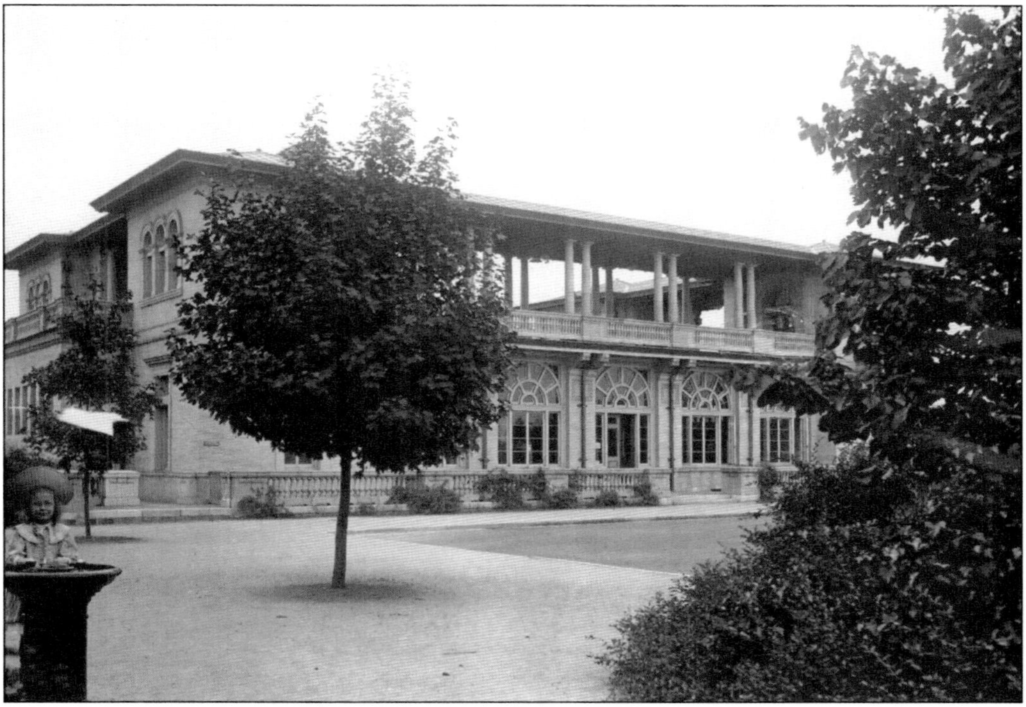

According to the "General Plan of Franklin Park," Refectory Hill was "a place for refreshments, to be principally served from the house shown, out-of-doors, under a large pergola, or vine-clad trellis, upon a terrace formed in the manner of the Playstead Overlook. From this terrace extensive sylvan prospects open, one of which will be later referred to. In the rear of the Refectory building, across a carriage-court, there is a circular range of horse-sheds for use of the visitors." (Courtesy of Historic New England.)

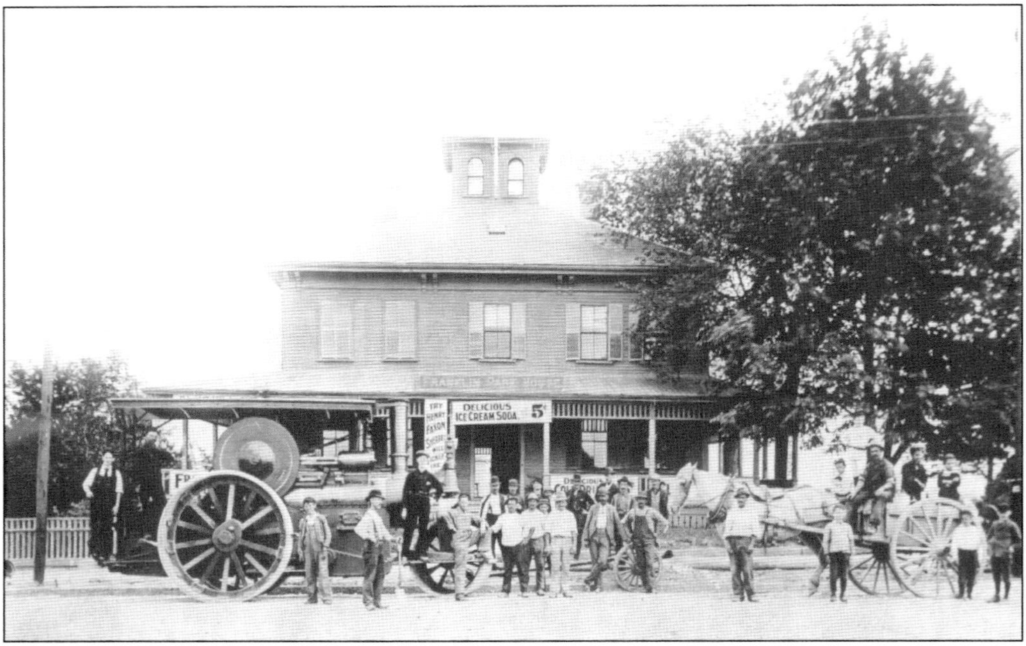

Frederick Law Olmsted provided for the refreshment of park users in all corners of Franklin Park from the beginning of construction. His 1883 preliminary plan called for the Sewall House to be "fitted up early in the season with a refectory and conveniences for refreshments of visitors to the park." This building provided the background for Maurice Prendergast's painting *Franklin Park, Boston*. (Courtesy of Historic New England.)

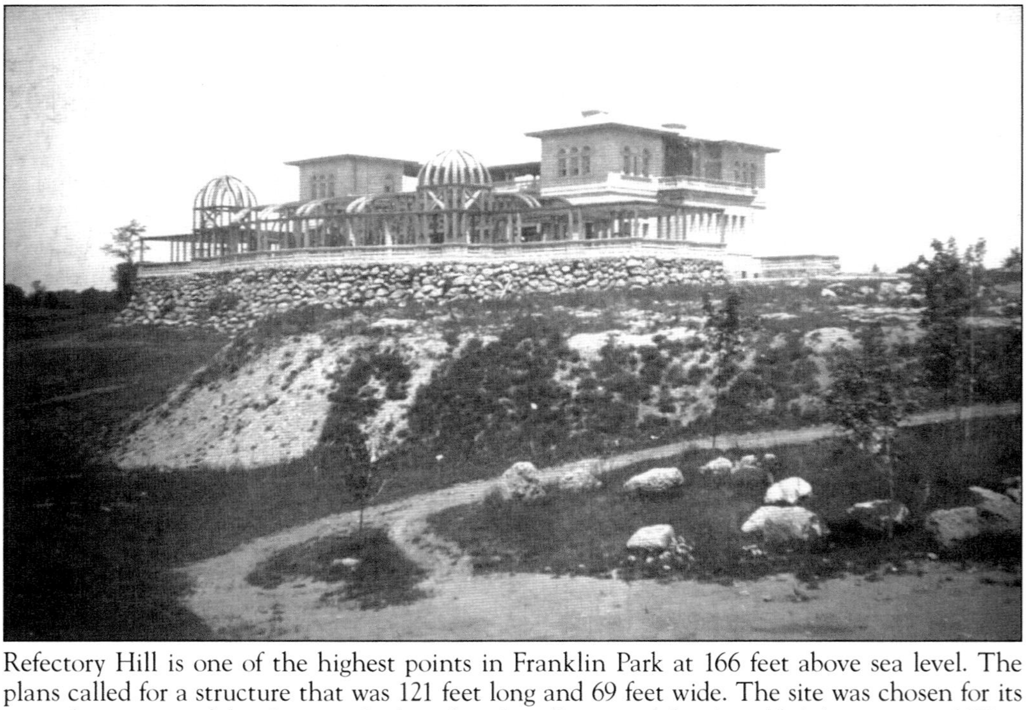

Refectory Hill is one of the highest points in Franklin Park at 166 feet above sea level. The plans called for a structure that was 121 feet long and 69 feet wide. The site was chosen for its immediate views of the Country Park and its far-off views of the Arnold Arboretum and West Roxbury. (Courtesy of the Boston Public Library Print Department.)

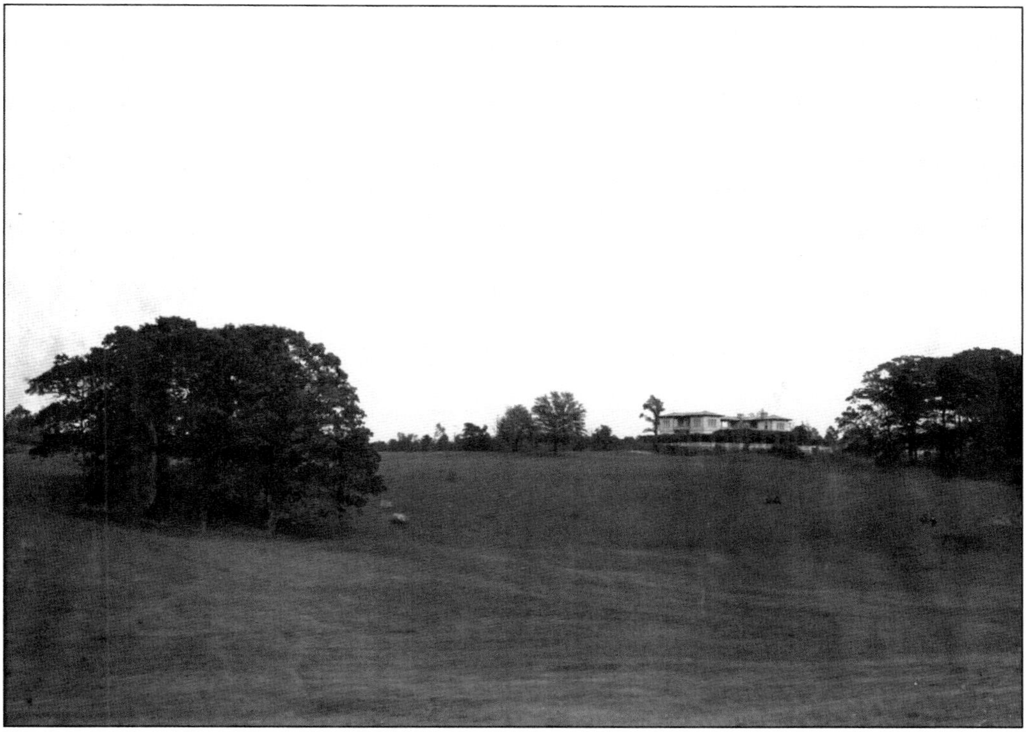

In 1891, the architectural firm of Hartwell and Richardson submitted its plans for the "most important building erected on the park" on the site of the former Gleason House. Due to delays in construction, the brick and terra-cotta structure finally opened on July 4, 1896. The Refectory was built in 1895. In 1896, the building was described as "the chief park restaurant, a building of elaborate design, with general restaurant, private dining rooms, pergola with trellised roof, and roof garden" by Edward Bacon in *Walks and Rides about Boston*. (Above, courtesy of the National Park Service, Frederick Law Olmsted National Historic Site; below, courtesy of Jerry Burke.)

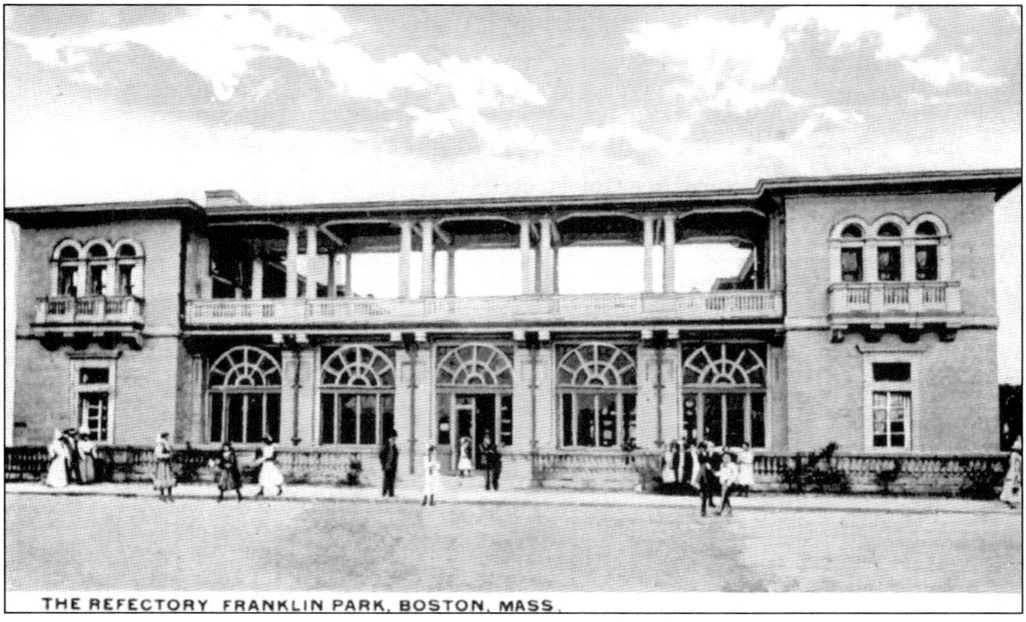

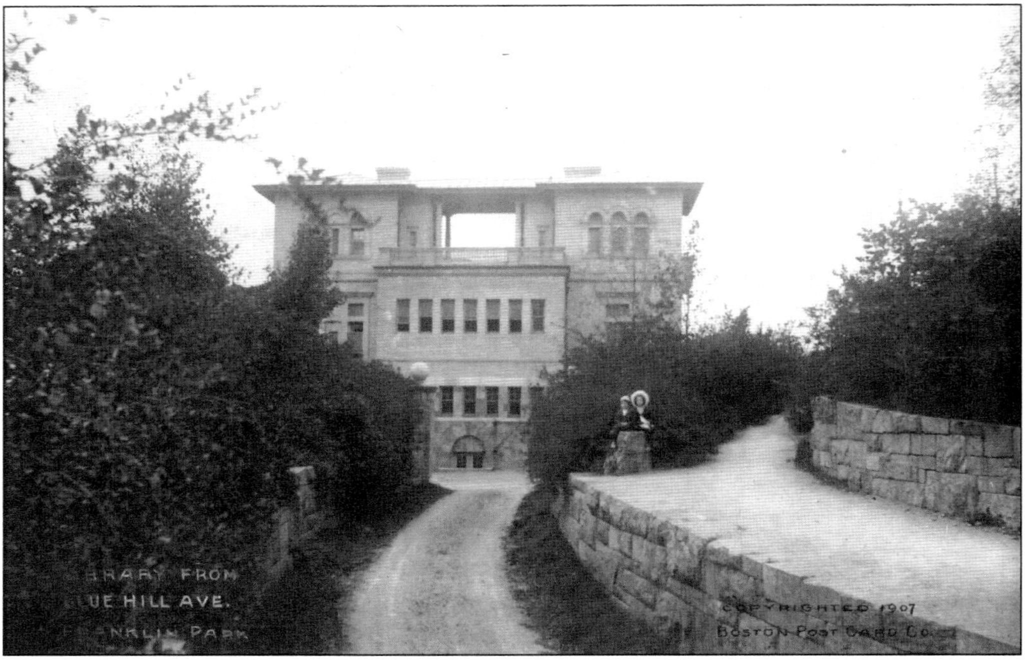

A Dorchester student, Falk Nathan, wrote about the Refectory for a school project in 1907. He described the building as an "open air library where books can be taken out and read on the veranda or balcony which faces the park. Here the air is always cool and reading in this quiet, cool spot makes it a pleasant pastime." He also noted that the "building was used as a consumptives' school but a complaint was issued that consumption was catching and the school had to be removed." (Above, courtesy of Historic New England.)

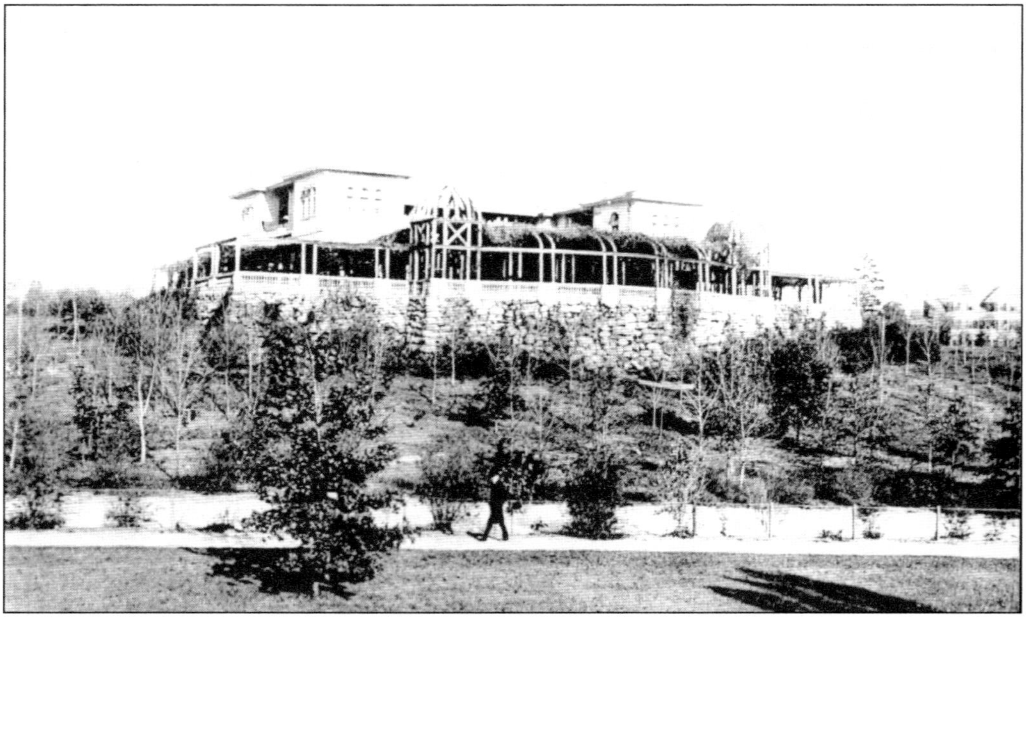

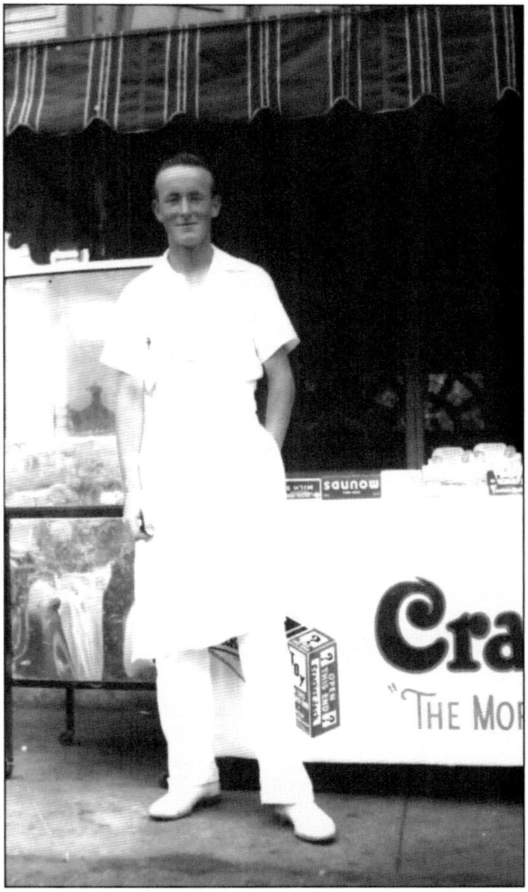

In 1905, the city found itself in the middle of a bidding scandal. The Boston park commissioners wanted the highest bidder to not only be able to pay the lease and make improvements but also to have the ability to support concessions, be qualified and responsible to the building, and follow the rules and regulations of the park commission. The bid system controlled concessions in all parts of the park, including the golf course and zoo. In 1928, the Burke family gained the right to operate concessions in the park and did so until 1971. (Courtesy of Jerry Burke.)

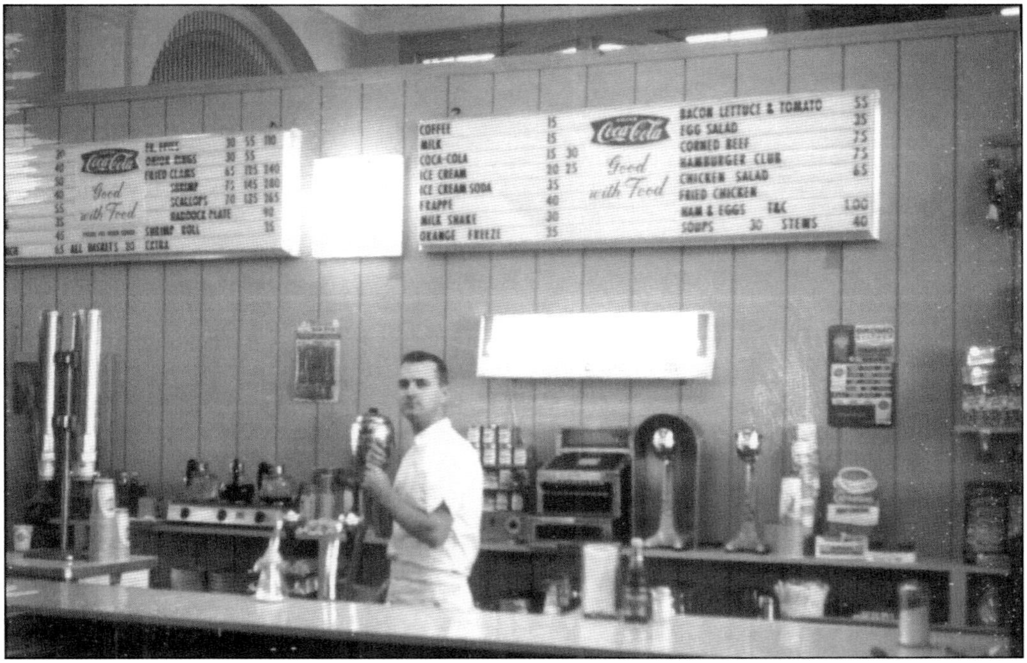

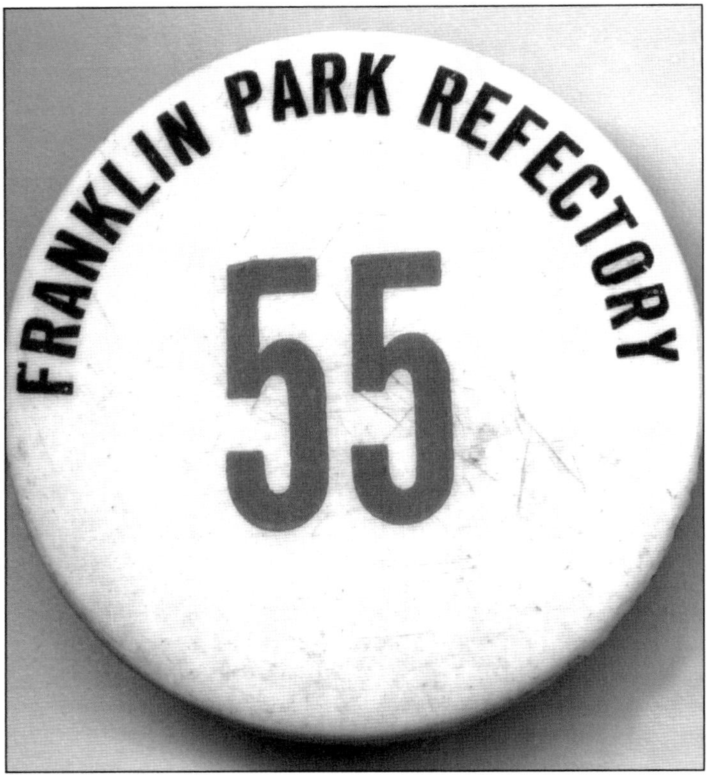

The concessions uniform included a long, white apron and an identification button. The button was the way that the boys would register at the beginning and end of each day of work and be known to the general public. At the beginning of the day, workers were responsible for inventorying their daily supplies and going to their posted assignments. Upon return to the Refectory to restock or at the end of the day, the inventory would be checked. The workers at the Refectory returned summer after summer to serve up snacks, balloons, and sodas within Franklin Park, at the Refectory, and at the zoo. (Courtesy of Jerry Burke.)

FRANKLIN PARK REFECTORY

Stand____________________ Date____________________

NO. PCS.	ARTICLE	Count	Price	Amount
	French Fried Corn			
	Sugar Corn			
	Molasses Bars			
	Pinwheels			
	Peanuts			
	Cracker Jacks			
	Potato Chips			
	Balloons & Sticks			
	Hot Dogs & Rolls			

Seasonal employment was enjoyable for many of the neighborhood boys. There was camaraderie among the Refectory workers, young and old. Bartenders knew their regulars and shared stories of families and friends. The younger boys who worked in the stands in the zoo sold balloons and were known to sneak peanuts to the elephants. (Courtesy of Jerry Burke.)

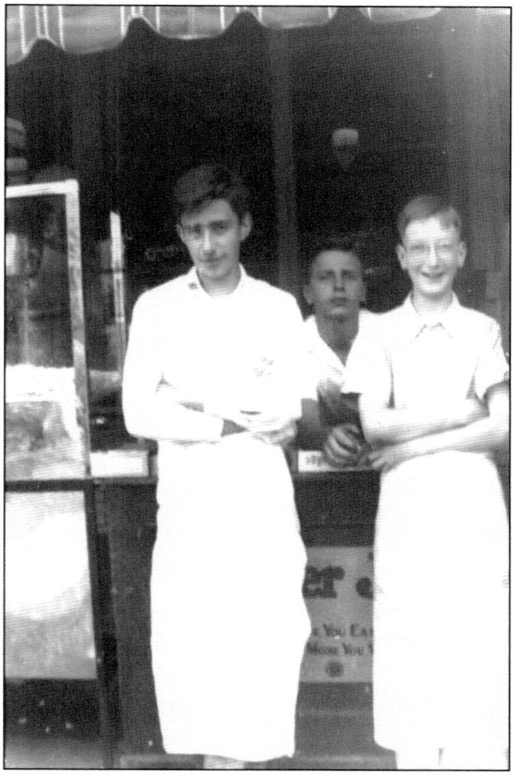

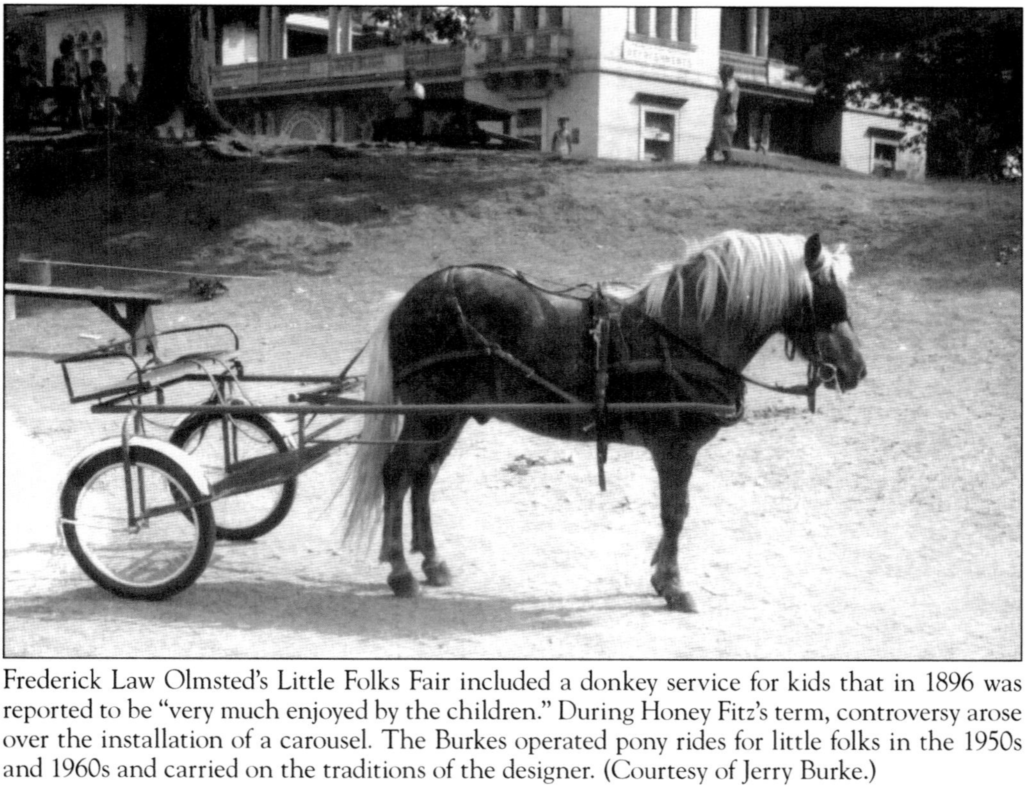

Frederick Law Olmsted's Little Folks Fair included a donkey service for kids that in 1896 was reported to be "very much enjoyed by the children." During Honey Fitz's term, controversy arose over the installation of a carousel. The Burkes operated pony rides for little folks in the 1950s and 1960s and carried on the traditions of the designer. (Courtesy of Jerry Burke.)

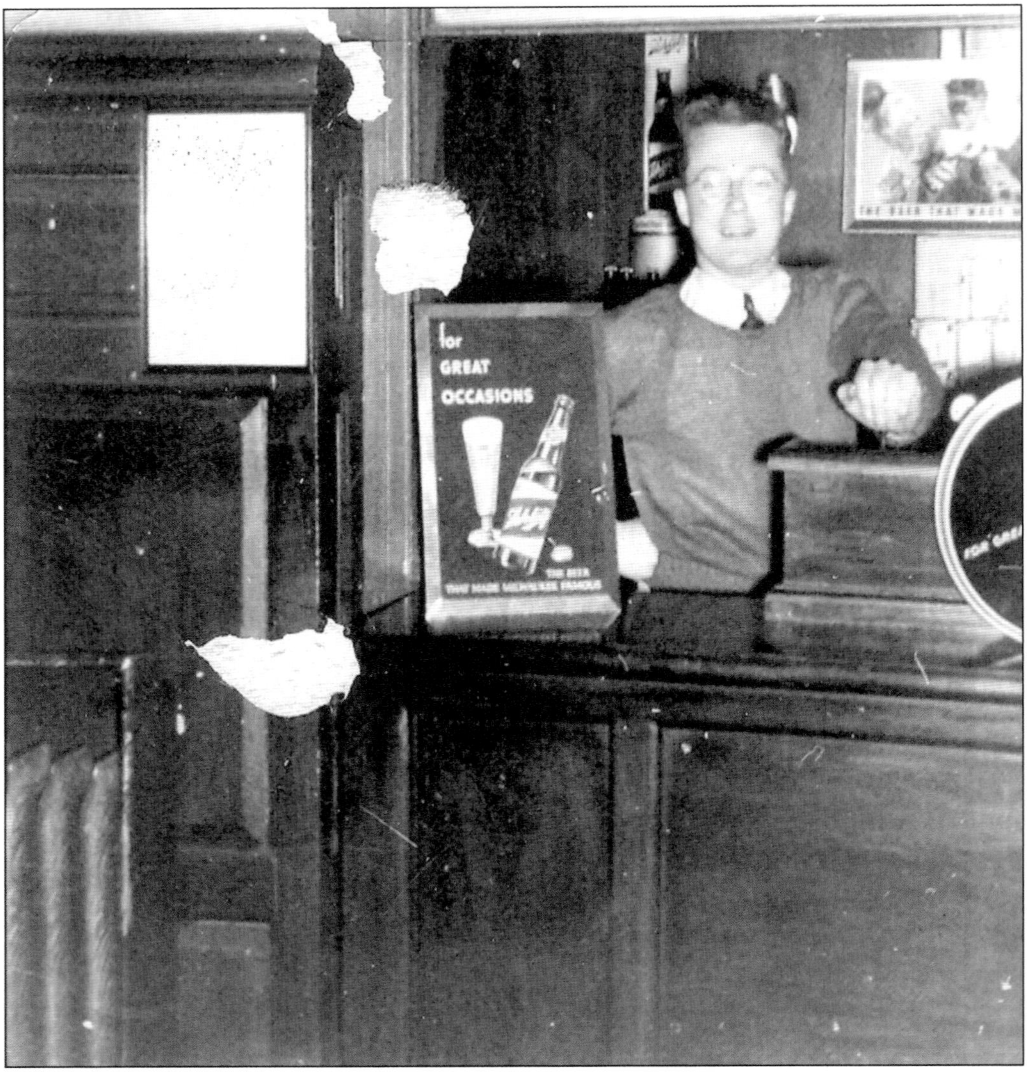

Operations were available by winning a bid with the City of Boston. The winning bidder was typically granted a five-year lease on the property and was responsible for improvements, quality food and service, and daily operations. William F. Dwyer was banned from selling peanuts near the elephant house in 1915 because he did not have the financial means to pay for the privilege. From 1928 to 1974, the Burke family of Jamaica Plain was responsible for concessions in the Franklin Park Zoo and on the golf course. Visitors could enjoy hot popcorn, tonic, peanuts, and Cracker Jacks from the bear dens to the Refectory. The Burke family employed hundreds of young men in the park as grill cooks, bartenders, and even Cracker Jacks peddlers. (Courtesy of Jerry Burke.)

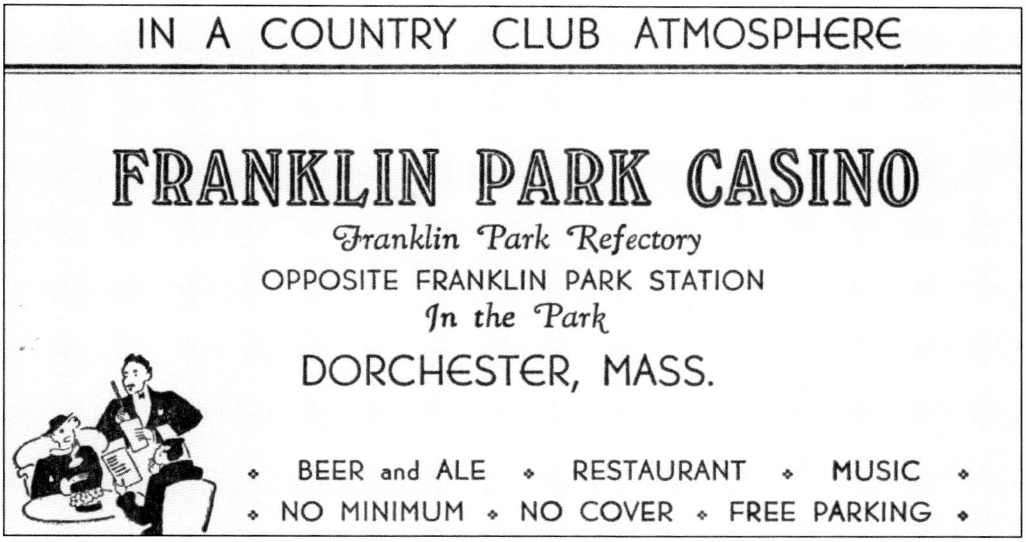

John Charles Olmsted called the design of the Refectory "a marked violation of our instructions . . . as to the relation of the design to the landscape. We did not intend to have a building of light-colored terra cotta, nor so showy in its details." The showy details would eventually mark the rebirth of the Refectory as a formal dining room and ballroom for the Franklin Park neighbors. The building was marketed as a ballroom and casino for evening events and a place to quench thirst of all kinds and have casual meals in the day. Through the 1940s and 1950s, the Refectory was the place to rent equipment for sporting in the park—including toboggans for the Schoolmaster Hill run. The park department used the building to capitalize on popular activities for a profit. (Courtesy of Jerry Burke.)

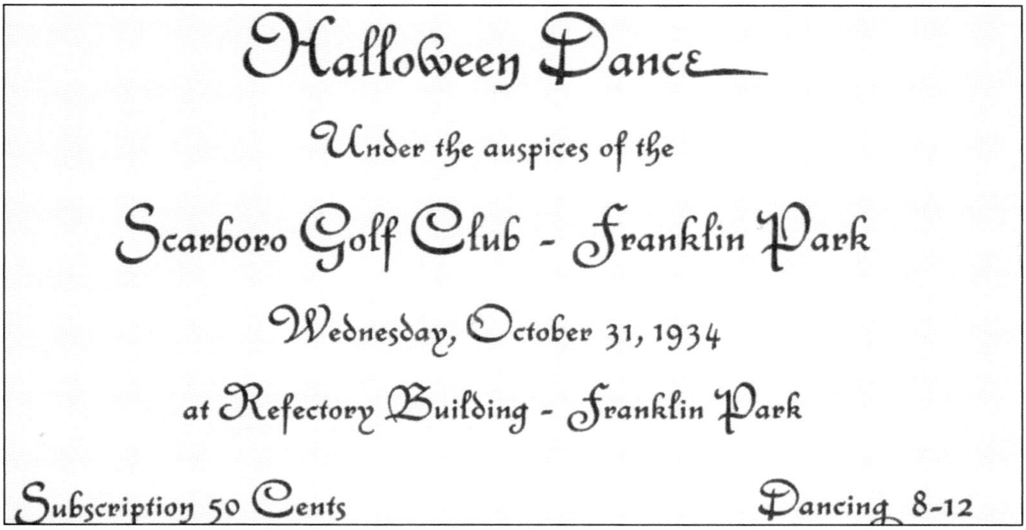
Halloween Dance

Under the auspices of the

Scarboro Golf Club - Franklin Park

Wednesday, October 31, 1934

at Refectory Building - Franklin Park

Subscription 50 Cents   Dancing 8-12

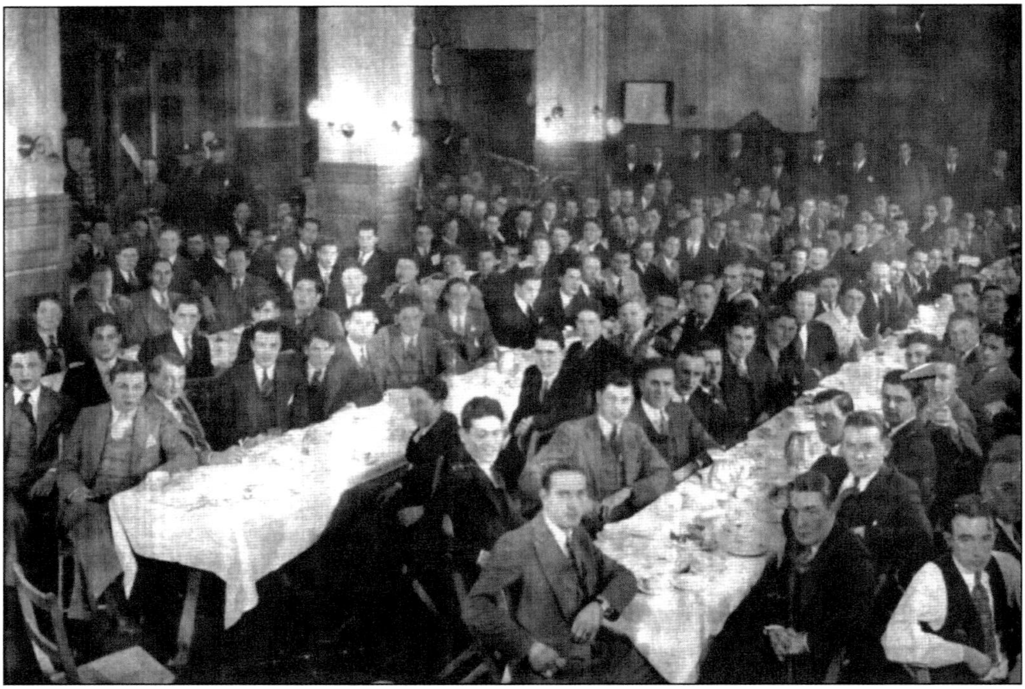

Sylvester Baxter described the Refectory as "a large restaurant with a private dining room and one of the most beautiful ball rooms in Boston." The ballroom hosted everything from galas to bachelor dinners to holiday dances throughout the 20th century. The Refectory was equipped with multiple kitchens and bars to accommodate all types of gatherings. (Courtesy of Jerry Burke.)

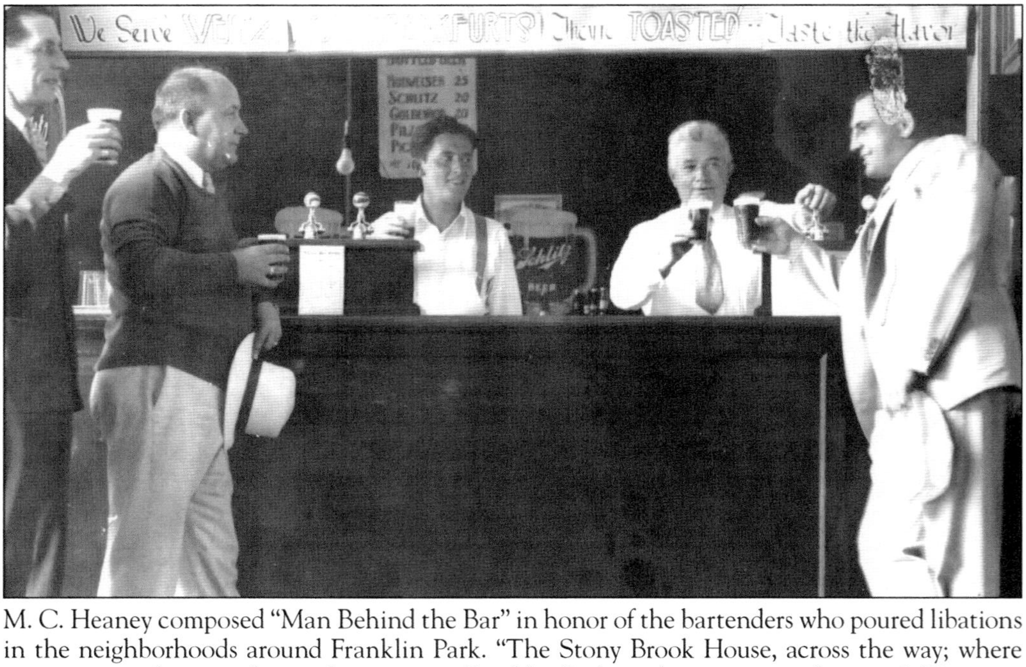

M. C. Heaney composed "Man Behind the Bar" in honor of the bartenders who poured libations in the neighborhoods around Franklin Park. "The Stony Brook House, across the way; where you can sit and rest; and view the scenes in Franklin Park; as the sun sets in the west." (Courtesy of Jerry Burke.)

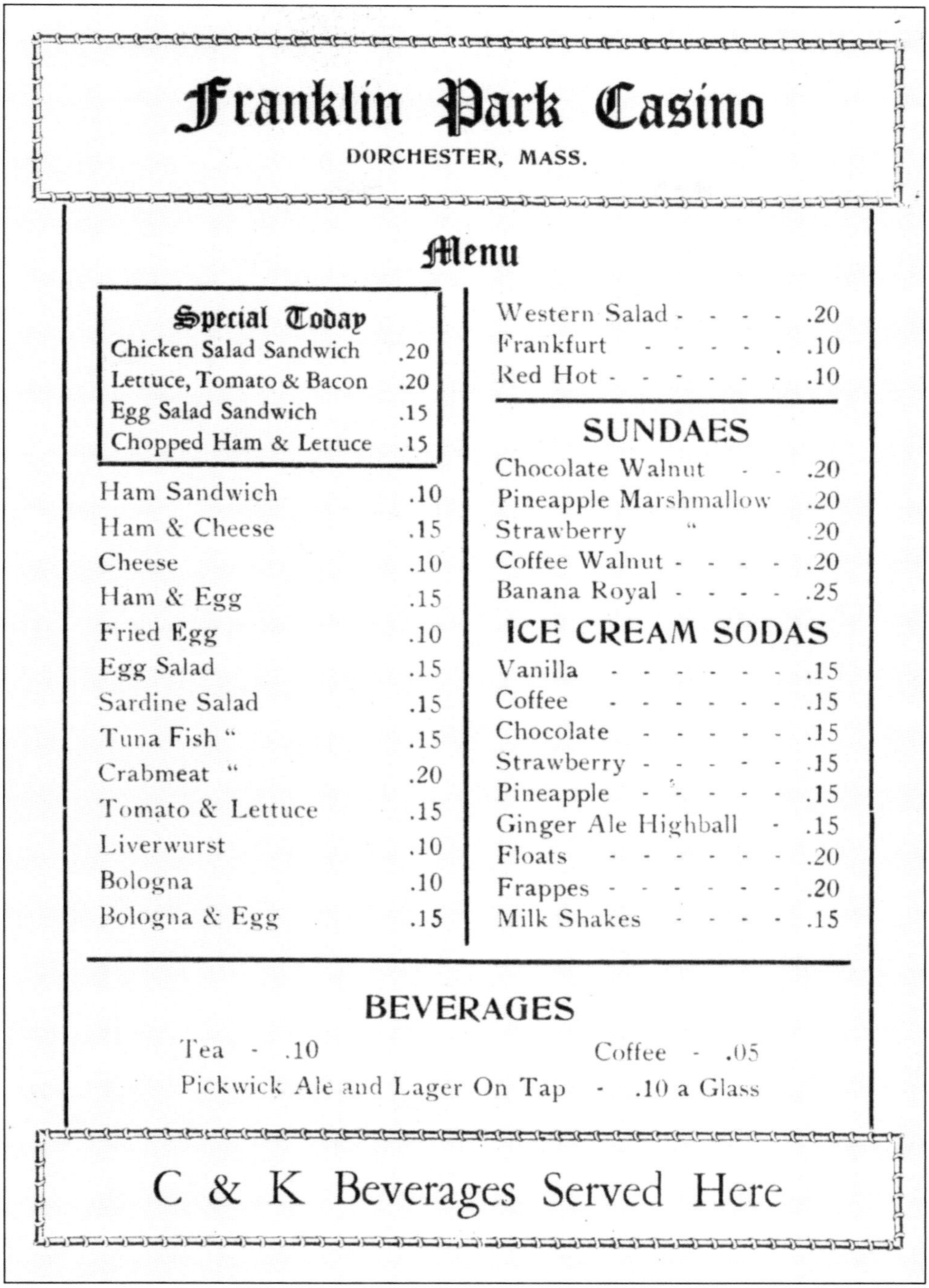

Franklin Park Casino

DORCHESTER, MASS.

Menu

Special Today

Chicken Salad Sandwich	.20
Lettuce, Tomato & Bacon	.20
Egg Salad Sandwich	.15
Chopped Ham & Lettuce	.15

Ham Sandwich	.10
Ham & Cheese	.15
Cheese	.10
Ham & Egg	.15
Fried Egg	.10
Egg Salad	.15
Sardine Salad	.15
Tuna Fish "	.15
Crabmeat "	.20
Tomato & Lettuce	.15
Liverwurst	.10
Bologna	.10
Bologna & Egg	.15

Western Salad - - - -	.20
Frankfurt - - - - - -	.10
Red Hot - - - - - - -	.10

SUNDAES

Chocolate Walnut - -	.20
Pineapple Marshmallow	.20
Strawberry "	.20
Coffee Walnut - - - -	.20
Banana Royal - - - -	.25

ICE CREAM SODAS

Vanilla - - - - - - -	.15
Coffee - - - - - - -	.15
Chocolate - - - - - -	.15
Strawberry - - - - -	.15
Pineapple - - - - - -	.15
Ginger Ale Highball -	.15
Floats - - - - - - -	.20
Frappes - - - - - - -	.20
Milk Shakes - - - - -	.15

BEVERAGES

Tea - .10 Coffee - .05

Pickwick Ale and Lager On Tap - .10 a Glass

C & K Beverages Served Here

Besides being a formal venue for big celebrations, lunch at the Refectory—either at the snack bar or on the terrace—was quite the affair for those lucky enough to live around the park. The menu from the 1940s shows an assortment of treats that was available. Lunch could be purchased for under $1 and included a chicken salad sandwich, a pineapple marshmallow sundae, and a chocolate frappe. One of the most talked about memories of the Refectory from the 1950s to the 1970s was the hot dogs—to many a trip to the park was not complete without that treat. (Courtesy of Jerry Burke.)

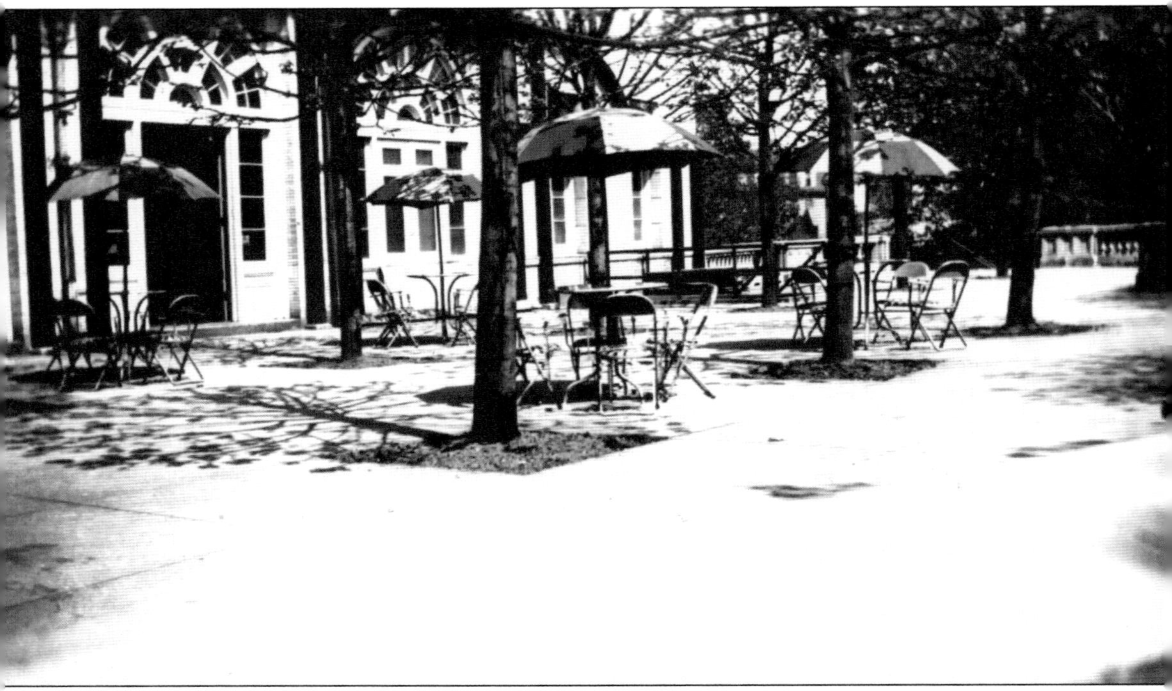

Falk Nathan described the veranda as "the back part of the library which is overhung with vines." *House and Garden* magazine wrote about the initial failure of the Refectory building in 1906. "Equally regrettable is the Refectory's failure as a restaurant. For a few years it conducted as such, then closed, and now the building is used as a branch of the Public Library. The question arises, why did it fail?" The Boston park commissioners conducted a small study. They cited incapable lessees without knowledge of finances, insufficient patronage by neighbors, and unfamiliarity with outdoor dining as reasons for the failure. The Refectory terrace, although unpopular in the first incarnation as a restaurant, was a popular place to enjoy a soda and hot dog on a summer afternoon. (Courtesy of Jerry Burke.)

Six

Ellicottdale, the Nursery, and Heathfield

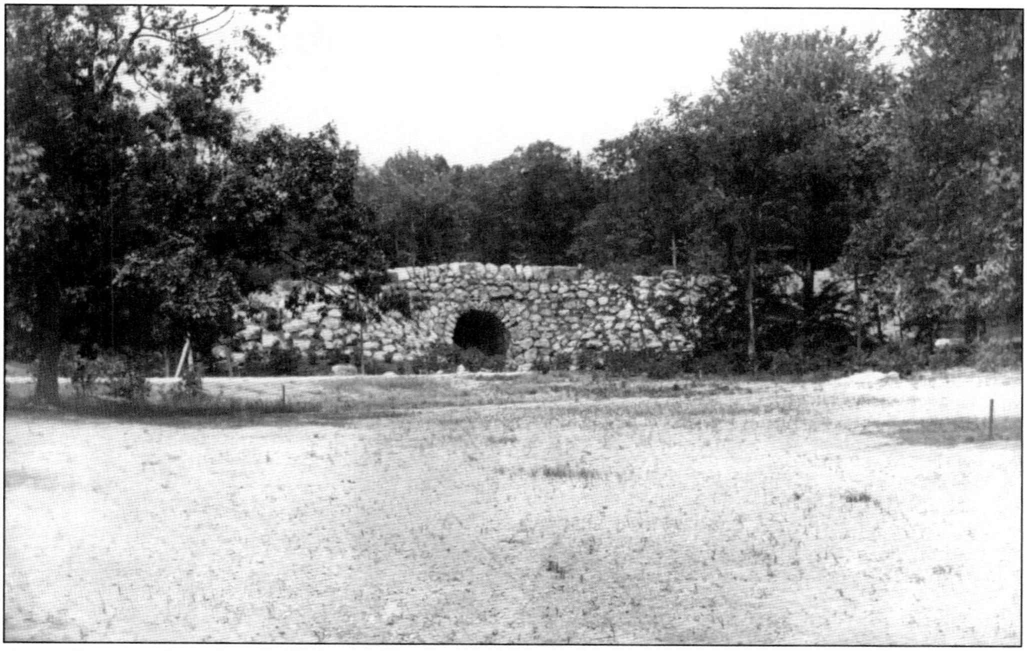

According to the "General Plan of Franklin Park," Ellicottdale "may be approached by a walk coming from Williams Street. The entrance at this point is arranged with a view to a terminus and turning place of a street railroad; and to avoid compelling women and children to pass through a throng of carriages, the walk from it to Ellicottdale passes the circuit drive of the Park by a subway."

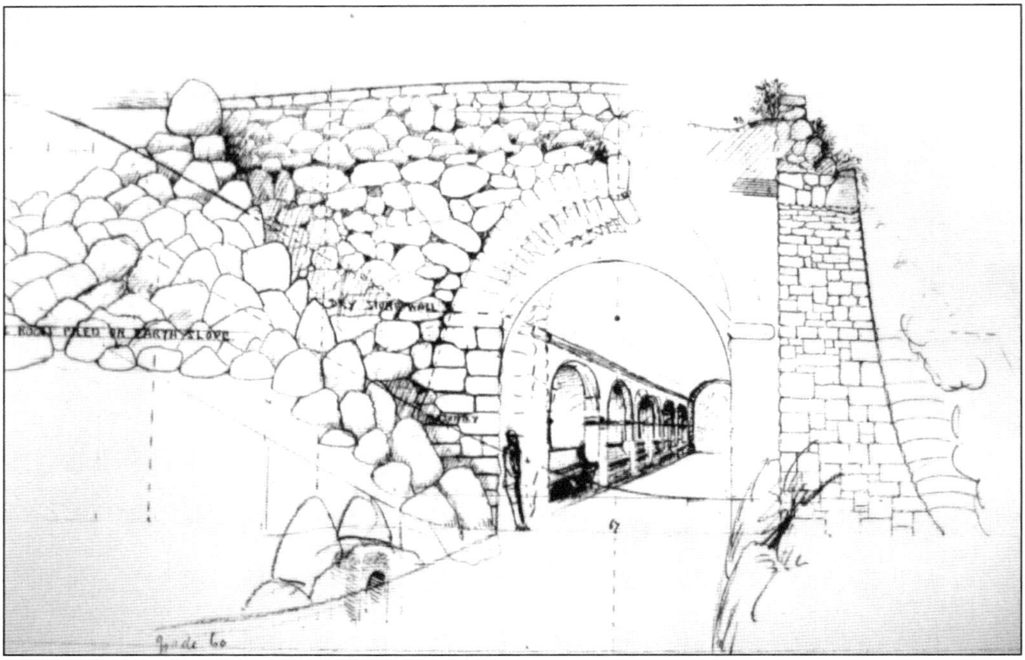

John Charles Olmsted designed Ellicott Arch not only to provide safe passage for pedestrians under Circuit Drive but also to frame the vantage of Ellicottdale. It also was a cool place to sit on a hot summer day. The completed archway measured 71 feet in length and was 15 feet wide. It was built between 1889 and 1890. (Courtesy of the National Park Service, Frederick Law Olmsted National Historic Site.)

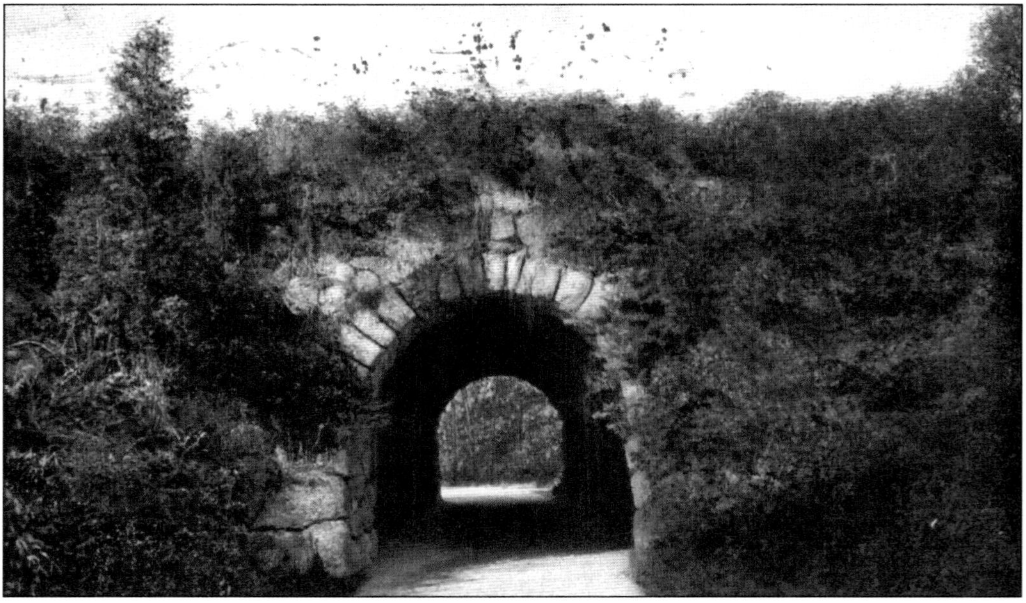

Ellicottdale is named for John Ellicott, who purchased four acres of land and a house on the Scarborough property for a summer home, which was located near today's 99 steps. For the remainder of the year, Ellicott resided in the South End of Boston and was a partner with the commission merchants E. D. Peters and Company. This section of the park was completed in 1890.

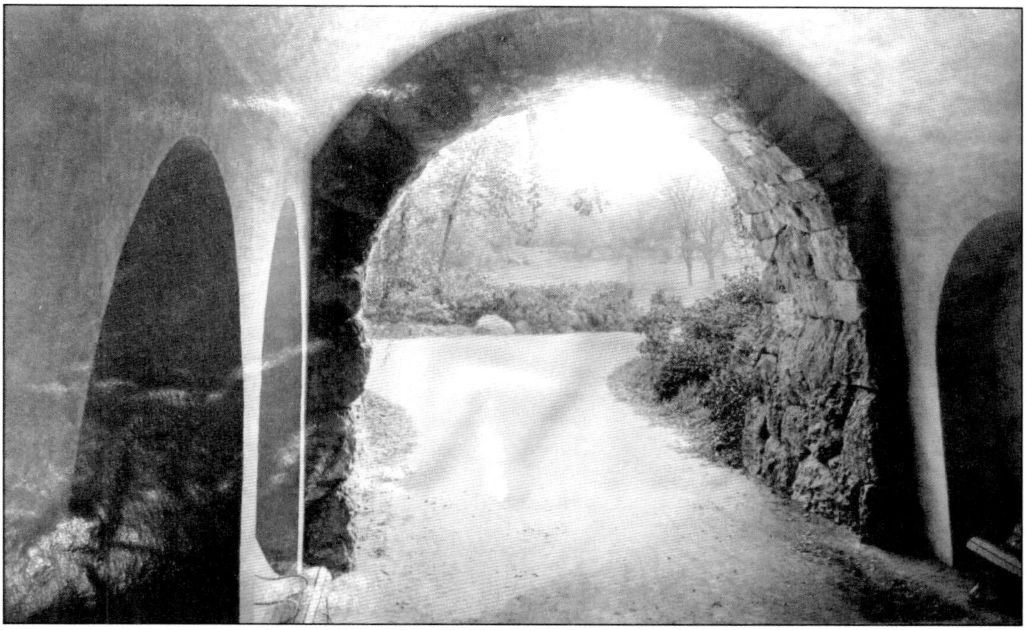

Frederick Law Olmsted planned, "Another small house is provided at which parties wishing to play [tennis and croquet] will obtain assignments of ground, and can leave outer garments and store or hire needed implements." City architect Edmund Wheelwright designed the building, located on the Wilderness side of the arch. The building caught fire in 1921 and was rebuilt. In 1945, the parks department razed it. (Courtesy of the National Park Service, Frederick Law Olmsted National Historic Site.)

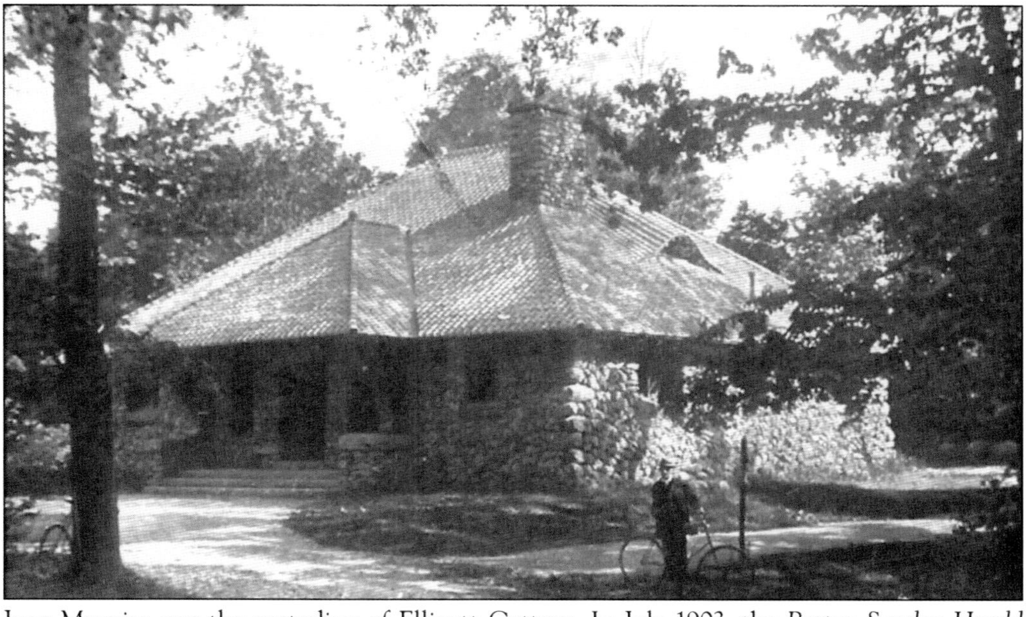

Jane Maguire was the custodian of Ellicott Cottage. In July 1903, the *Boston Sunday Herald* reported, "Both sexes are supplied with dressing, bath, and toilet rooms, all gratis. . . . The towels, good ones, too, and as many are needed, are furnished free to the players, and this in itself is a big item, as anyone connected with a tennis club knows." (Courtesy of the Dorchester Historical Society.)

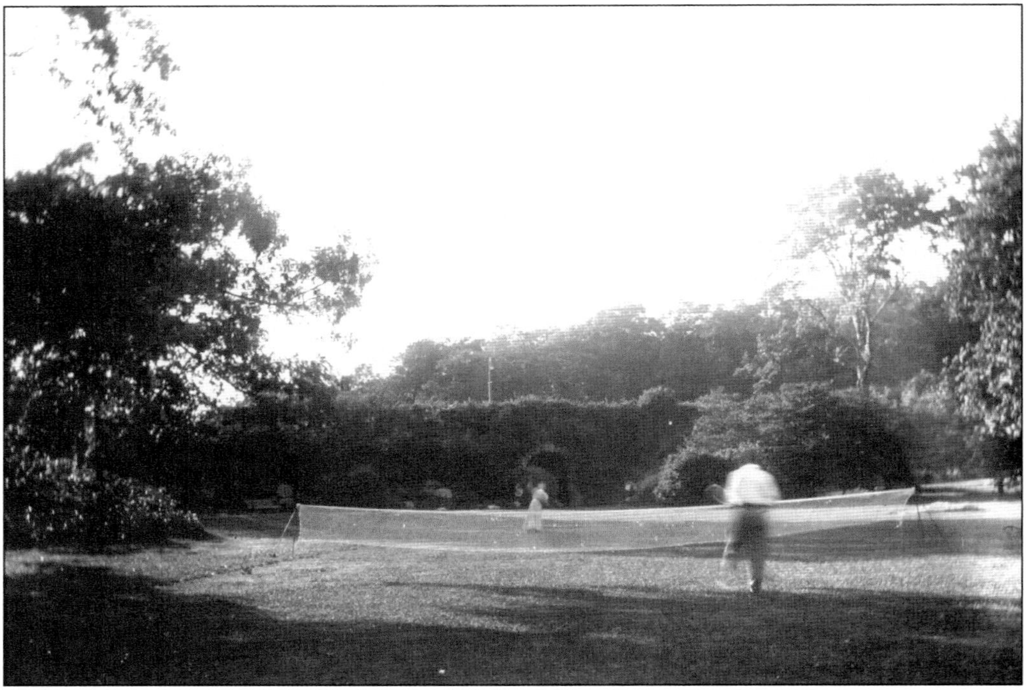

Plans for active recreation in Ellicottdale called for lawn tennis and croquet on the flat grounds. Tennis was by far the most popular choice. By 1900, there were 42 courts in the area. On Sundays and holidays, through the warm months, the courts were filled through the daylight hours. Both the cottage custodian and the greenskeeper in Ellicottdale maintained the courts and enforced the rules of play. Players were required to wear rubber-soled shoes, so as to not ruin the turf, which was meticulously maintained. There was no time limit unless others were waiting to play. If that was the case, it was courteous to play a set and allow others the pleasure. (Courtesy of the National Park Service, Frederick Law Olmsted National Historic Site.)

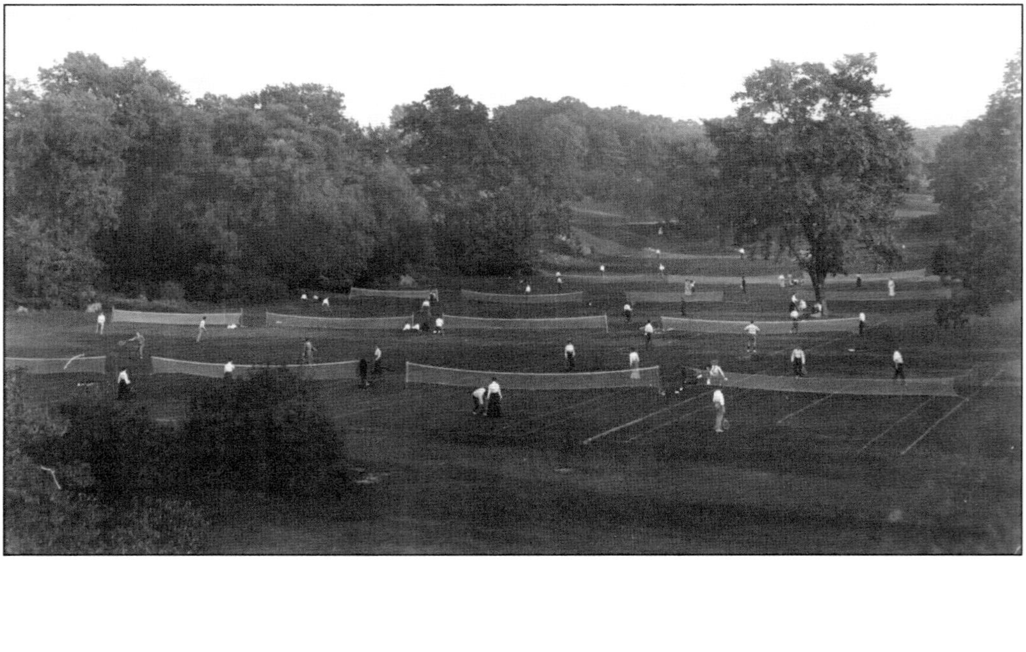

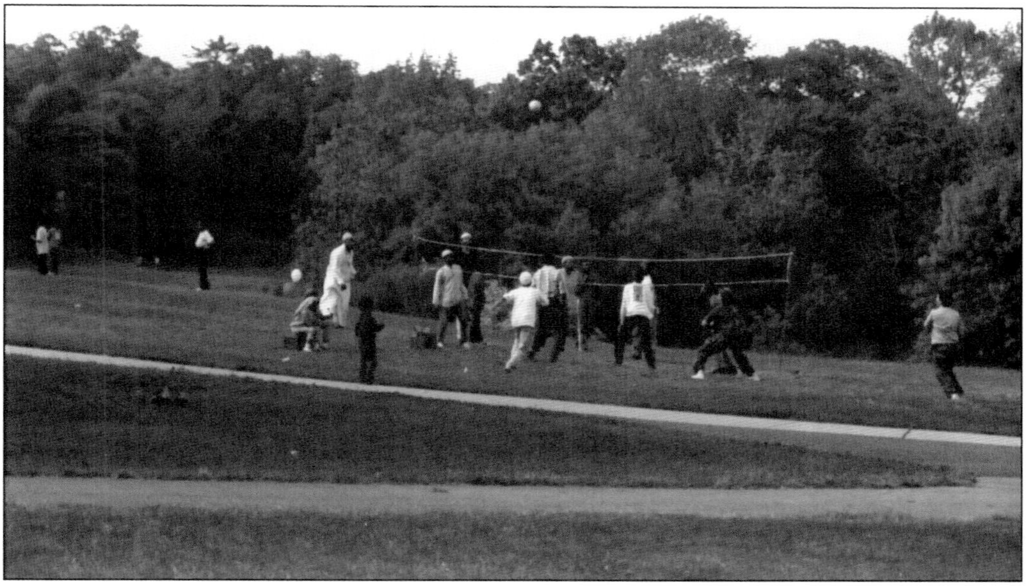

As lawn tennis declined in popularity in the mid-20th century, Ellicottdale was used for other sports. The flat surface was ideal for another net sport—volleyball. Tournaments occurred almost daily in the warm summer months. Frederick Law Olmsted's plans did not call for active recreation in this area of the park, but it remains popular. (Courtesy of the Franklin Park Coalition.)

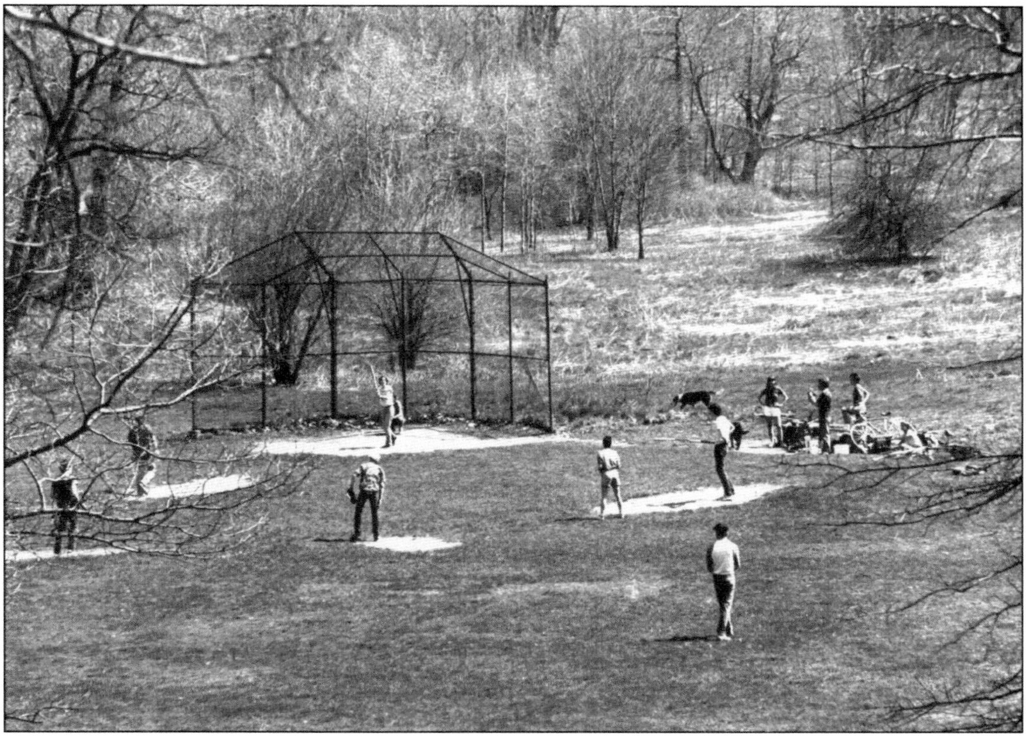

In 1903, Jamaica Plain residents petitioned to bring back baseball and to play football on the Playstead. In 1945, a baseball diamond was added to Ellicottdale. Older players typically used the four baseball diamonds on the Playstead, and the diamonds in Ellicottdale were reserved for Little League players and spectators. (Courtesy of the Franklin Park Coalition.)

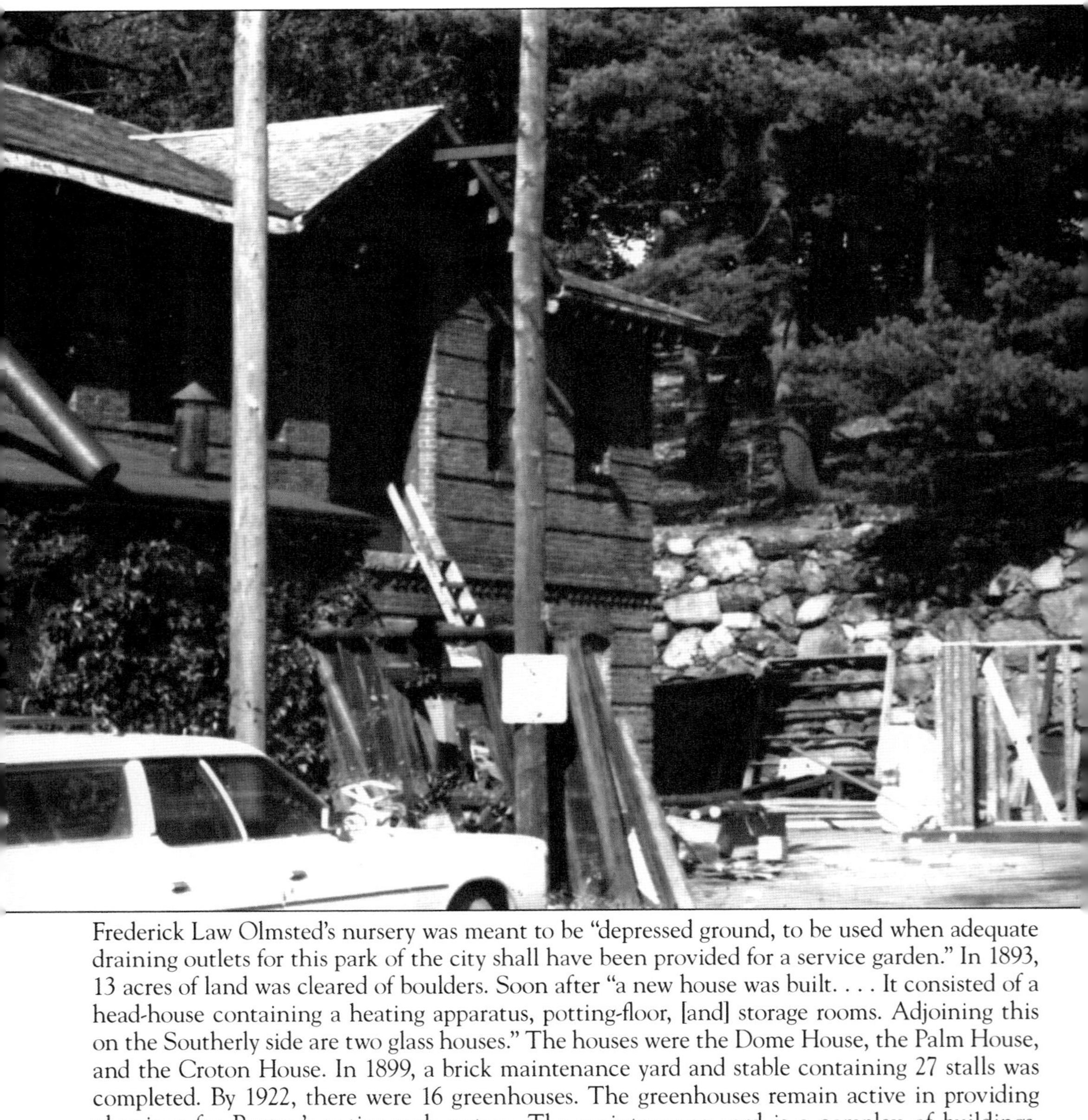

Frederick Law Olmsted's nursery was meant to be "depressed ground, to be used when adequate draining outlets for this park of the city shall have been provided for a service garden." In 1893, 13 acres of land was cleared of boulders. Soon after "a new house was built. . . . It consisted of a head-house containing a heating apparatus, potting-floor, [and] storage rooms. Adjoining this on the Southerly side are two glass houses." The houses were the Dome House, the Palm House, and the Croton House. In 1899, a brick maintenance yard and stable containing 27 stalls was completed. By 1922, there were 16 greenhouses. The greenhouses remain active in providing plantings for Boston's entire park system. The maintenance yard is a complex of buildings, stables, and departments, including the Boston Parks and Recreation Department and the mounted park rangers. (Courtesy of the Franklin Park Coalition.)

The City of Boston first employed women to maintain the greenhouses and plantings in the early part of the 20th century. By the middle of the century, gardening in both greenhouses as well as labor in the maintenance yard was considered men's work. Leslie Jones had a flair for photographing Bostonians in places where they enjoyed life and also the places where they worked. Franklin Park was a place for both labor and leisure. At right, Michael Crehan was photographed on March 13, 1951, preparing for St. Patrick's Day with over 2,400 shamrock plants. The greenhouse foreman, John Keane, was photographed in June 1951. (Courtesy of the Boston Public Library Print Department.)

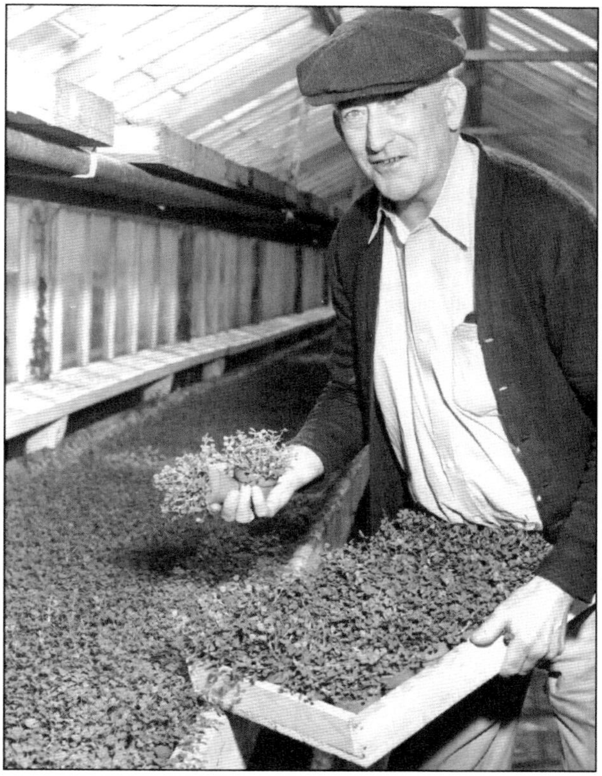

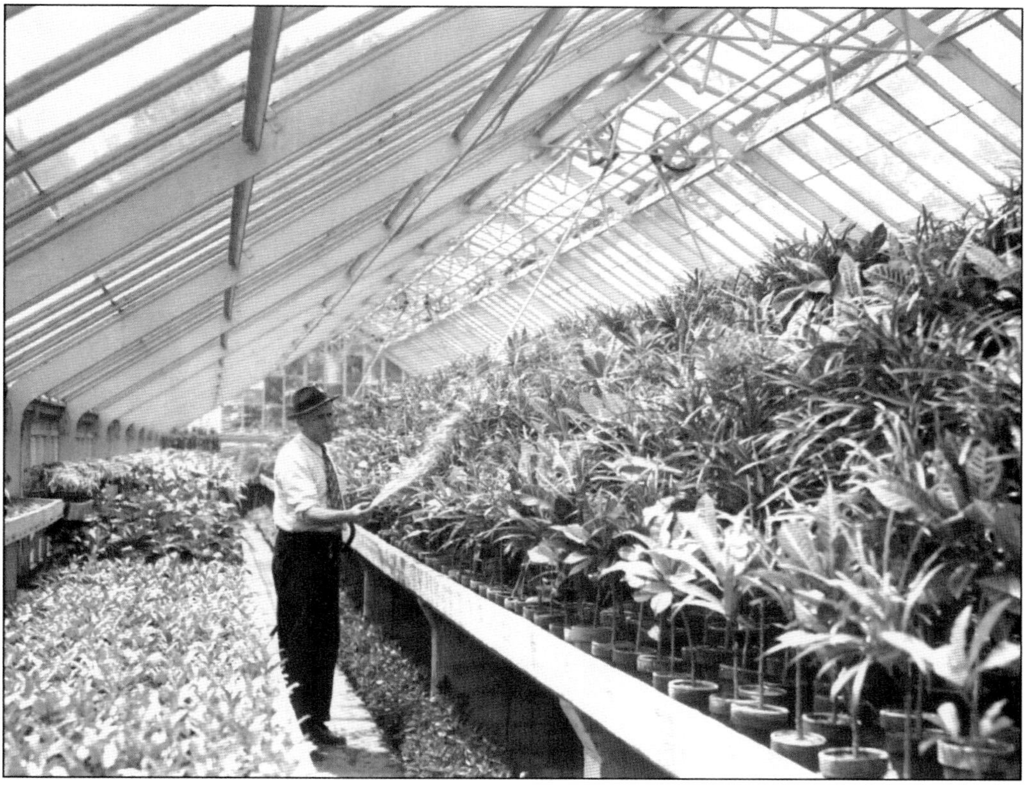

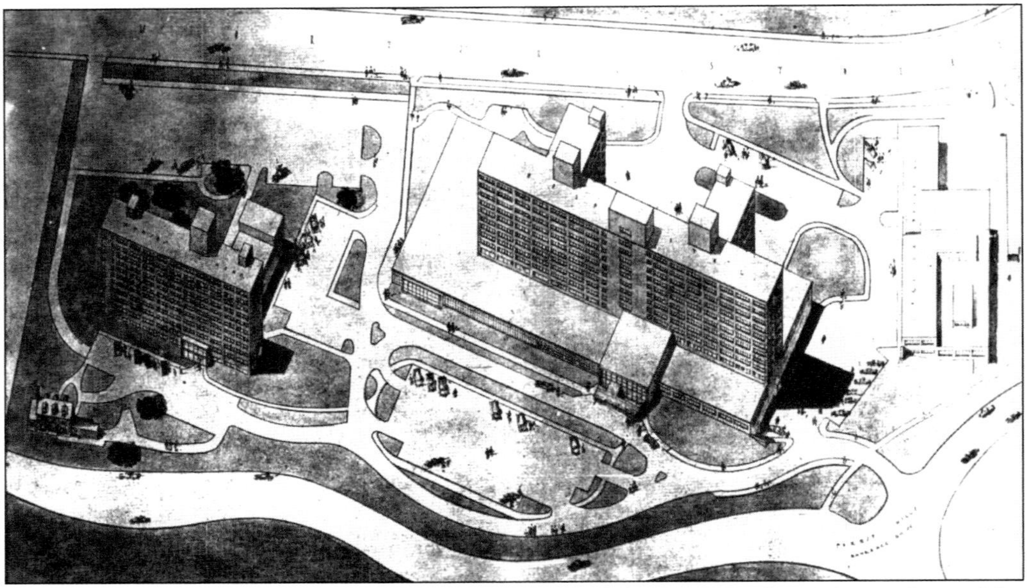

Heathfield was named for the Heath family that occupied the property along Morton Street. The Lemuel Shattuck Hospital was built in this area of Franklin Park. The hospital was named for a Boston bookseller and publisher who was responsible for spurring the creation of the nation's first board of public health. In 1944, the State of Massachusetts assumed the responsibility to care for patients considered chronically ill. In 1949, the City of Boston made this land available to the state. Construction started in 1951 and continued until the hospital opened in 1954. The hospital has provided a number of services, including dialysis and AIDS treatment, when other hospitals did not have the capacity to help these patients. The hospital also houses services for the Massachusetts Department of Corrections and a shelter for patients. (Courtesy of the Lemuel Shattuck Hospital.)

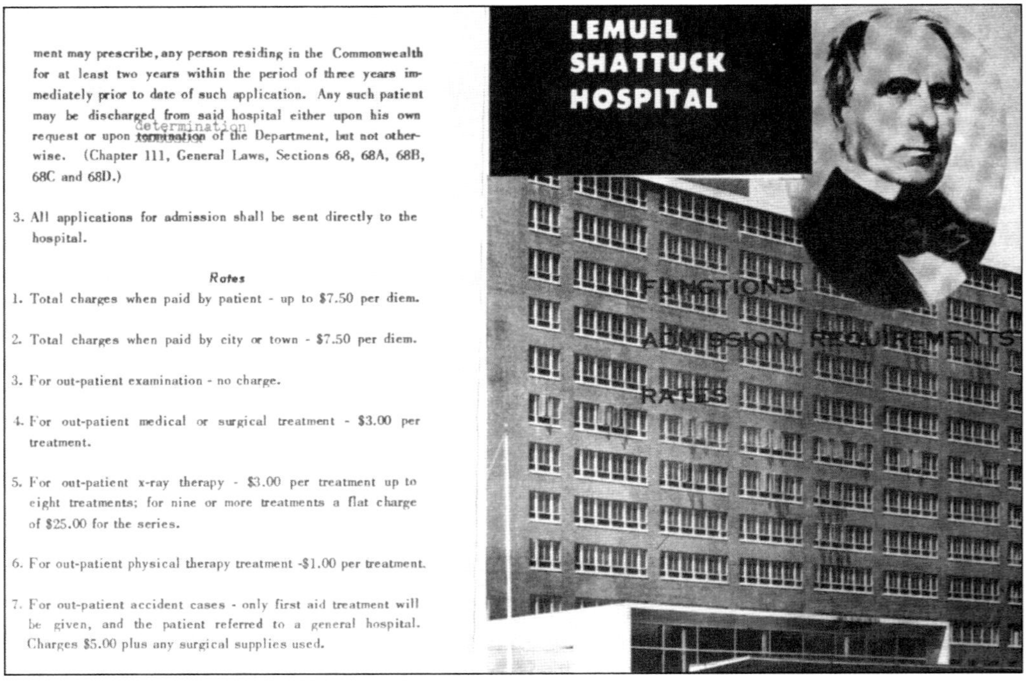

ment may prescribe, any person residing in the Commonwealth for at least two years within the period of three years immediately prior to date of such application. Any such patient may be discharged from said hospital either upon his own request or upon determination of the Department, but not otherwise. (Chapter 111, General Laws, Sections 68, 68A, 68B, 68C and 68D.)

3. All applications for admission shall be sent directly to the hospital.

Rates

1. Total charges when paid by patient - up to $7.50 per diem.
2. Total charges when paid by city or town - $7.50 per diem.
3. For out-patient examination - no charge.
4. For out-patient medical or surgical treatment - $3.00 per treatment.
5. For out-patient x-ray therapy - $3.00 per treatment up to eight treatments; for nine or more treatments a flat charge of $25.00 for the series.
6. For out-patient physical therapy treatment -$1.00 per treatment.
7. For out-patient accident cases - only first aid treatment will be given, and the patient referred to a general hospital. Charges $5.00 plus any surgical supplies used.

LEMUEL SHATTUCK HOSPITAL

FUNCTIONS

ADMISSION REQUIREMENTS

RATES

Seven

Border Grounds and Parkways

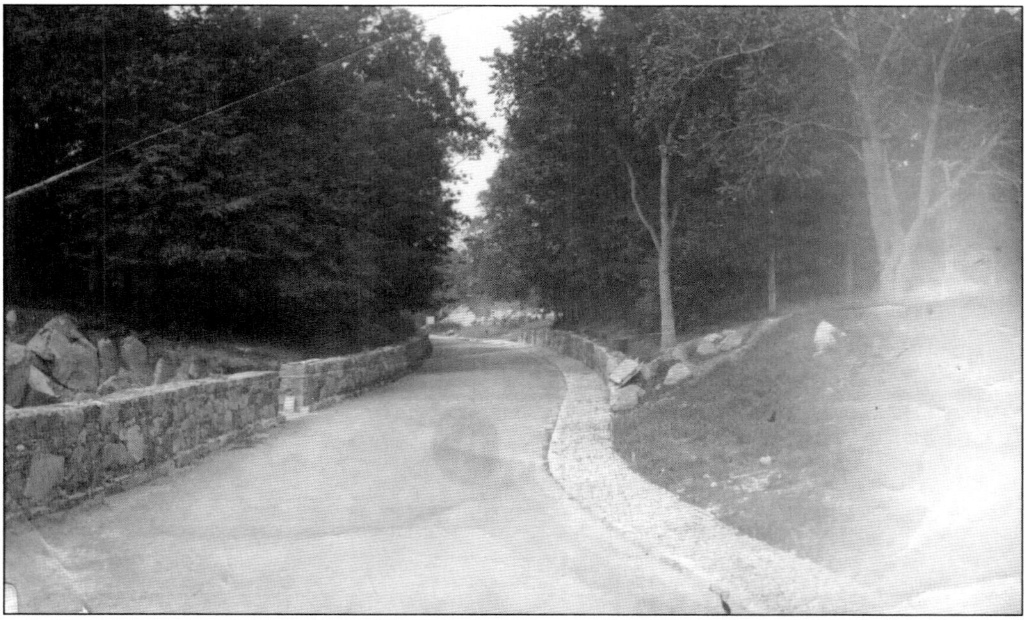

Glen Road was completed in August 1892. According to the "General Plan of Franklin Park," it was planned as a "public convenience that the park should be divided by a road crossing it from Blue Hill Avenue to Forest Hills Street." This road was designed to separate the active and passive sections of Franklin Park. Today Glen Road is blocked to vehicles, and much of the area has been deconstructed and planted over with grass.

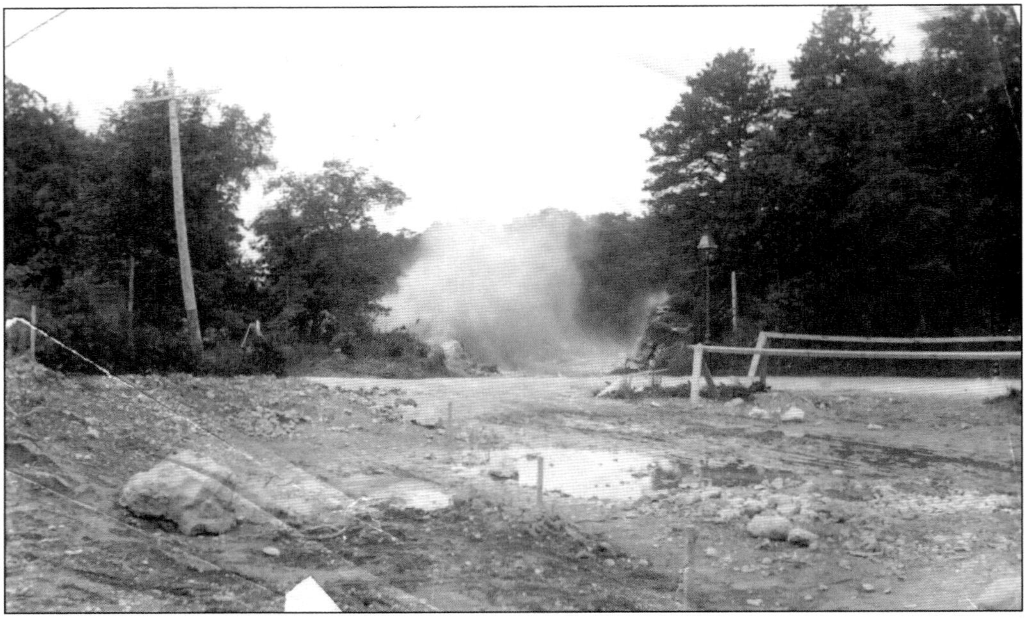

The construction and design of roads started in the 1880s and has continued to be a source of controversy. As part of the urban renewal plans for the neighborhoods surrounding Franklin Park in the 1950s and 1960s, the Southwest Corridor plan was developed. This plan would have replaced the Orange Line with an eight-lane highway that was constructed to be close to downtown Boston and connect with Route 128. Neighborhood protests against demolishing homes and businesses were great, and the plan was never achieved. The el was moved underground, and the area was turned into green space, including playgrounds, a bicycle path, and a community garden. According to the Heart of the City database, this was the first time in U.S. history that construction funds allocated for a major expressway had been redirected to a transit project.

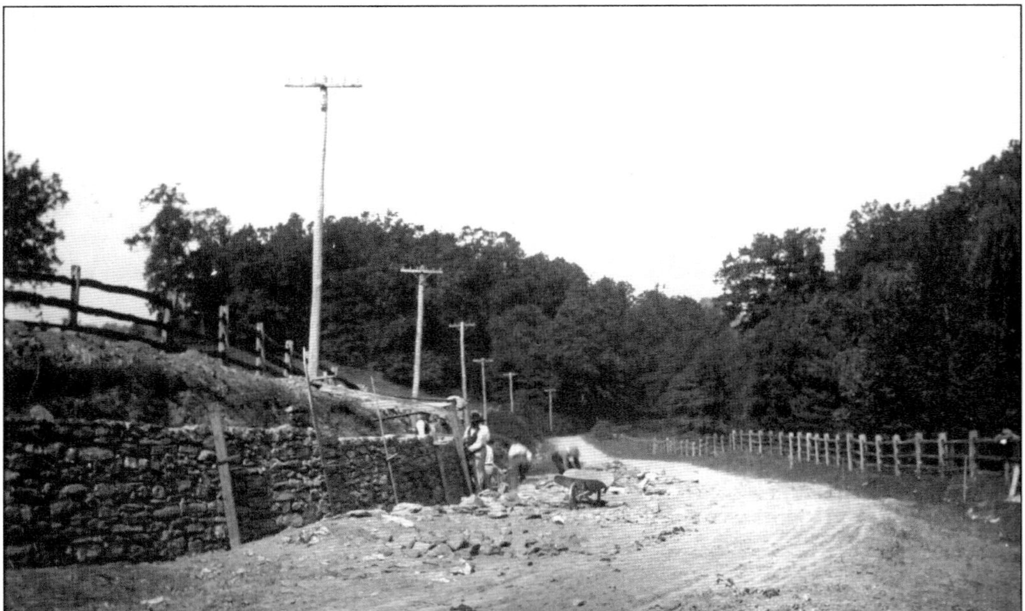

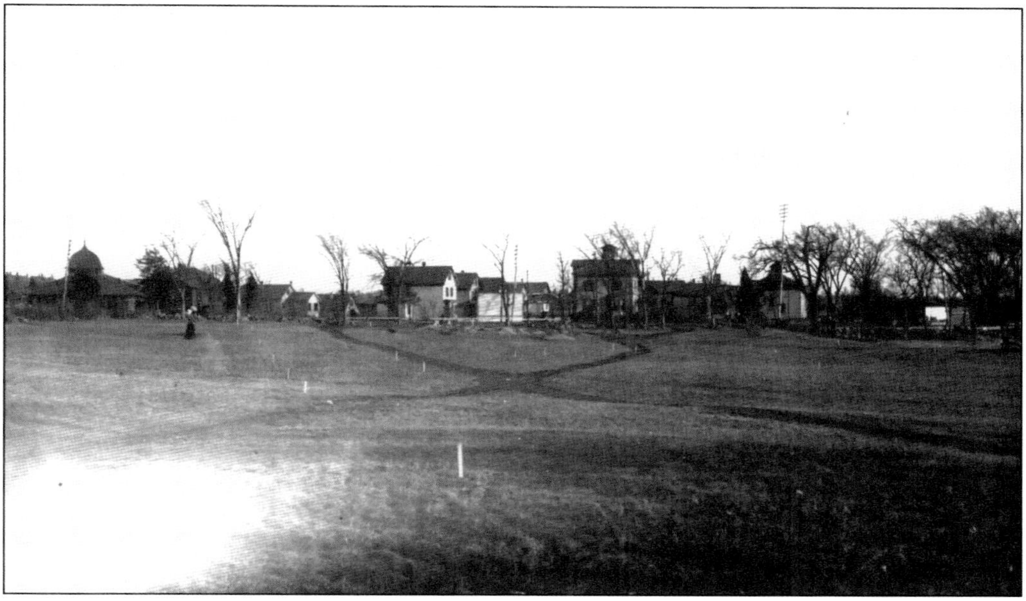

According to the 1889 annual report, "The roads and walks of the park have been designed less with a purpose of bringing the visitor to points of view at which he will enjoy set scenes or landscapes than to provide for a constant mild enjoyment of simply pleasing rural scenery while in easy movement, and this by curves and grades avoiding unnecessary violence to nature."

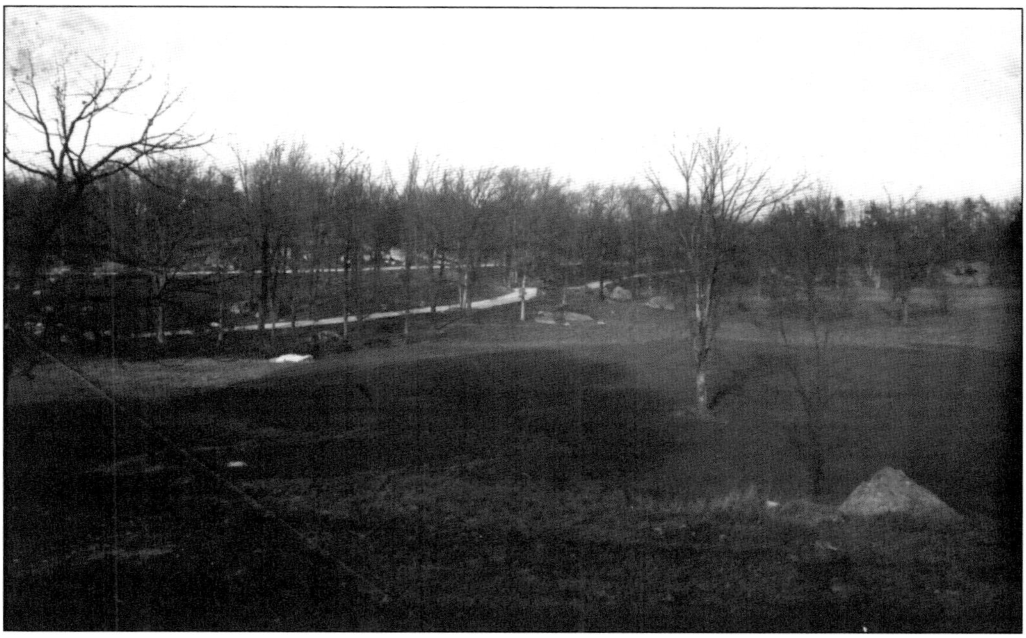

Circuit Drive is the loop around the park that was completed with fill from the excavation of Scarboro Pond. According to the *Boston Daily Globe* of October 2, 1891, Circuit Drive was a "wide, heavily macadamized avenue that girdles the park and is completed from Refectory Hill to Scarboro Hill. Circuit Drive was planned to be two and a half miles in length.

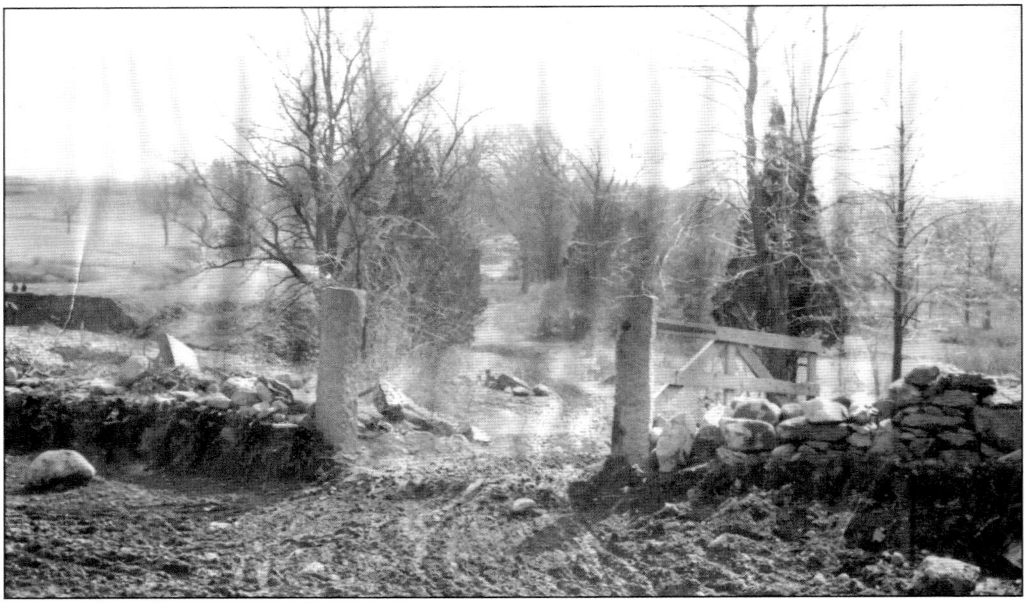

The Humboldt Avenue entrance was completed in 1889. This entrance to the park was part of an old Shawmut tribe trading trail that extended from Boston to Plymouth. Seaver Street was named for the family that occupied farmland in the Long Crouch Woods area of the park. Long Crouch was the original name of Seaver Street. (Courtesy of the National Park Service, Frederick Law Olmsted National Historic Site.)

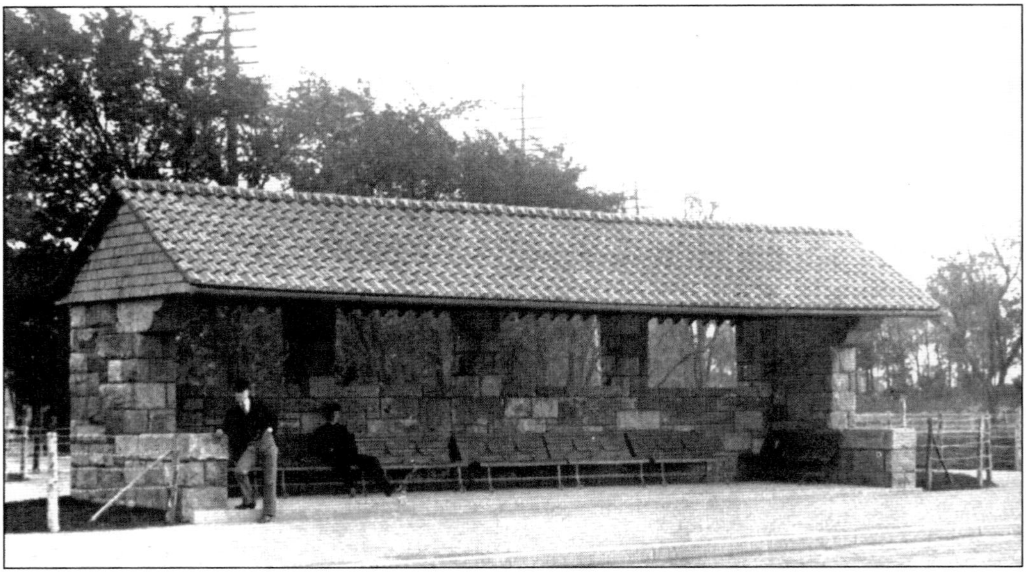

Frederick Law Olmsted's plans have generally outlasted the age of the carriage paths and footpaths in the park. The only building structure that remains from Olmsted's era is the Blue Hill Avenue structure. According to Sylvester Baxter's *Boston Park Guide*, "A handsome shelter of stone, with tiled roof, is provided here for passengers waiting to take the carriages." The carriage shelter at Peabody Circle is a wood and stone historic structure designed by the architectural firm Sturgis and Cabot. One hundred years ago, the carriage shelter allowed park visitors to take horse-drawn carriage rides through the park for 25¢. The shelter was restored around 1980. (Courtesy of the Dorchester Historical Society.)

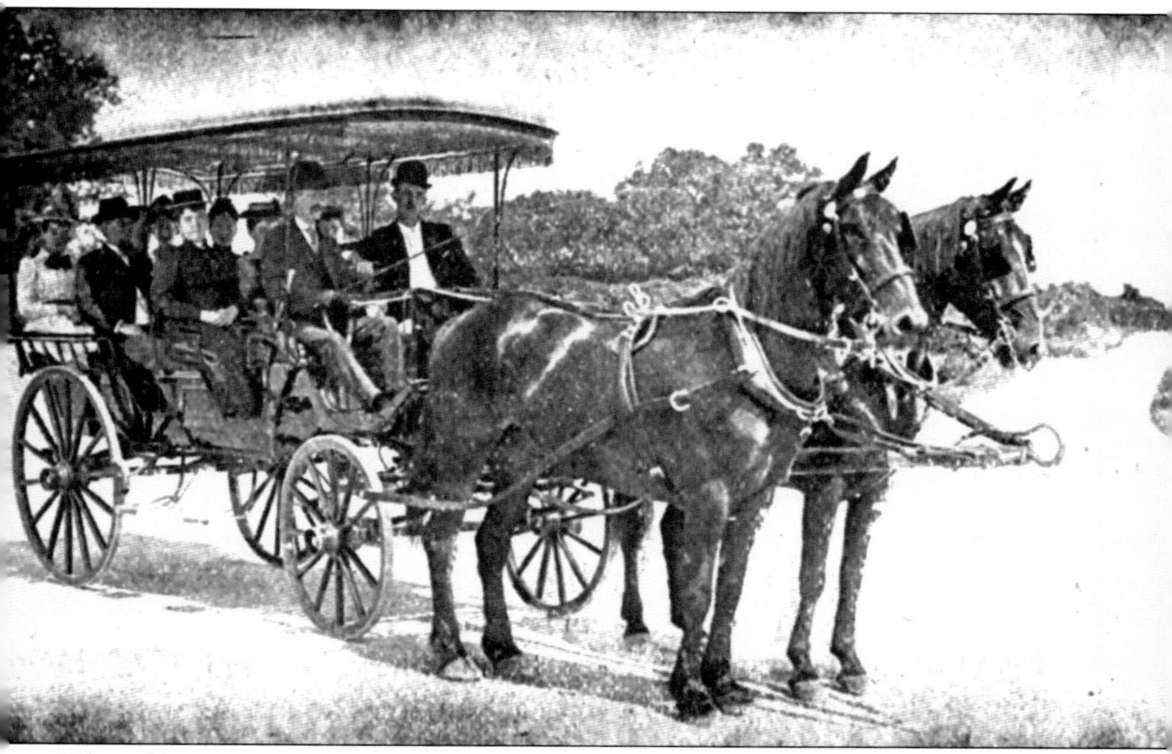

"The public carriage service, established by the park commissioners, marked the beginning of a new stage of development of our park system." Carriage service began in 1887, when sufficient roadways were completed for the five-mile jaunt through the park. For 25¢, riders were able to enjoy a "delightful drive" and observe the new developments in Franklin Park. The Franklin Park Carriage Service brochure described the route available to riders who used Bacon and Tarbell's service. A carriage "with limited company of strangers" passed through the planned Greeting and turned onto Pierpoint Road to face the Playstead and the overlook. From there the old Native American trail was pointed out, and the ride continued through the Valley Gates with the Country Park as the vista. The ride continued on Circuit Drive with stops for the Wilderness and a viewing of the Blue Hills, followed by Ellicottdale and Nazingdale. The carriage continued up Schoolmaster Hill and then returned to its starting point on Blue Hill Avenue. The guided ride took approximately one hour. (Courtesy of Historic New England.)

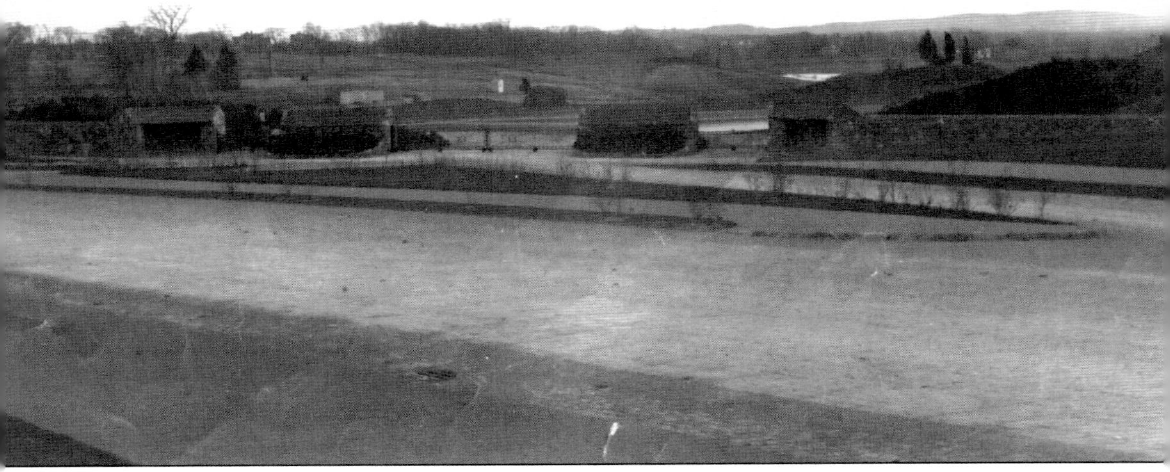

Frederick Law Olmsted did not overlook the idea of security within park borders. Oil lamps were installed on some paths in 1891. Stone and iron gates were installed at the Blue Hill Avenue entrance and the Forest Hills entrance, and the Valley Gates were installed to separate the active and passive sections of the park. The architectural firm of Walker and Best designed the gates in 1889. The gates were to be closed at sundown, but it is said that the gates never closed. In 1901, they were removed. In his 1905 report on the continued construction of the Boston Park System, John Charles Olmsted criticized the removal of the Valley Gates. "The yielding to the characteristic American hatred of restraint, and willingness to take chances of robbery and even murder, this theory of shutting the greater half of the park during the latter half of the night has been abandoned, even to the extent of tearing down the gateway." Two of the four stone buildings remain from the 1889 Valley Gates construction.

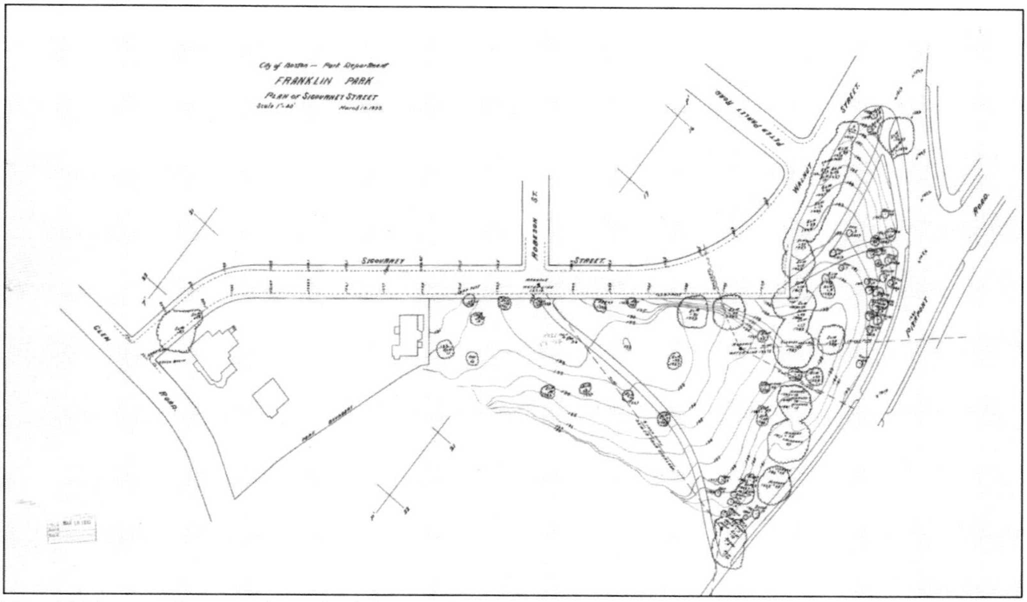

The 1886 annual report described the need to extend Sigourney Street. "The Board recommends that the streets running through the park lands be discontinued as public ways, and that Walnut Street be continued through Sigourney Street, outside the park limits." It was believed this would facilitate safe passage for pedestrians and carriages within the park. (Courtesy of the National Park Service, Frederick Law Olmsted National Historic Site.)

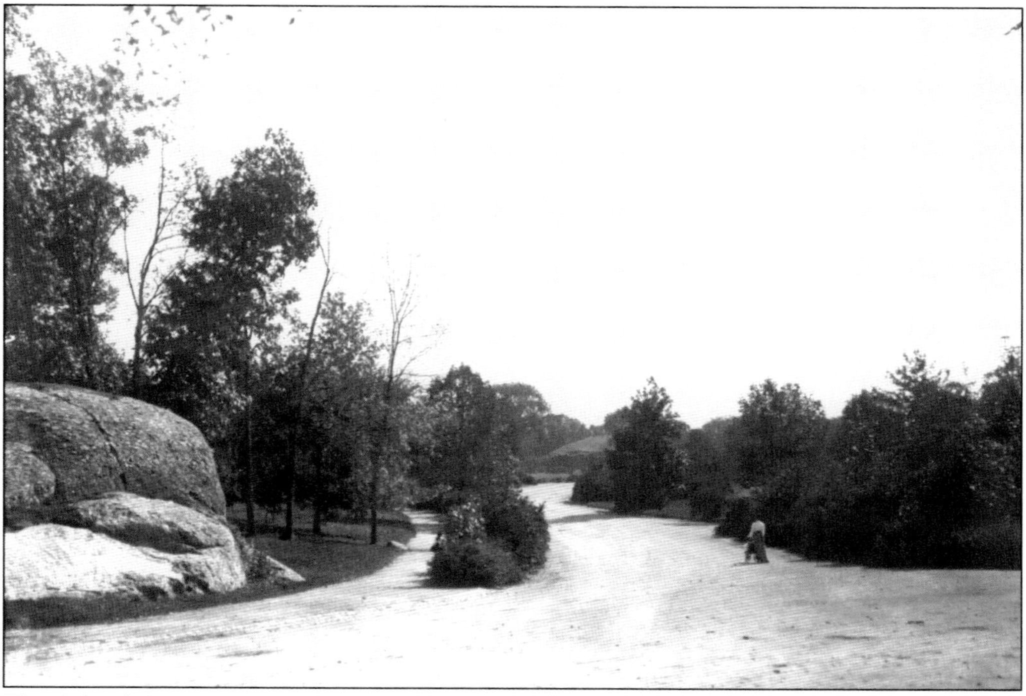

The School Street entrance of the park was designed to connect to Pierpoint Road near the Playstead and to create easy access to that section of the park. The plan for the area called for the "rides and walks come together" and to be "designed closely planted with low bushes." (Courtesy of the National Park Service, Frederick Law Olmsted National Historic Site.)

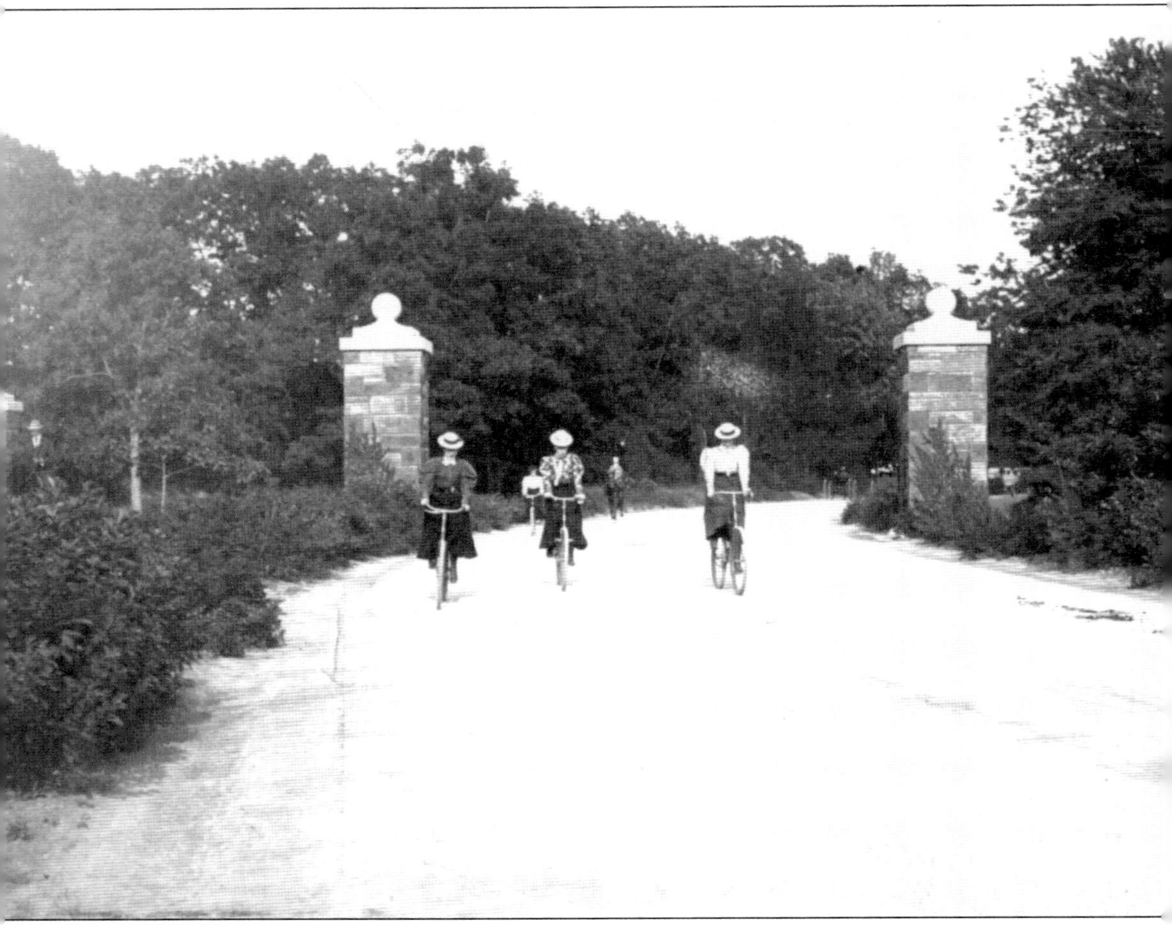

The border grounds were designed to shield park users from the outside world. The neighborhoods around Franklin Park represented a variety of social classes and living situations, and Frederick Law Olmsted believed that these would change in Boston much like they had in other cities. When the park was constructed, its surroundings included large estates, middle-class homes and businesses, and light industry. By the dawn of the 20th century, the area was lower-class triple-decker homes and apartment buildings. The shrubs and plantings were meant to keep street noises and actions out of the park and provide a sense of isolation. In 1899, park neighbors publicly complained about these plantings and called for their removal. Park neighbors were incensed about the closure of ways that were convenient to their homes. (Courtesy of the National Park Service, Frederick Law Olmsted National Historic Site.)

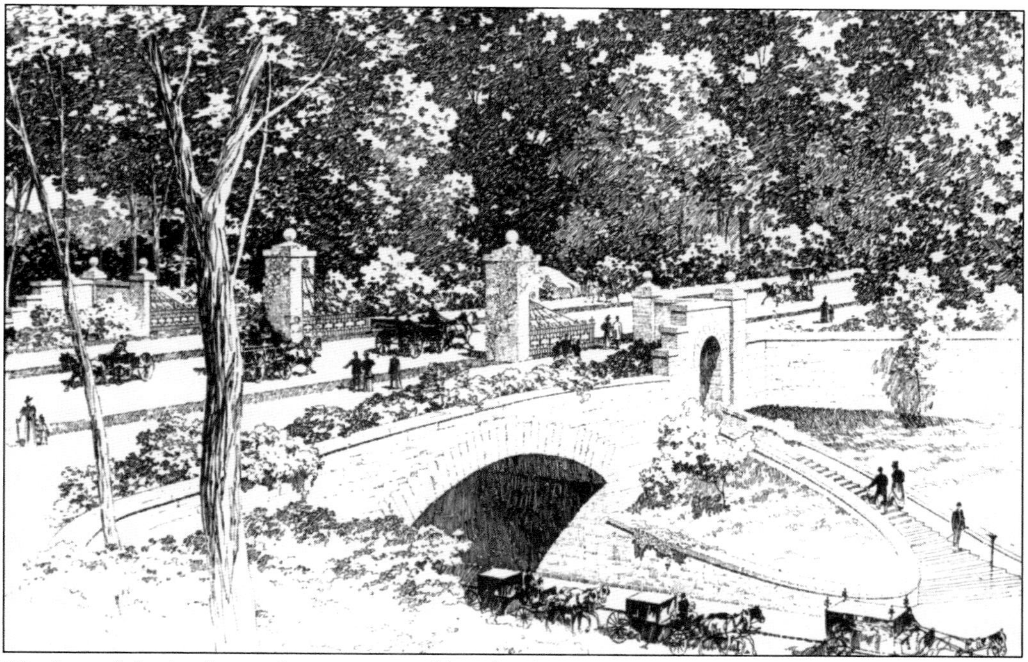

The last of the bridges to be constructed by Shepley, Ruttan, and Coolidge in the park was the Funeral Bridge. The bridge was designed to "avoid travel interruption of pleasure travel by funeral processions, and to improve passage around the park." The cost of the bridge was $50,920, and opening ceremonies occurred on August 2, 1896. In 1925, a rotary, designed by Arthur Shurtleff, was added to the end of Circuit Drive and near the Funeral Bridge to assist with the growing flow of automobile traffic. The Forest Hills Overpass, which connects the Arnold Arboretum and Franklin Park, changed the original plan for the Arborway and was completed in 1953. (Courtesy of the National Park Service, Frederick Law Olmsted National Historic Site.)

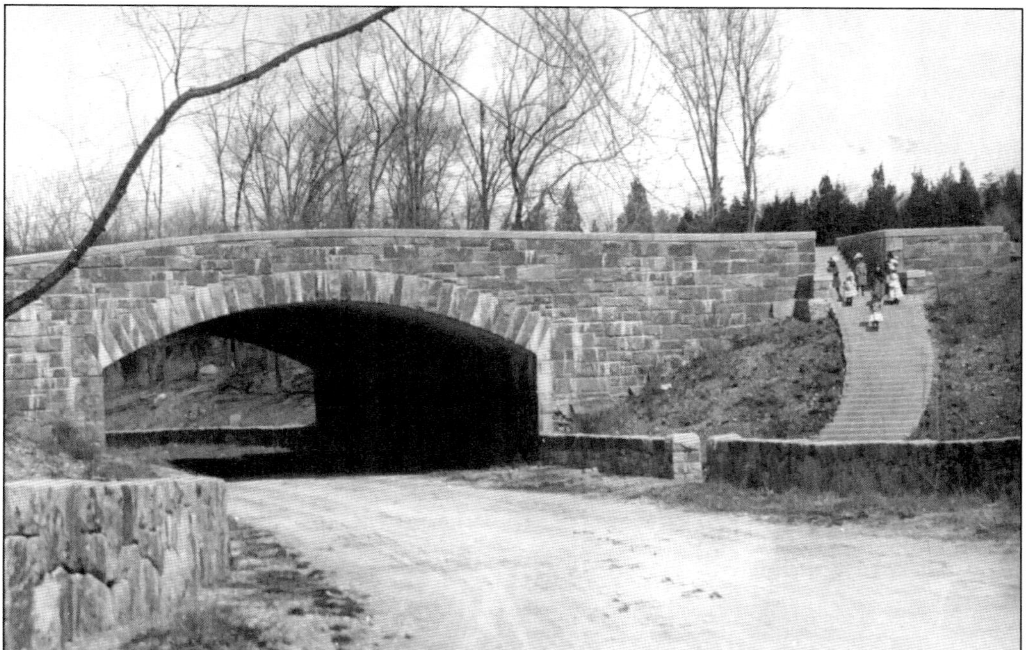

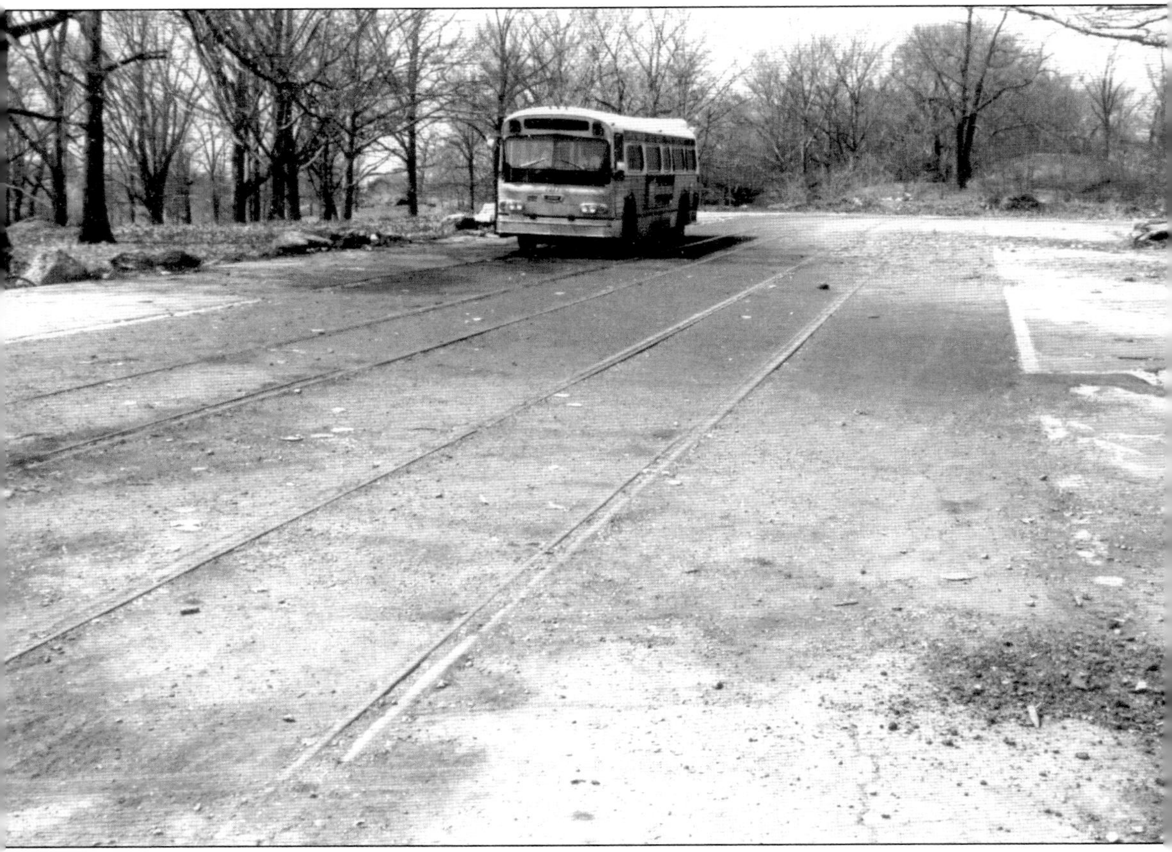

No Massachusetts Bay Transportation Authority (MBTA) stations offer direct access to Franklin Park. In his design plans, Frederick Law Olmsted demonstrated that dependable, regional transportation was essential to the success of Franklin Park. He provided two streetcar turnarounds at Pierpoint Road and Peabody Circle in hopes of luring the MBTA to extend service to the entrance to the park. In his "Notes on the Plans for Franklin Park," he stated, "By this route a thousand men could, in half an hour, be transferred in a body from the Common to the Playstead." The train was never extended, but the elevated Orange Line, built in 1909, offered stops at Forest Hills and Green Streets that made the park accessible for only 5¢. On September 18, 1915, the *Christian Science Monitor* praised the streetcar system leading to Franklin Park in 1915. Peabody Circle remains the most used stop in the park for today's MBTA buses. The road was named for Robert Peabody, the parks commissioner responsible for the construction of the zoo. (Courtesy of the Franklin Park Coalition.)

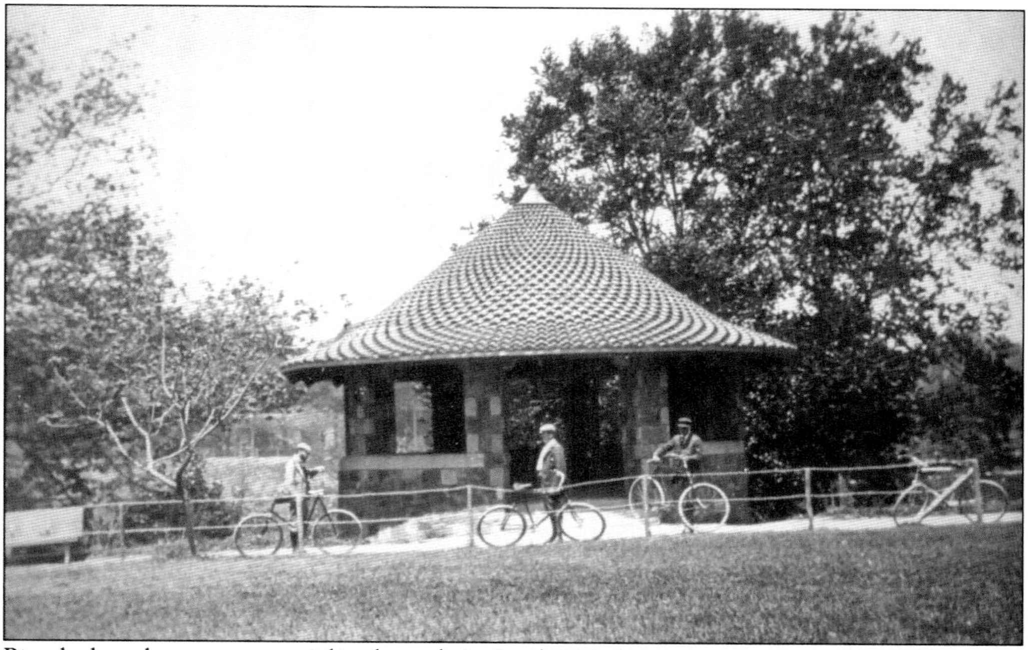

Bicycles have been controversial in the park. In April 1895, there were an estimated 25,000 bicyclists who used the pathways in the park. Olmsted stated that this type of usage disturbed the general peace of the park. Criticism by Olmsted and others did not stop bicyclists. A Fourth of July race in 1895 attracted thousands of bicyclists and became an annual event. (Courtesy of the Franklin Park Coalition.)

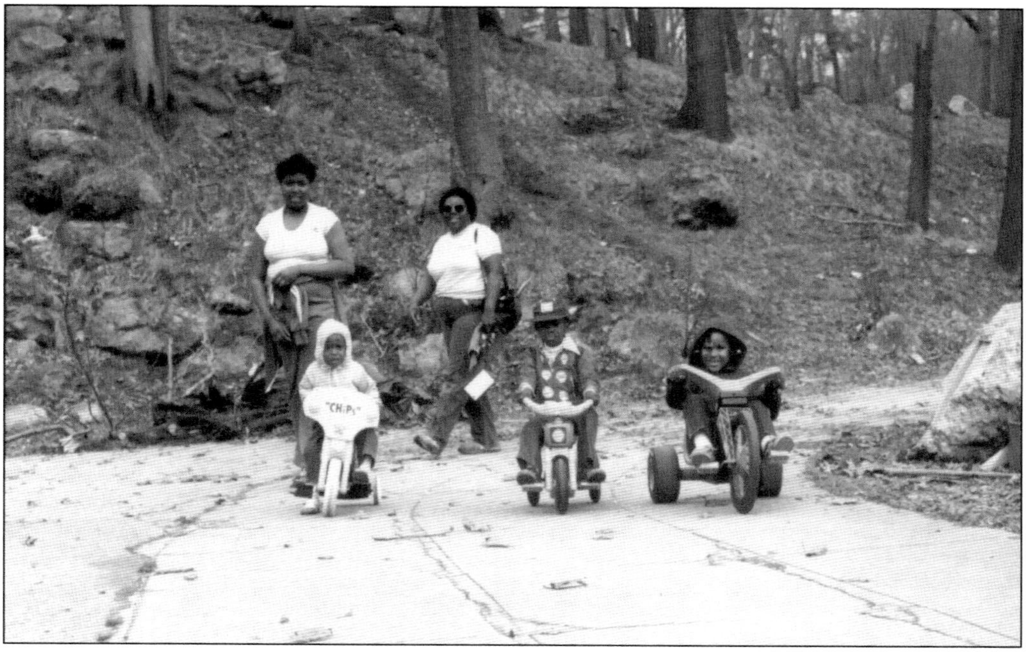

Traffic within the boundaries of the park has also been a consistent source of controversy. On October 28, 1895, 5,526 carriages, 51 saddled horses, and 2,368 bicycles entered the park from 1:00 p.m. until 7:00 p.m. The advent of automobiles added a new level of strain to Franklin Park's roadways and users. (Courtesy of the Franklin Park Coalition.)

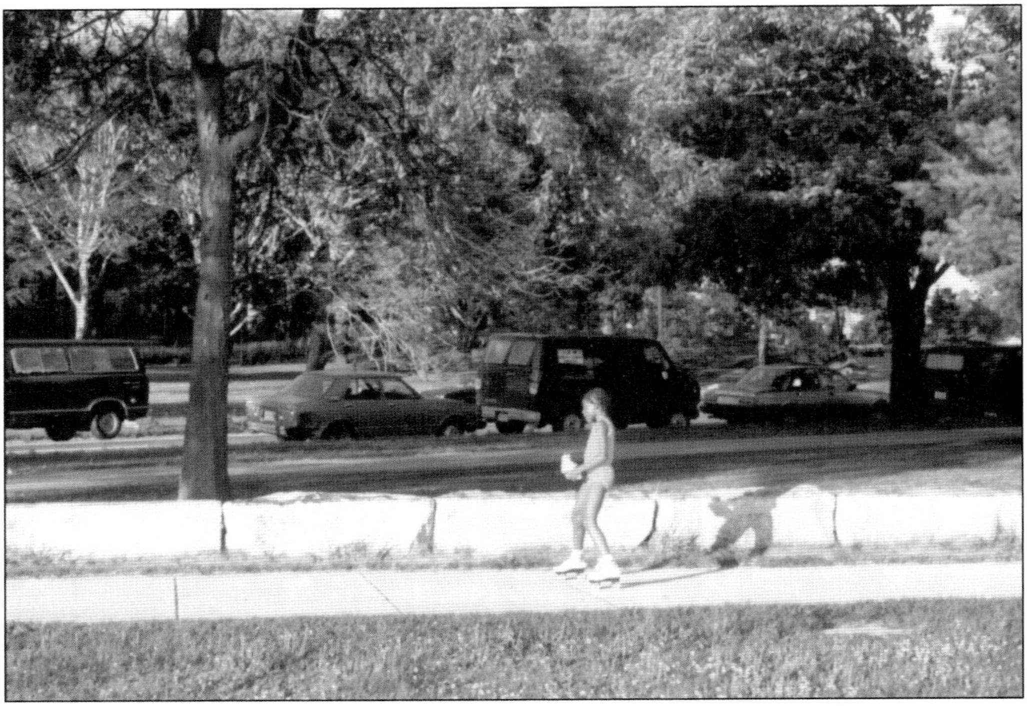

Many decided that closing the roadways was a necessity for the safety of pedestrians. In 1972, the City of Boston closed all roads to vehicles except Glen Road and Circuit Drive. The law did not stop cars from driving illegally through the park. The Franklin Park Coalition fought for the installation of granite blocks for all areas of the park except Circuit Drive. (Courtesy of the Franklin Park Coalition.)

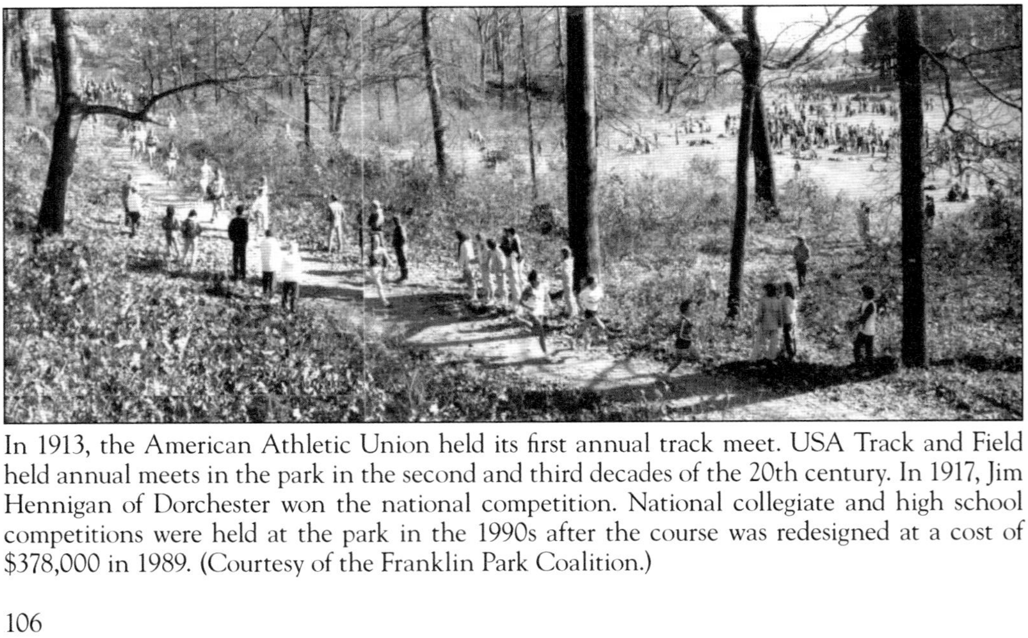

In 1913, the American Athletic Union held its first annual track meet. USA Track and Field held annual meets in the park in the second and third decades of the 20th century. In 1917, Jim Hennigan of Dorchester won the national competition. National collegiate and high school competitions were held at the park in the 1990s after the course was redesigned at a cost of $378,000 in 1989. (Courtesy of the Franklin Park Coalition.)

Eight

THE FALL AND RISE OF FRANKLIN PARK

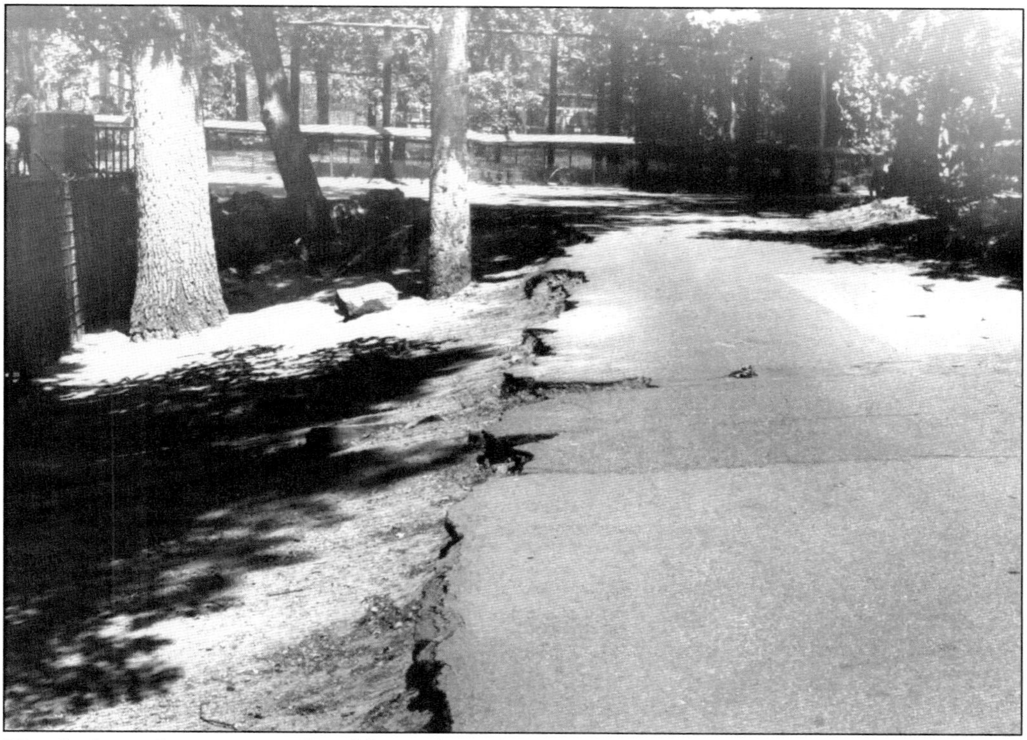

The decline of attention in Franklin Park in the 1960s and 1970s was blamed on many factors. Some said the park's size was unattractive. Others blamed the fact that a small percentage of population lived around the park. Others blamed the social and economic conditions around the park for the neglect. In 1969, Elma Lewis and Thomas Atkins started a campaign to draw attention to Franklin Park. (Courtesy of the Franklin Park Coalition.)

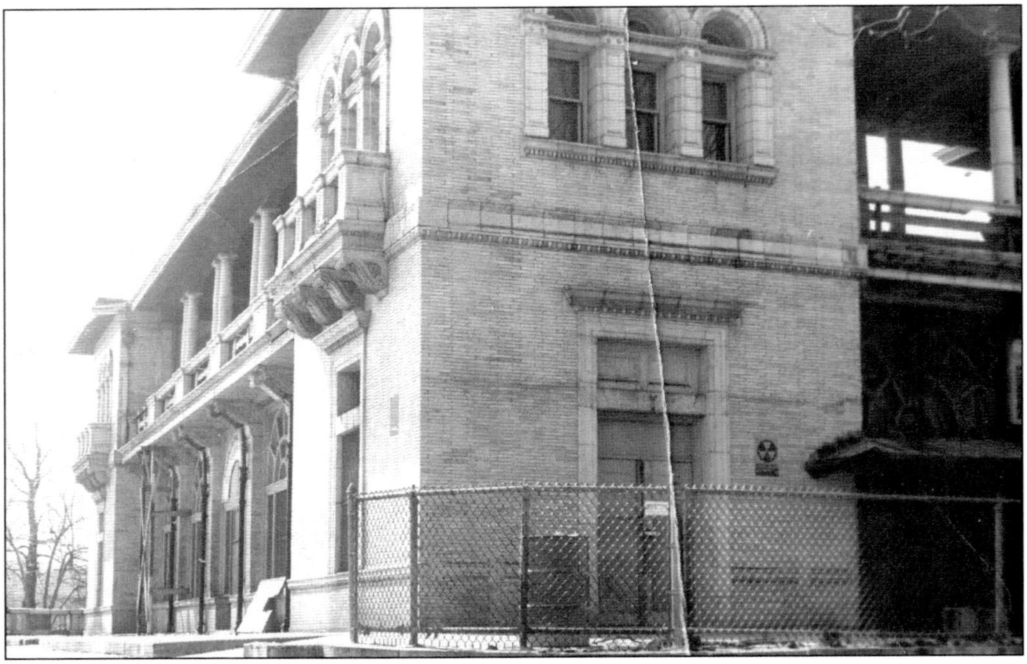

The last person to operate the Refectory as a restaurant and entertainment venue was Jerry Burke. In 1971, the Burke family decided to not renew the lease on the family business with the City of Boston. Some of the reasons for the decision to close were related to the danger of operating the business in the park and the decline of business that was consistent with the decline of attendance in Franklin Park. A 1972 feasibility study for the area suggested the removal of the building and the construction of parking garages for the zoo, which was undergoing renovations. The public was displeased with this plan. In 1976, the building was razed without public hearings. (Courtesy of Jerry Burke.)

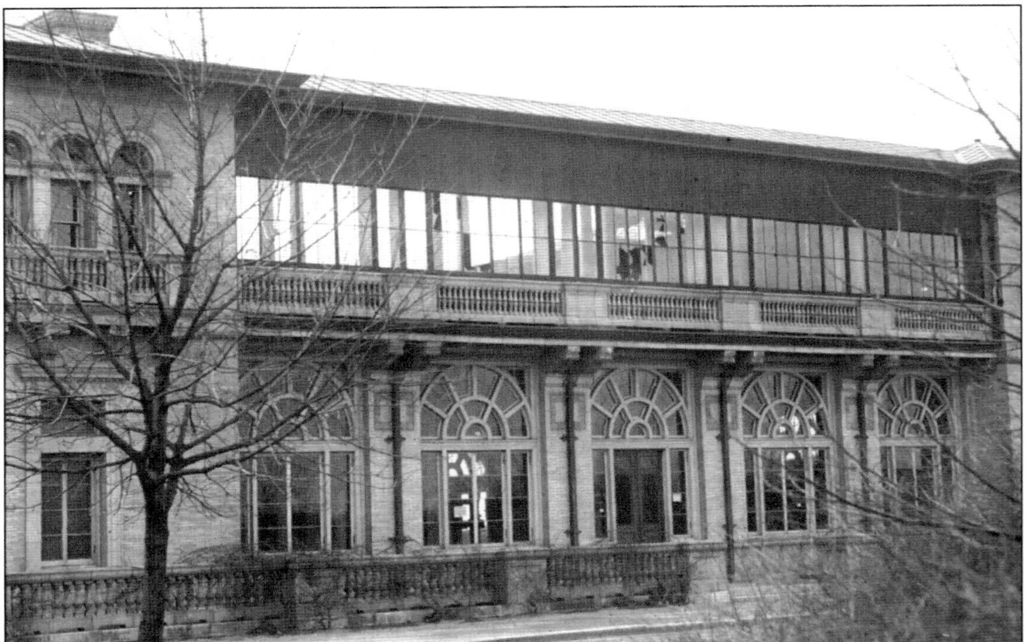

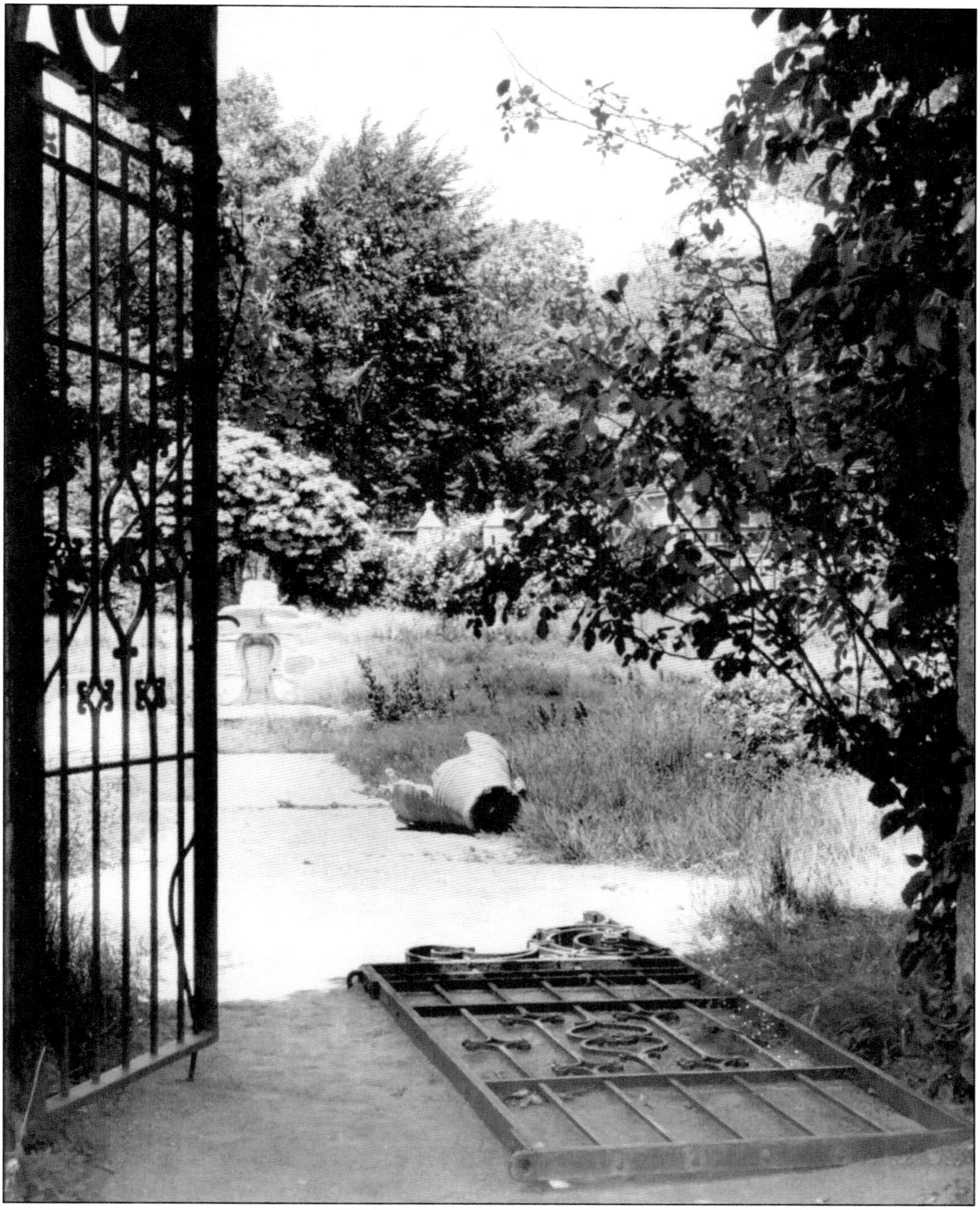

The Boston park commissioners published a special report in 1925 for Mayor James Michael Curley. The report noted that priorities within the borders of Franklin Park included "the acquisition of new parks and playground areas and the improvement of old areas." During Curley's reign, there were improvements to the park, such as the installation of the rose garden, but by 1978, when Mark Jay Mirsky wrote "In Search of Franklin Park" for the *Boston Globe Magazine*, many of these improvements had been neglected or vanished. According to Mirsky, neighbors around the park "followed the Puritan lead in trooping to the Museum of Fine Arts, to Isabella Gardner's palace, to the symphony for their sense of culture, but this remarkable asset of Boston was forgotten." Many city officials agreed that Franklin Park was not receiving the appropriate share of city funding. (Courtesy of the Boston Public Library Print Department.)

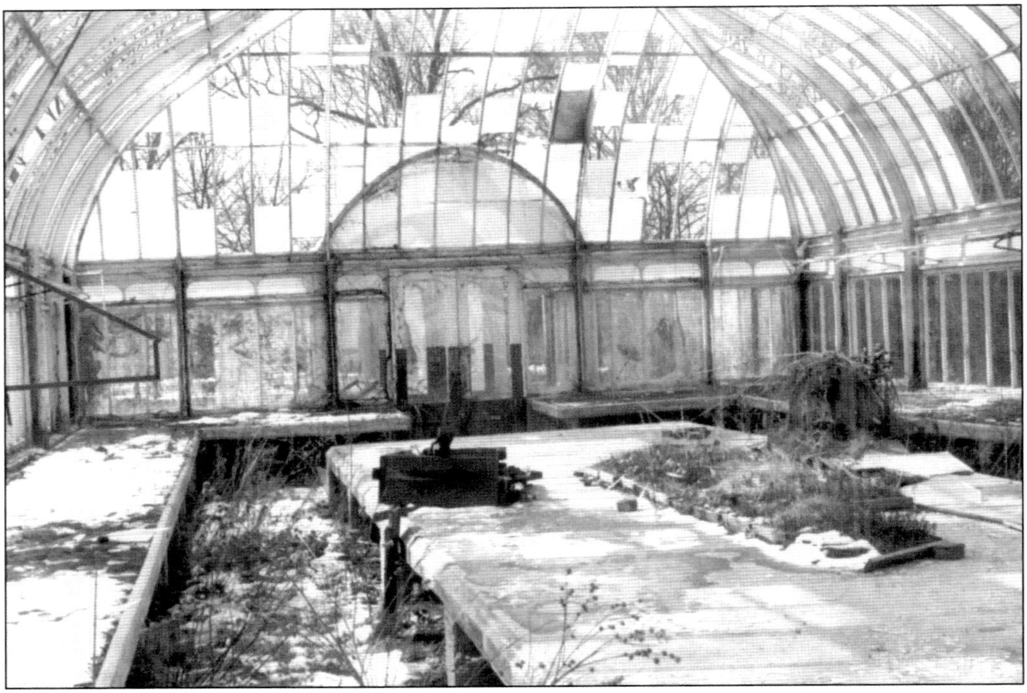

In a 1975 letter to Mayor Kevin White, the Franklin Park Commission proclaimed the proposed removal of the greenhouses in the park as "another gross insult . . . perpetuated against [the park] and the surrounding neighborhoods. A statement by him reported in the Boston Globe, July 24, to 'move a 40 by 70 foot greenhouse to roughly the [Public] Garden's Boylston Street border' is most offensive. The fact that the source of that beautification for Boston's 'show parks' is housed in the one park that needs it most, is itself, a sign of disrespect for the surrounding neighborhoods. To now remove this greenhouse indicates to us that any hope to indeed restore Franklin Park is indeed lost and that your promises are indeed not to be taken seriously." (Courtesy of the Franklin Park Coalition.)

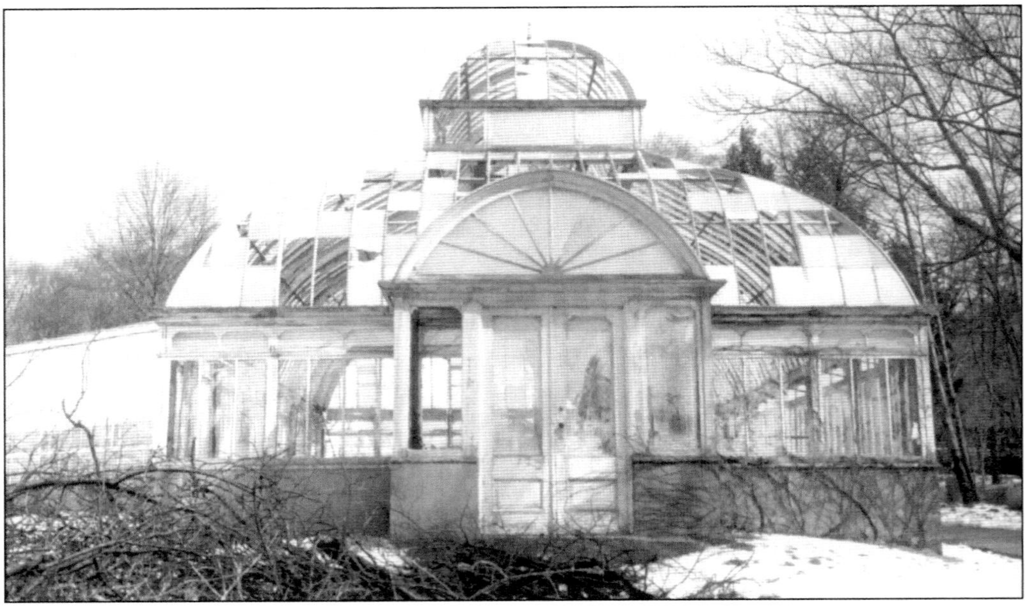

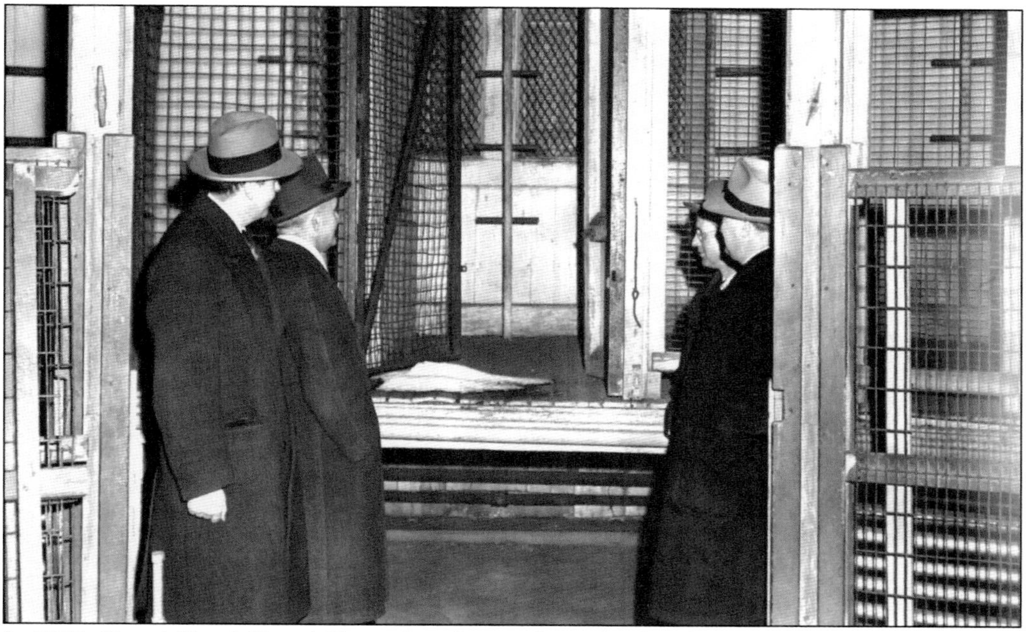

In 1954, Shurcliff and Shurcliff were hired to perform the first feasibility study of the zoo. The firm suggested reducing the size from 89 to 58 acres. It also suggested reducing the exhibit space within the 58 acres. "If the zoo had been built as planned, there would have been little unused space between the exhibits, and hence no complaints would have been made about walking the long distances between them." (Courtesy of the Boston Public Library Print Department.)

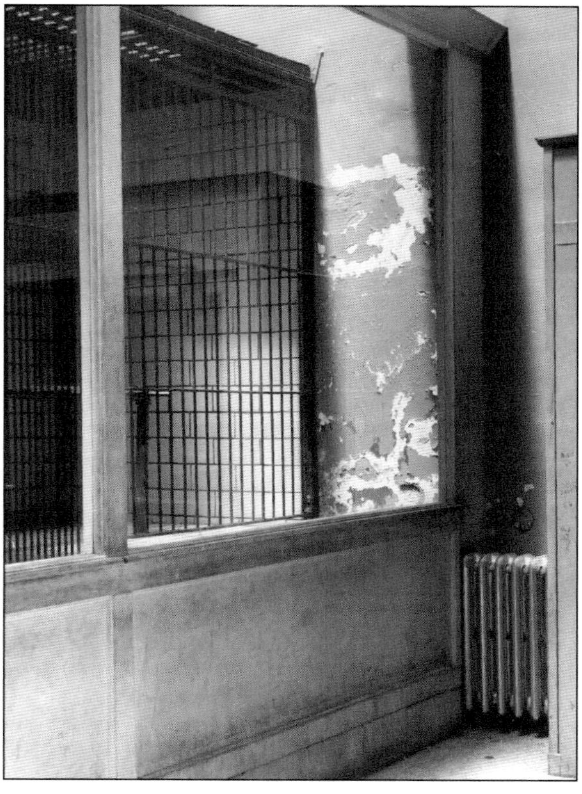

Control of the zoo was transferred to the MDC in 1957 because the zoo was viewed as a feature that benefited the region. The MDC then transferred operations to the Boston Zoological Society, an agency responsible for the Stone Zoo and the Franklin Park Zoo. Many believed the best animals were transferred to the Stone Zoo, while the fixtures in Franklin Park's zoo fell into disrepair. (Courtesy of the Boston Public Library Print Department.)

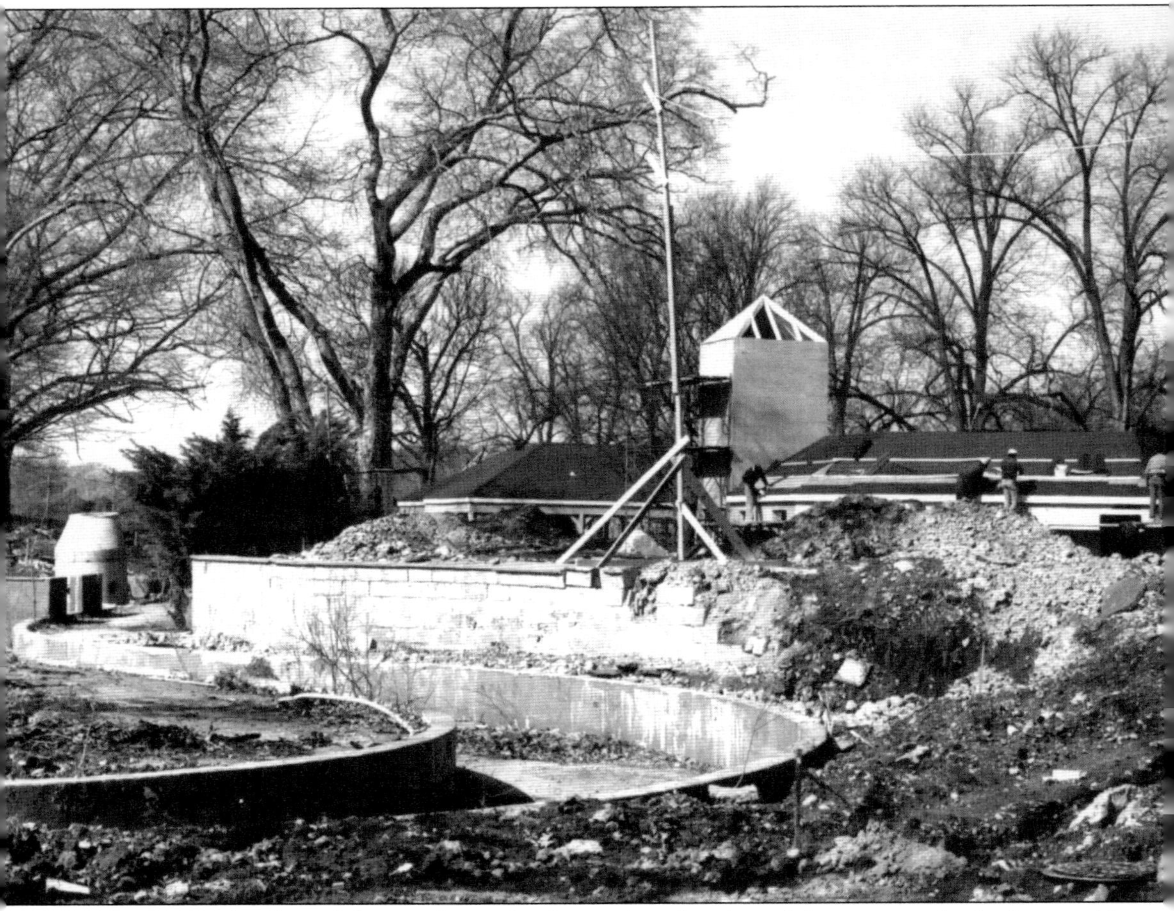

The Boston Zoological Society boasted a diverse board and an ability to raise funds that would benefit both zoos. There were many changes that culminated with the grand reopening in 1989. Many issues had to be resolved in the 20-year process, including the removal of historic yet decrepit buildings, increased parking areas and traffic control, and breaking the fears of regional zoo visitors who did not live in the neighborhood. (Courtesy of the Franklin Park Coalition.)

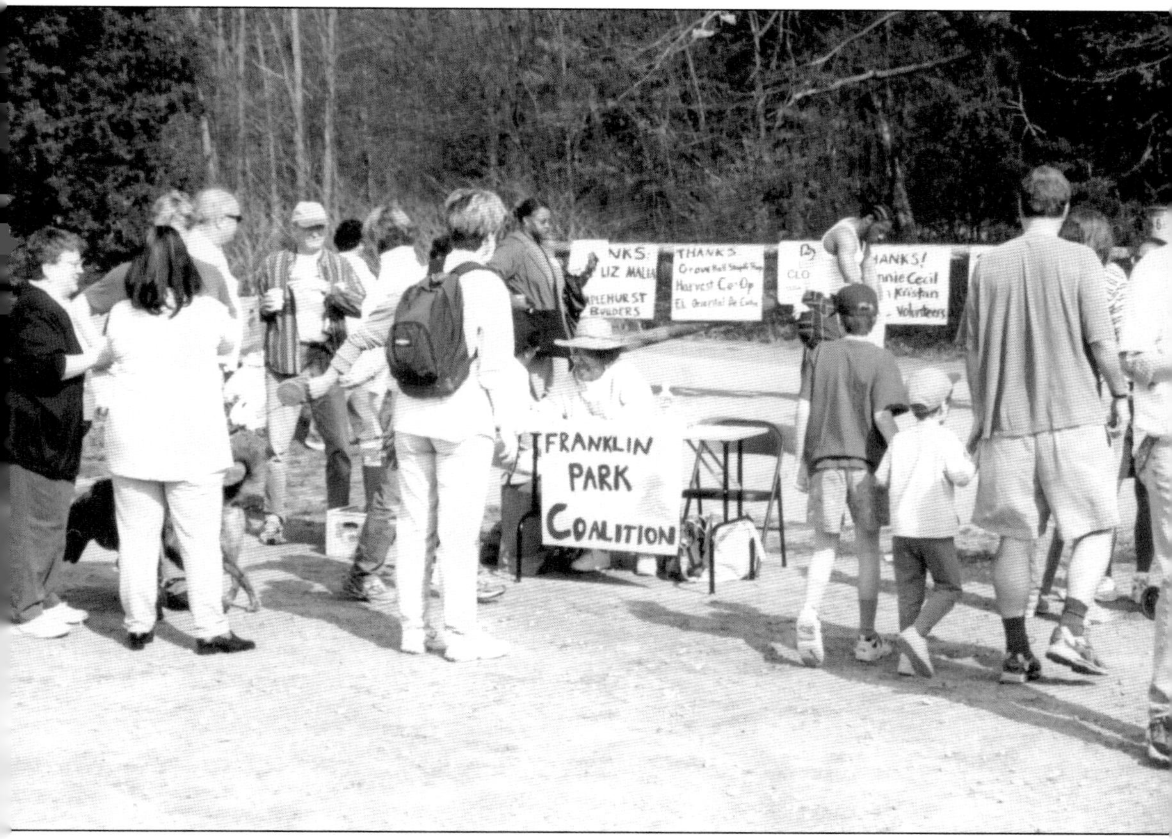

A group that advocated for Philadelphia's Fairmount Park inspired the Franklin Park Coalition. This group proved that local control could be effective in completing projects. The Elma Lewis School of Fine Arts was involved in funding tree removal and maintenance and other landscape projects. In 1971, the Franklin Park Advisory Committee was formed. By 1975, the Franklin Park Commission was established. The commission was responsible for producing publications, enlisting volunteers, and securing funding to support projects. The newly formed commission sent a petition to the mayor stating, "We, the undersigned local and regional citizens and users of Franklin Park, do hereby urge that you and the Parks and Recreation Dept. take all necessary actions to reverse the deterioration of Franklin Park. We further urge that Franklin Park be given the priority status and the definitive budget it deserves and requires, e.g. ordinances for proper use of the parks and regulations governing automobile access could and should be immediately enforced. Maintenance of the park, gradd-cutting, and daily removal of debris should be done as well. We await your response." (Courtesy of the Franklin Park Coalition.)

Franklin Park Coalition

EYES ON THE PARK

message line 983-9192

Phone in your observations of
Franklin Park vehicular impact.

PLANNING TRANSPORTATION FOR THE FUTURE.

(leer el reverso.)

Any vice could be bought in Franklin Park. "If the trunk was open—beer or whiskey. If the hood was open—dope." The Franklin Park Coalition recognized the ineffectiveness of the police to work within the park. Originally the group partnered with Roxbury Crime Commission to assuage crime. Eyes on the Park cards were passed out to empower park users to report issues. (Courtesy of the Franklin Park Coalition.)

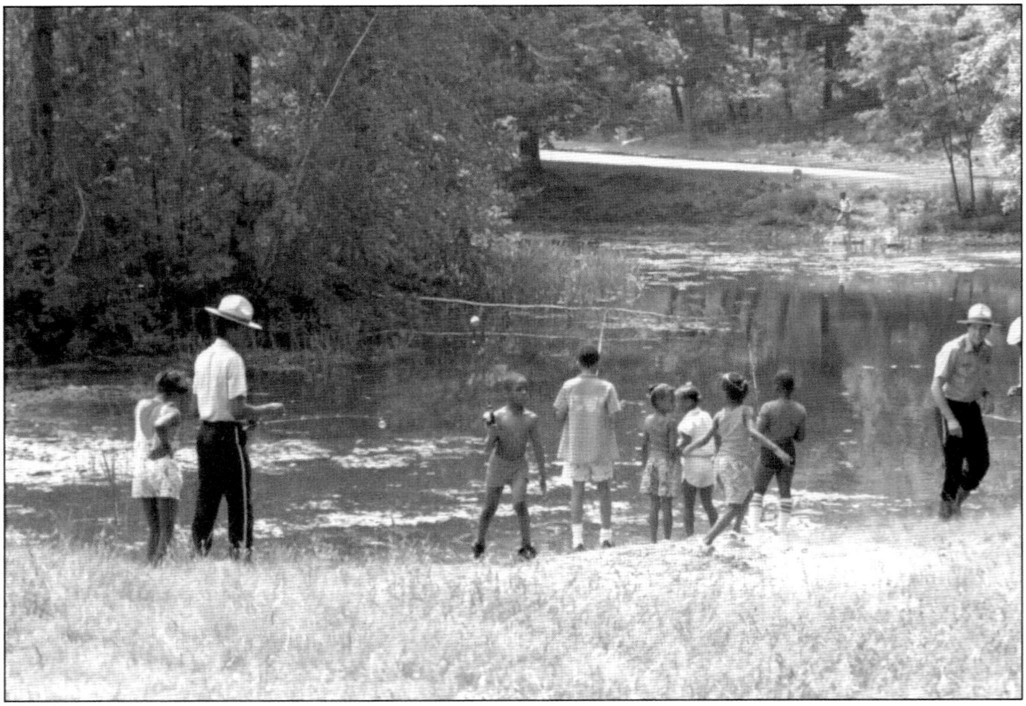

In 1978, the park police were disbanded in Franklin Park. Many believed that uniformed officials added to the tensions in the park and neighborhoods surrounding it. The Boston Police Department was left to assign patrolmen to the park who understood the neighborhood, although the program was futile. In 1984, the Boston Park Rangers became a fixture once again. (Courtesy of the Franklin Park Coalition.)

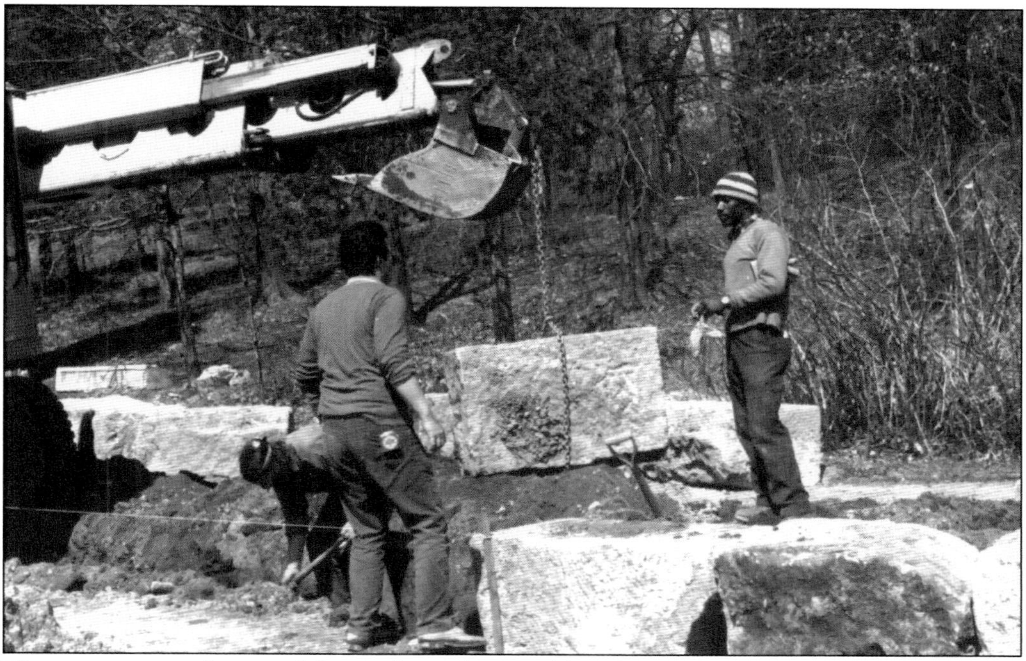

The controversy of automobiles in the park is as old as the automobile. Cars had no enforced restrictions. They compacted the grass in the Playstead, spilled gasoline in the Wilderness, and were sunk to the bottom of Scarboro Pond. In 1981, granite blocks were installed, and in 1982, parking was banned on the Playstead. By 1984, the park was closed to automobiles except for Circuit Drive. (Courtesy of the Franklin Park Coalition.)

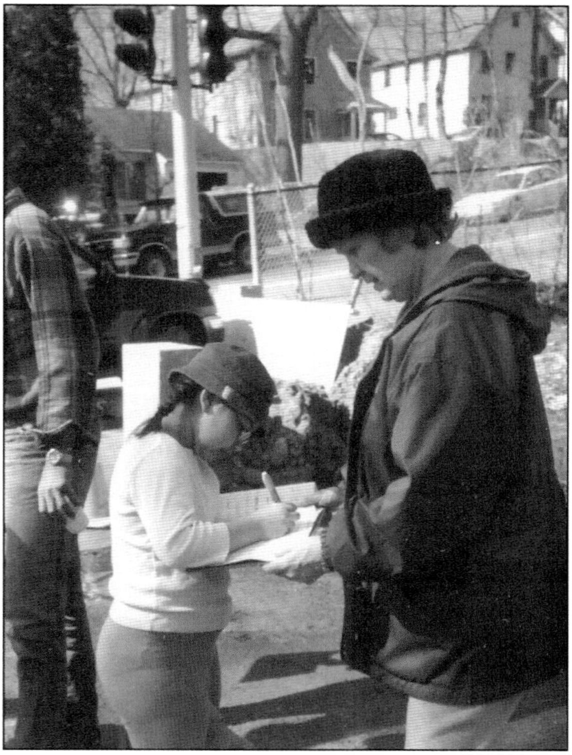

Franklin Park remained an important place for recreation and education. Local schools have been able to use the park for science and art projects and physical education. The Playhouse in the Park program has provided free summer entertainment to camps and day care centers. Suzanne Monk is helping to get a youngster involved in the park. (Courtesy of the Franklin Park Coalition.)

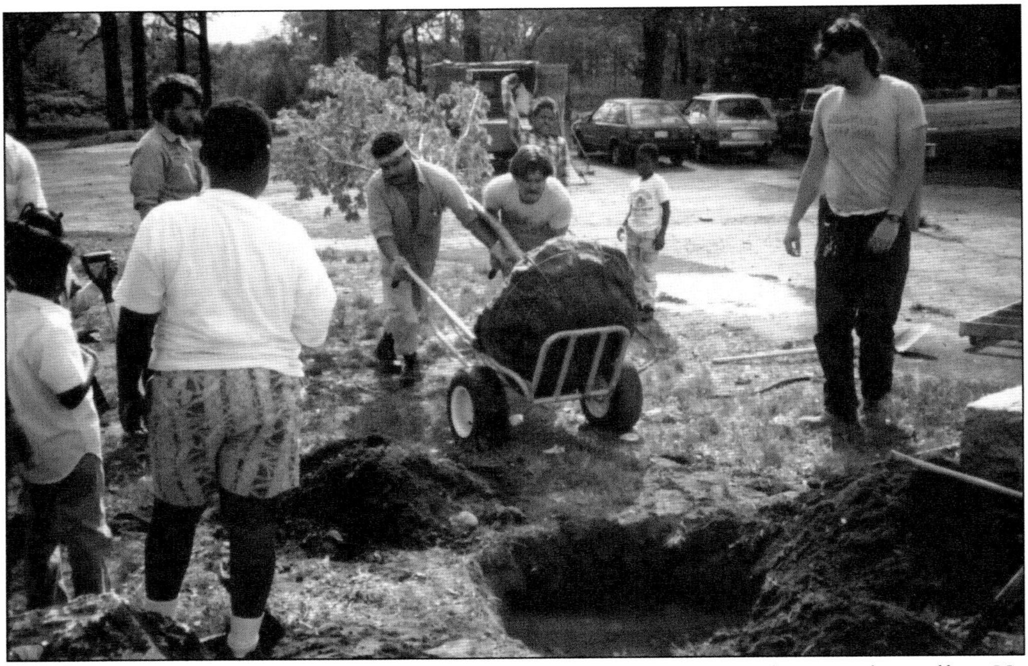

Frederick Law Olmsted's plans for Franklin Park were never meant to take immediate effect. He stated that it was a "question of time and of a wholesomely restrained ambient when they shall be seen." Years of neglect harmed many of the original plantings. There was "not a penny to replant the dying trees in a masterpiece of landscape art." (Courtesy of the Franklin Park Coalition.)

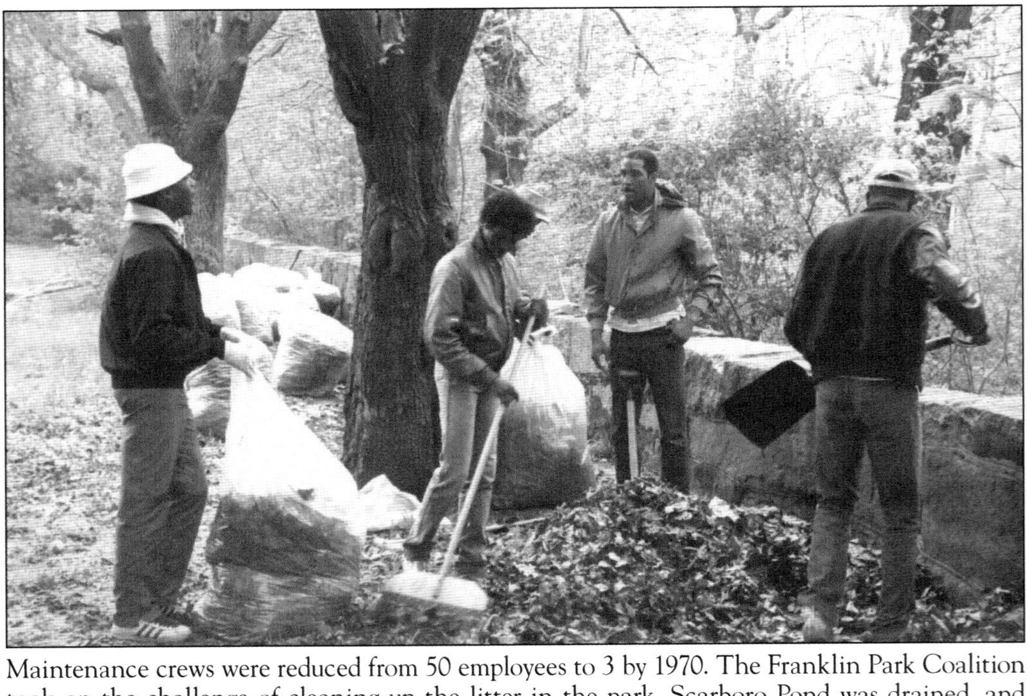

Maintenance crews were reduced from 50 employees to 3 by 1970. The Franklin Park Coalition took on the challenge of cleaning up the litter in the park. Scarboro Pond was drained, and it is storied that trash included city fixtures, thousands of golf balls, burglar tools, boats, and household appliances. (Courtesy of the Franklin Park Coalition.)

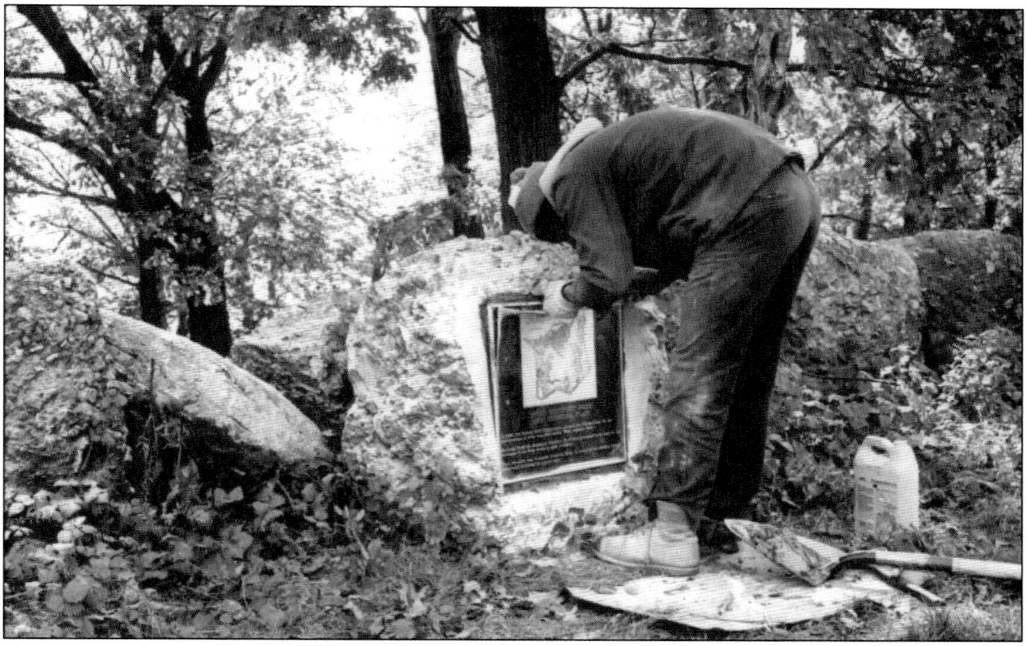

Franklin Park needed to be saved from developers and neglect. Louisa Day Hicks proposed building a new English High School campus in the area that is the Wilderness. In 1971, the Emerald Necklace was designated a national historic landmark. In 1980, the Boston Landmarks Commission designated Franklin Park a historic landmark. Both designations saved the park from a number of proposals and increased historic interest in the park. In 1984, the Department of Environmental Management established the Olmsted Historic Landscape Preservation Program to study the history and develop a master plan for park rehabilitation. The Franklin Park Coalition hung signs to specify uses in different areas around the park and installed maps and pictures in pudding stone boulders to signify historically important areas. (Courtesy of the Franklin Park Coalition.)

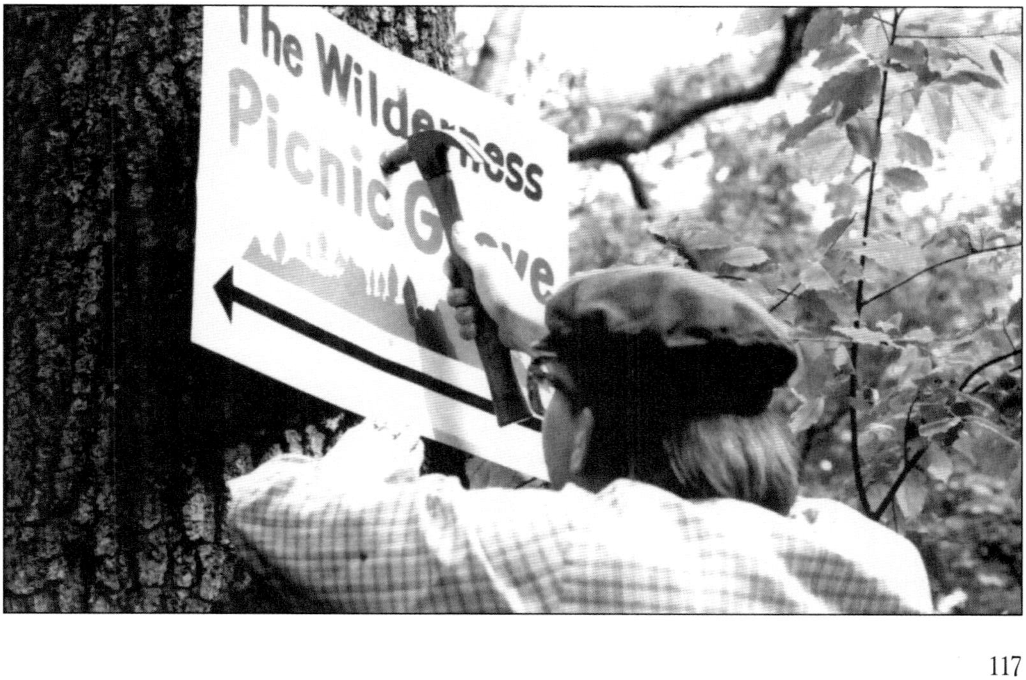

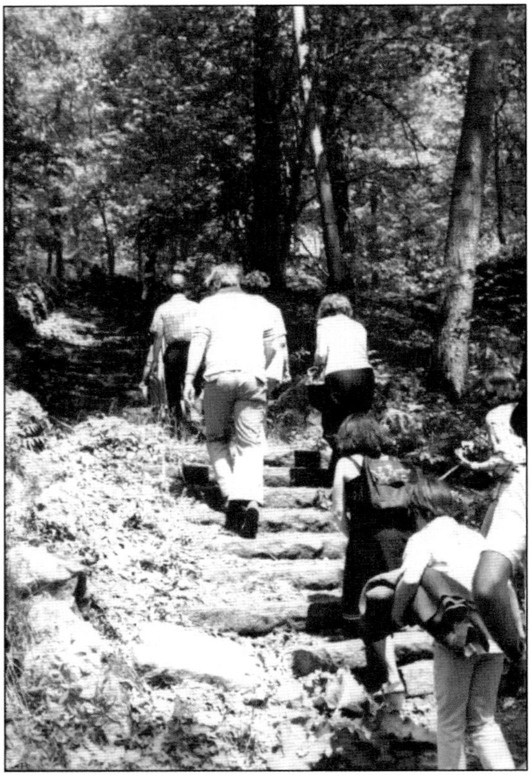

The Victorian Society's New England chapter sponsored the Franklin Park Coalition's first walking tour on May 30, 1976. Richard Heath, the director of Franklin Park from the late 1970s into the 1980s, used the *Franklin Park Bulletin* as another outlet to share the park's history and to capture the thoughts of park users. (Courtesy of the Franklin Park Coalition.)

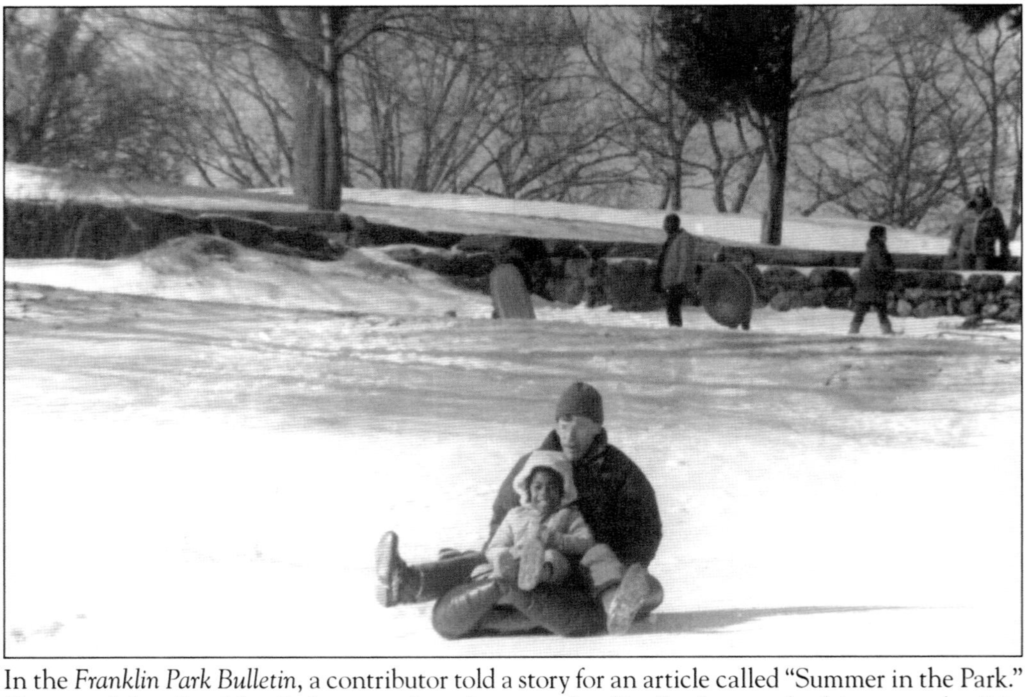

In the *Franklin Park Bulletin*, a contributor told a story for an article called "Summer in the Park." She stated that Franklin Park was a place that gave families "a place to do things together." In the mornings she ran while her husband and son golfed. Many other families enjoyed sports, barbecues, and live music throughout the summer. (Courtesy of the Franklin Park Coalition.)

Nine

PARK USERS

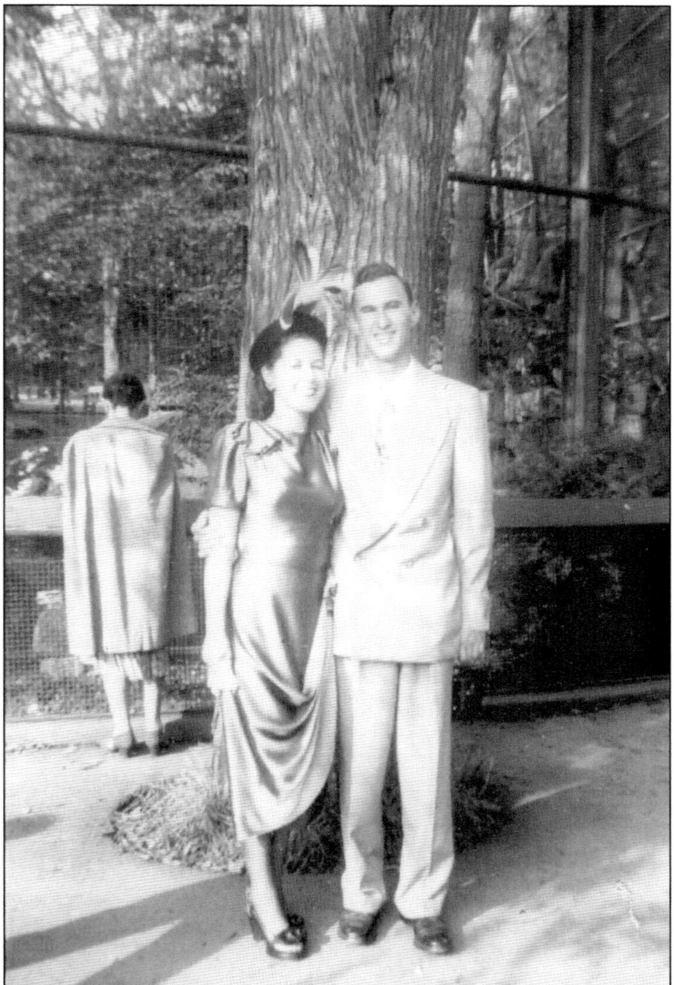

Bostonians, as taxpayers, have always been the true owners of Franklin Park. Holidays were often spent in the park, including Passover and Easter Sunday. Shep Wolsky and his wife, Ann, enjoy a stroll in the zoo on a holiday afternoon. (Courtesy of Shep Wolsky.)

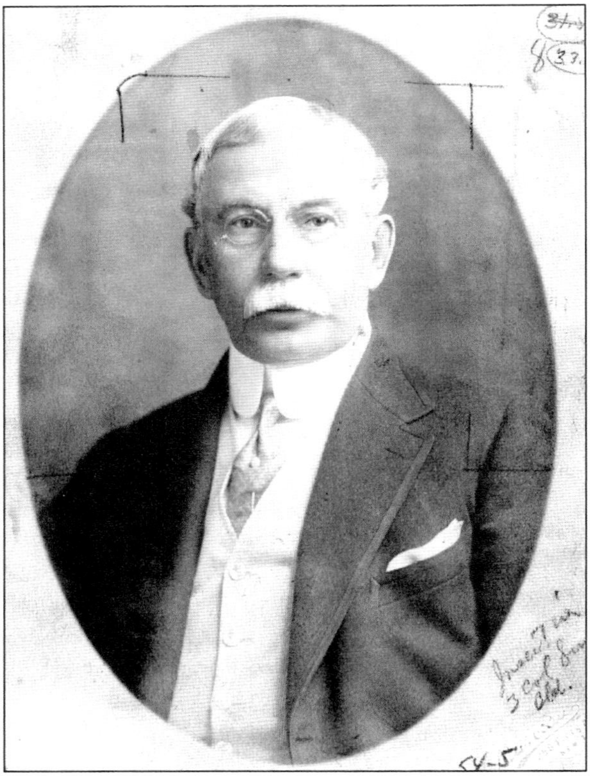

George Robert White died in 1922. He left a substantial fund to the City of Boston to "create works of public utility and beauty." The White Fund endowed a variety of projects in Franklin Park, including zoo structures, Schoolboy Stadium, and a community development center. (Courtesy of the Boston Public Library Print Department.)

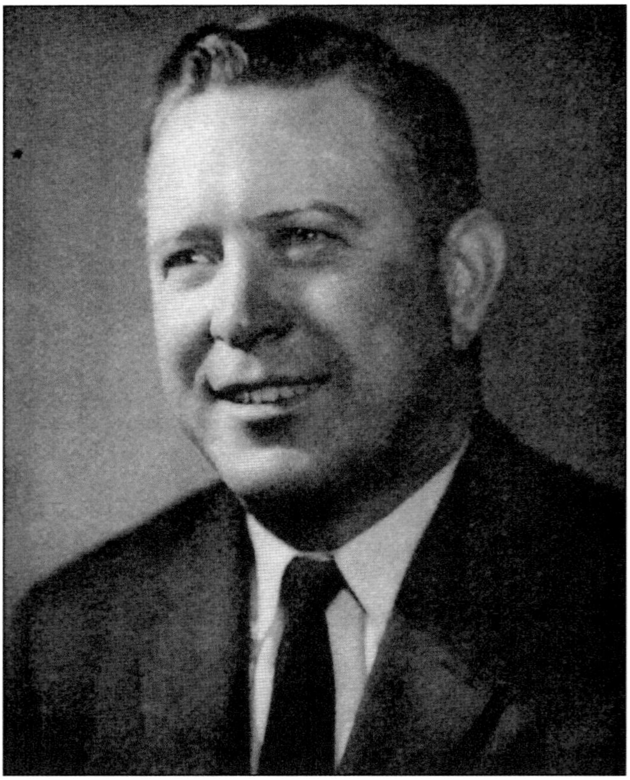

William J. (Billy) Devine was a lifelong Boston resident and the commissioner of the Boston Parks and Recreation Department from 1964 to 1967. At a time when many were fearful of the park, Devine continued promoting the golf course in Franklin Park, established charitable tournaments, and improved the park. The links were renamed in his honor in 1967. (Courtesy of Jerry Burke.)

The longtime director of the Franklin Park Coalition, Richard Heath, propelled the advocacy group through the 1980s. He was an ardent spokesperson for the continued attention for the park from the local government. His scholarly work on the history of Franklin Park is an invaluable resource in a number of sources. (Courtesy of the Franklin Park Coalition.)

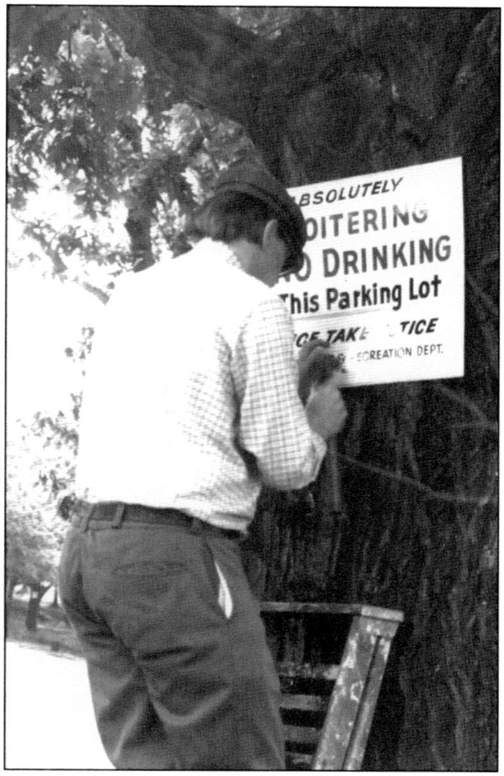

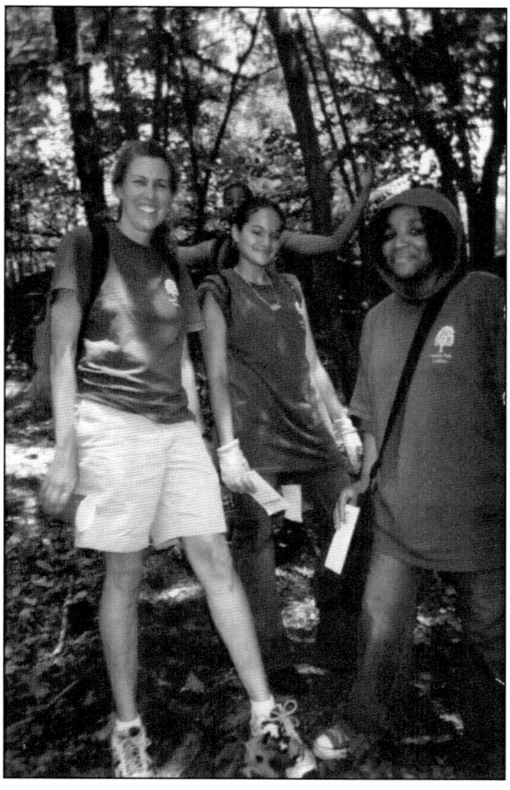

Christine Poff (left) has been the director of the Franklin Park Coalition since 2002. She has been active in the reinstatement of Elma Lewis's Playhouse in the Park and the Summer Youth Crew as well as extending the scope of fund-raising for the park and managing a variety of stewardship groups within the park. (Courtesy of the Franklin Park Coalition.)

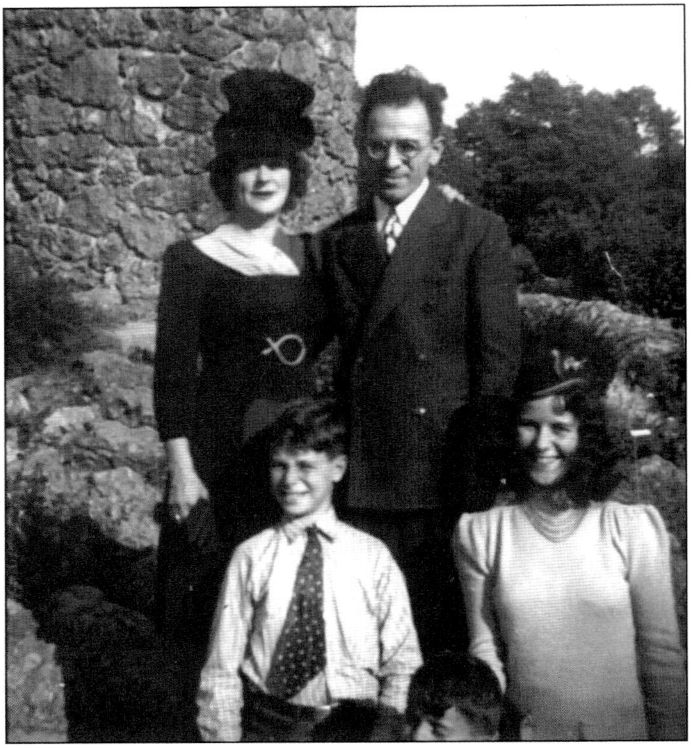

The demographics of the neighbors in Franklin Park around the 1940s and 1950s were mainly Jewish and Irish. Both groups had their "sides" of the park and activities they partook in. Here the Zolot family, with mother Esther, father George, brothers Herb and Mel, and sister Ann, celebrates Rosh Hashanah in 1941 with a visit to Franklin Park. (Courtesy of Shep Wolsky.)

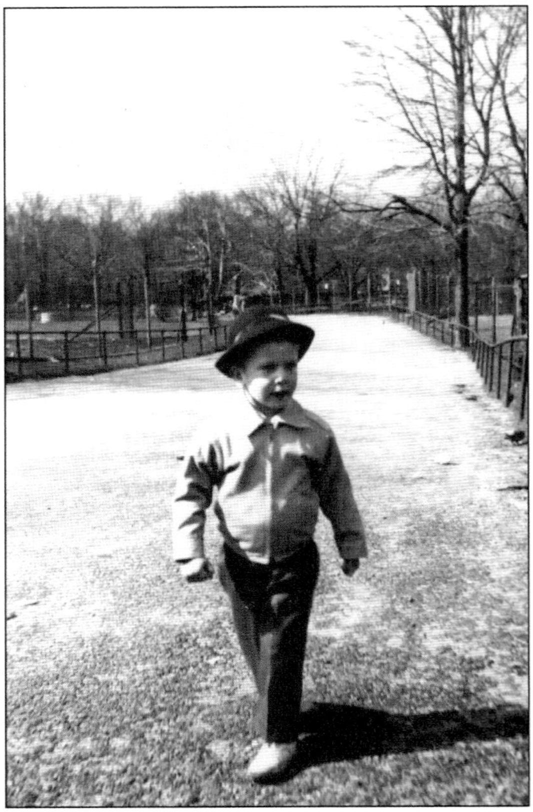

Stephen Kadish was the owner of Kay Bee Antiques on Boylston Street in Boston. He is pictured here at age seven, enjoying an afternoon at the Franklin Park Zoo. According to his brother, the park was a great place to grow up and become more independent. (Courtesy of Peter Kadish.)

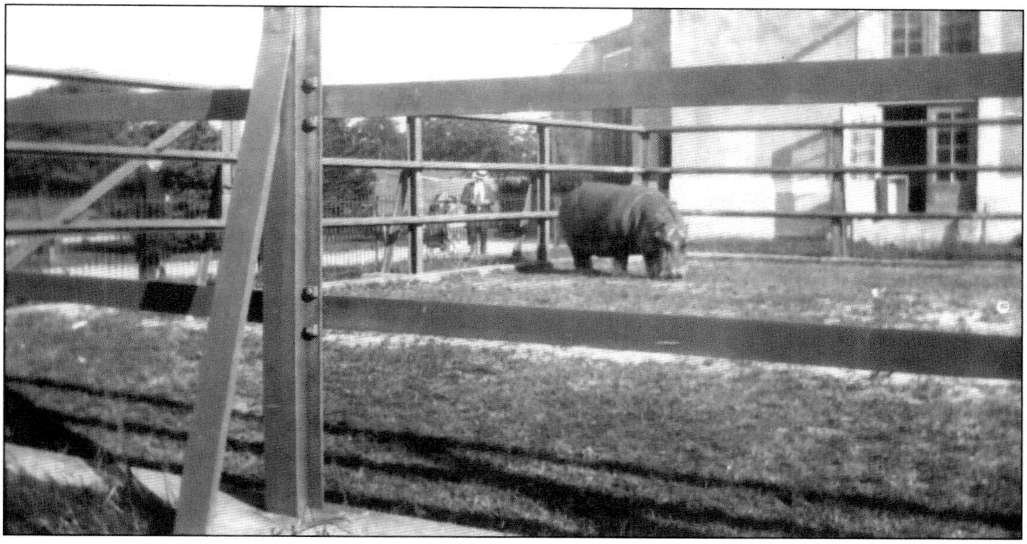

Photographers for the Boston Postcard Company and other businesses captured important moments in the history of Franklin Park. Some individuals would purchase postcards of family and friends to show their good times on vacation, while other postcards were mass-produced and sold. This postcard was never sent, but the original owner marked the occasion of Happy's arrival on the back of the card: "Baby Hippopotamus Age 4 years."

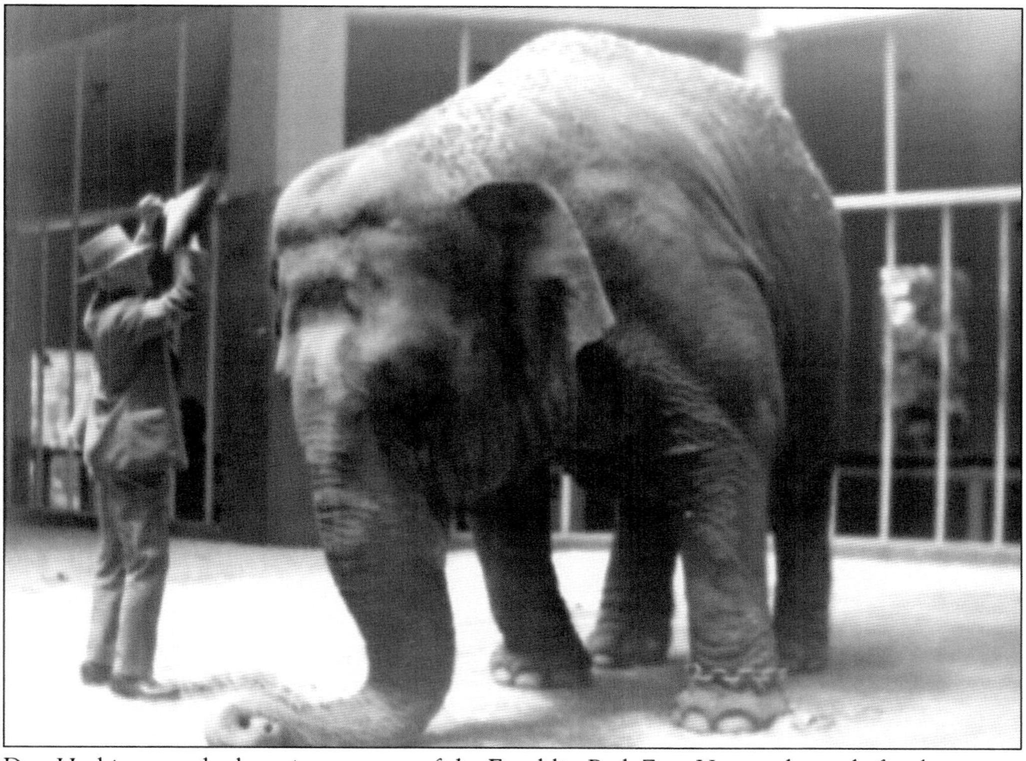

Dan Harkins was the longtime curator of the Franklin Park Zoo. He cared greatly for the proper operations of the zoo and led employees by example. Here he is shown sweeping Tony as part of the daily ritual in the elephant house. His journals detail the care of zoo animals through the middle of the 20th century. (Courtesy of the Boston Public Library Print Department.)

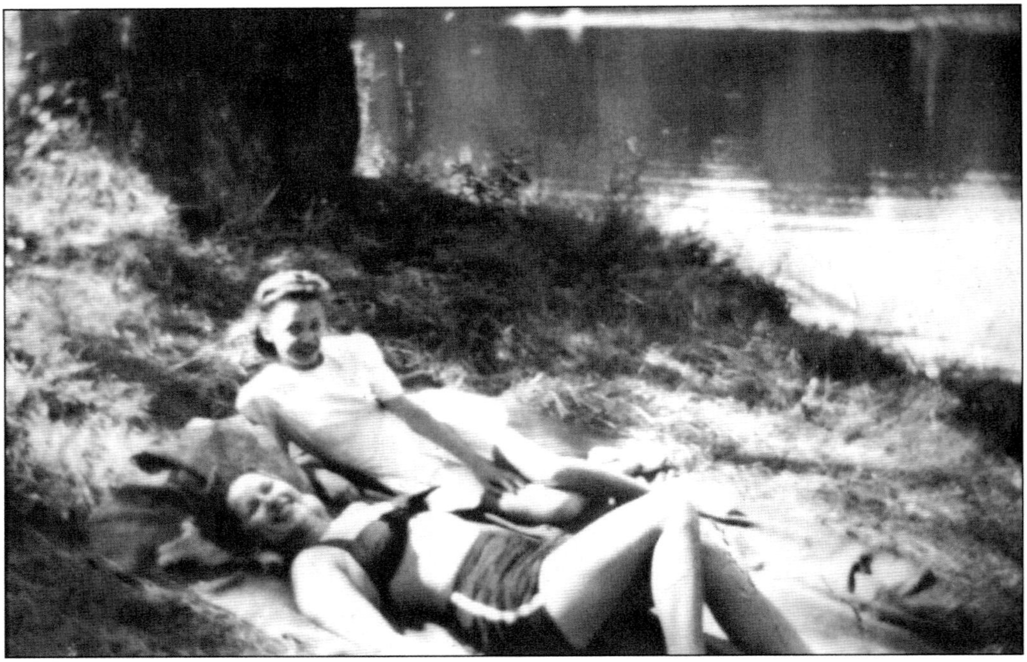

Recreation for ladies in Franklin Park, in the Victorian mind-set, was to be passive. It included leisurely walks, spectating, and riding in carriages. This idea changed drastically through the 20th century as women became more active within the boundaries of the park. Whether it is softball, rugby, golf, or running, the park has proven to be a place for all to enjoy. Here Ann Zolot and Shirley Rice are enjoying a leisurely afternoon of sunbathing on the shore of Scarboro Pond. Leslie Jones photographed Ruth McGaffigan of Stoneham on the bridle path in 1954. (Above, courtesy of Shep Wolsky; below, courtesy of the Boston Public Library Print Department.)

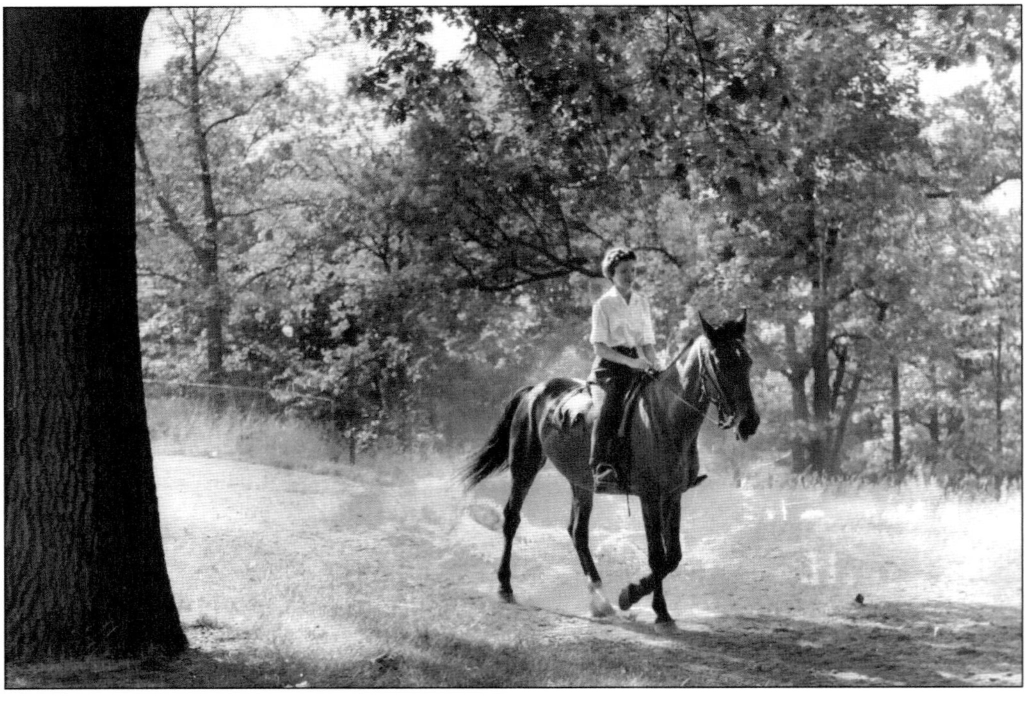

Officers James Maguire and Daniel Meanly were on patrol in the park in the summer of 1941 when a member of the staff photographed them behind the Refectory. Through the 1960s and 1970s, the Boston Police Department had orders to be "hands-off" within Franklin Park. (Courtesy of Jerry Burke.)

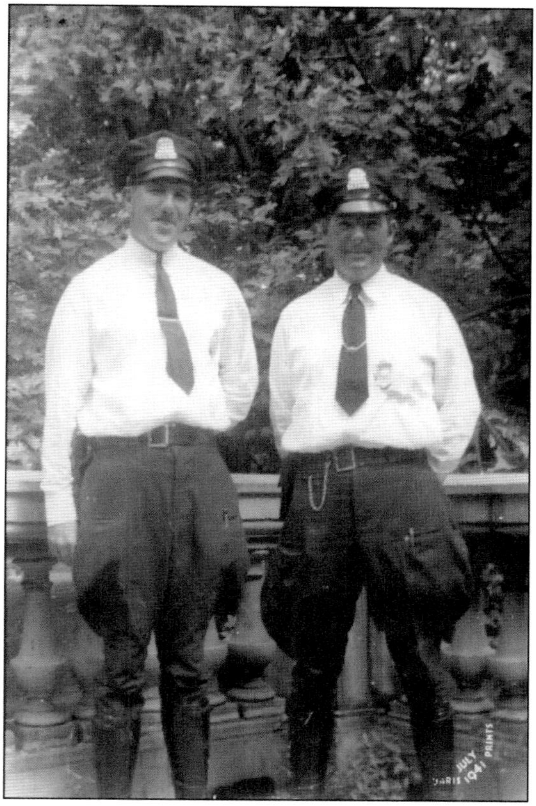

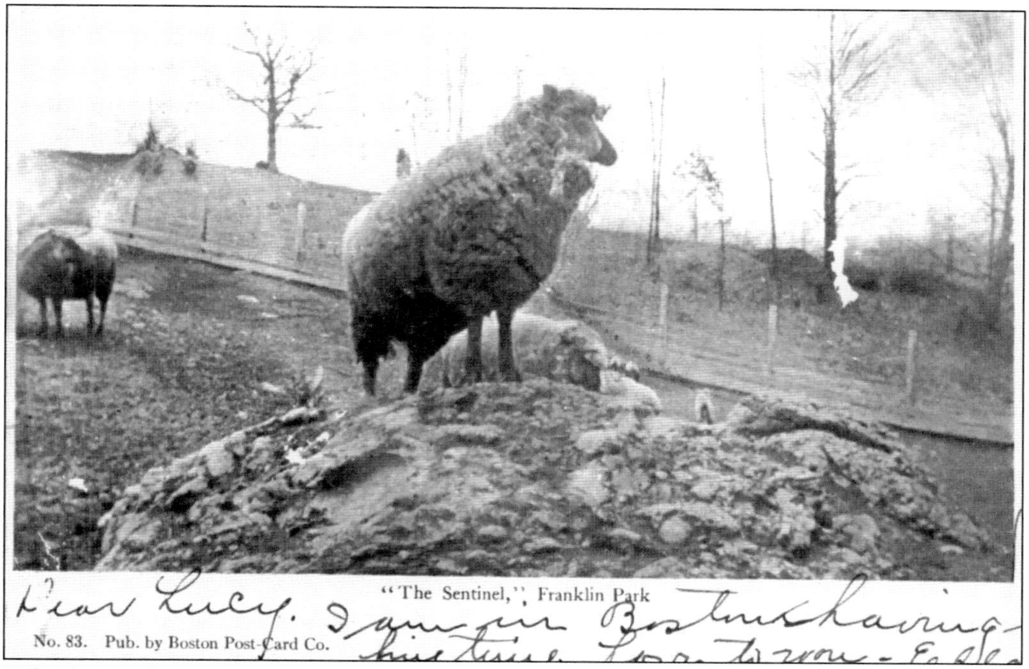

"The Sentinel" was sent to Lucy Williams in Western Springs, Illinois. The author wanted her to know that she was "in Boston having a fine time." The sheep were a special attraction in the park before they moved to Franklin Field.

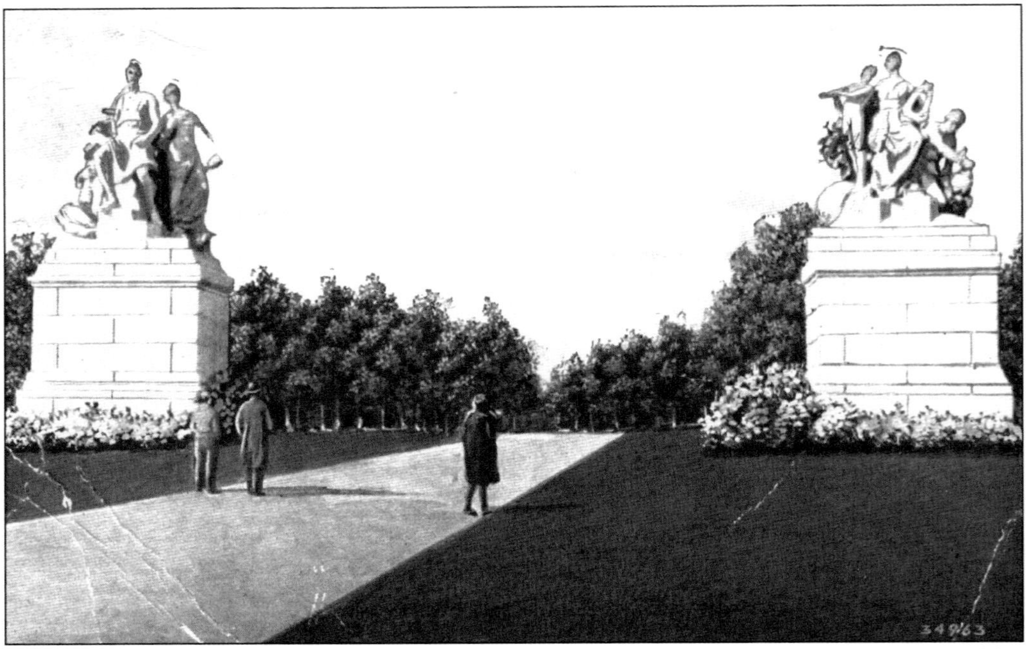

"Dear Mother and Dad; Having a swell time. Please send me some money. Sapo." Franklin Park was a place for young students to spend their spare time playing baseball, golfing, and enjoying other activities through the years. In a city with so many colleges, this young man wrote something timeless.

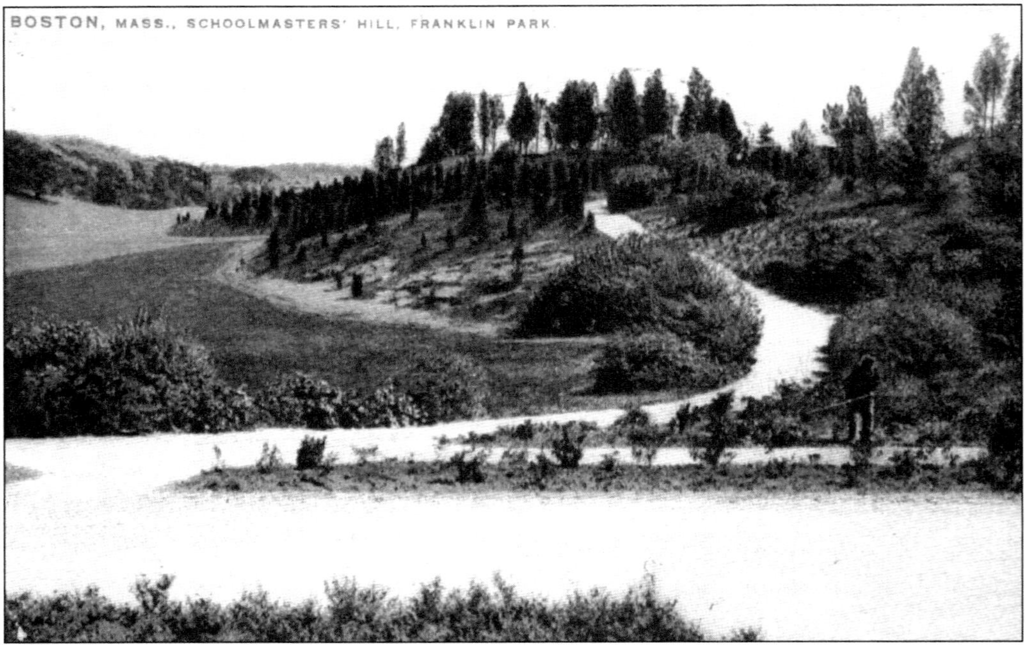

Mrs. A. A. Mattern wrote to Mrs. Albert Green of West Rush, New York, to let her know about the hot weather in Boston. Despite that, the family was managing to "have a good time." Franklin Park, especially after the construction of the zoo, was viewed as a vacation destination for New Englanders from near and far—the urban respite that Frederick Law Olmsted intended it to be.

Selected Bibliography

Beveridge, Charles E. *The Papers of Frederick Law Olmsted*. Vol. I. Baltimore: Johns Hopkins University Press, 1977.

———. *The Papers of Frederick Law Olmsted*. Vol. VII. Baltimore: Johns Hopkins University Press, 2007.

———. *The Papers of Frederick Law Olmsted*. Supplementary Series I. Baltimore: Johns Hopkins University Press, 1997.

Hasenfus, Nathaniel J. *Marie Visits the Zoo*. West Roxbury, MA: Heffernan Press, 1953.

Heath, Richard, and Cynthia Zaitzevsky. *Modified Historic Structures and Furnishings Report*. Boston: Department of Environmental Management, May 1986.

Hepburn, Perry Dean. *Franklin Park Zoo Inventory*. Boston: Metropolitan District Commission, 1967.

Nolen, John. "Frederick Law Olmsted and His Work: Franklin Park." *House and Garden*. July 1906.

Olmsted, Frederick Law. *Civilizing American Cities: Writing on City Landscapes*. Edited by S. B. Sutton. Boston: DaCapo, 1997.

———. "Master Plan for Franklin Park, Job 918."

Parks for the People: Proceedings of a Public Meeting Held at Fanueil Hall, June 7, 1876. Boston: Franklin Press, 1876.

Study and Report on the Establishment of Management Plans for the Operation of Franklin Park, A. Boston: Boston Parks and Recreation Department, 1972.

Zaitzevsky, Cynthia. *Franklin Park Bibliography*. Boston: Department of Environmental Management, April 1986.

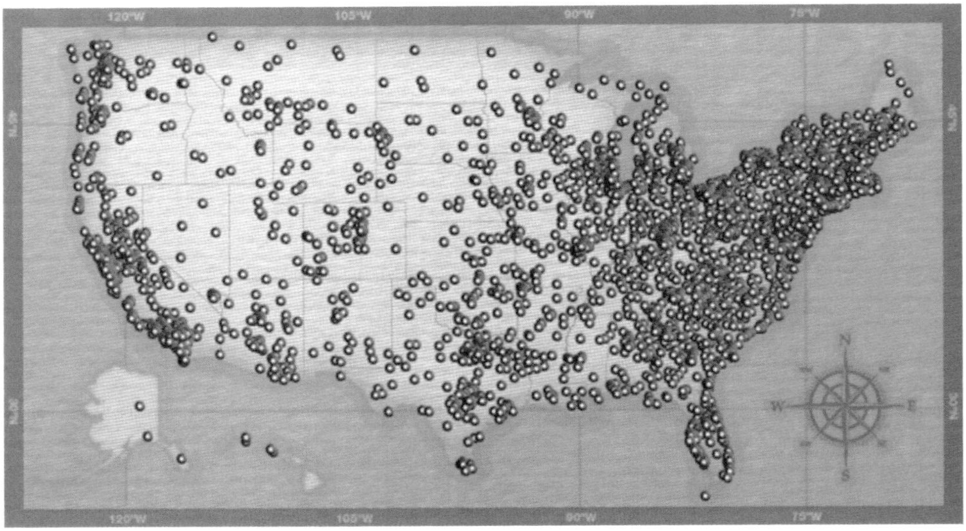